AFTER THE CORINTHIAN
WOMEN PROPHETS

SEMEIA STUDIES

Steed V. Davidson, General Editor

Editorial Board:
Eric D. Barreto
Jin Young Choi
L. Juliana M. Claassens
Gregory Cuéllar
Katie B. Edwards
Jacqueline Hidalgo
Shively T. J. Smith

Number 97

AFTER THE CORINTHIAN WOMEN PROPHETS

Reimagining Rhetoric and Power

Edited by

Joseph A. Marchal

Atlanta

Copyright © 2021 by SBL Press

All rights reserved. No part of this work may be reproduced or transmitted in any form or by any means, electronic or mechanical, including photocopying and recording, or by means of any information storage or retrieval system, except as may be expressly permitted by the 1976 Copyright Act or in writing from the publisher. Requests for permission should be addressed in writing to the Rights and Permissions Office, SBL Press, 825 Houston Mill Road, Atlanta, GA 30329 USA.

Library of Congress Control Number: 2021940691

Contents

Acknowledgments vii
Abbreviations xi

Still After: Reintroducing the Corinthian Women
    Prophets at Thirty
    Joseph A. Marchal 1

Hearing Wo/men Prophets:
    Intersections, Silences, Publics
    Shelly Matthews 47

The Celebrity Paratexts: The 1 Corinthians 14 Gloss Theory
    before and after *The Corinthian Women Prophets*
    Jorunn Økland 69

Reading Paul Obliquely: Reading against the Grain in a
    Latourian Pluriverse
    Cavan Concannon 99

Alternative Futures, Ephemeral Bodies: Untouching
    the Corinthian Women Prophets
    Joseph A. Marchal 123

The Writing Continues: The Women Are Still There
    in 2 Corinthians
    Arminta Fox 145

Out of House and Home: Early Christian Community
    as Public *Ekklēsia*
    Anna Miller 165

A Posthumanist Lens on Paul and Corinthian Agency
    Antoinette Clark Wire 195

Contributors 215
Ancient Sources Index 219
Modern Authors Index 225
Subject Index 227

Acknowledgments

Time is a … queer thing, to put it mildly.
 I sit here revising and updating these acknowledgments more than a year now into a global pandemic, and all of its associated, or just exacerbating apocalypses. This has been "the longest March," for so many of us, with so many losses, only some of which we have had the opportunity to even initially acknowledge. We remain *after*, or in pursuit of a better, more just world, but we are otherwise hardly *after*, or past persistent kyriarchal conditions, even as these differ in some key ways from the kyriarchal conditions faced by the Corinthian women prophets. Those times when I was still in classrooms with students, or in churches, synagogues, or the streets with friends, grappling with both these pasts and our presents, somehow feel like both yesterday and a lifetime ago. I hope enough of us survive this, because too many of us have not, underscoring that we should do much more than aspire to "get back to normal," given the dehumanizing and debilitating conditions that passed for normal before we completed this book about our *after*.
 Any energy or insight I have to contribute in either past or present times were made possible and, thus, irrevocably shaped by my time learning with and from Antoinette Wire and her work, which began most formally before the turning of this century, but preceded my move to Berkeley and Oakland by several years. My introduction to Dr. Wire came through the book that provokes this volume, *The Corinthian Women Prophets*, and it powerfully charged and deepened my commitment to intersectional and interdisciplinary feminist projects, informed by reflexive approaches to the rhetoric of the past and the present. Anne's ongoing generosity and curiosity inspires me and too many scholars to count, so this volume is one, compelling, yet inadequate indicator of this inspiration and broader impact, specifically of her landmark project, first published in 1990. This collection, then, is not a Festschrift per se, particularly since another student, colleague, and friend of Anne's (and then, in turn, of

mine, in a characteristic duplication of our advisor's generosity), Holly Hearon, capably steered one sterling example of this genre to publication in 2004. Rather, the thirtieth anniversary of its publication is an occasion to be both retrospective and prospective about a range of fields and approaches that *The Corinthian Women Prophets* have touched, or still might. The idea for the volume goes at least as far back as a special session at the 2015 Society of Biblical Literature Annual Meeting, cosponsored by the Feminist Hermeneutics of the Bible, Paul and Politics, and Rhetoric and New Testament program units, on the twenty-fifth anniversary of its publication. We then owe a particular debt to the steering committees of these three units, and particularly those who co-organized that session with me, Margaret Aymer and Todd Penner, for their own brands of generosity, with a number of colleagues (once more, including me, among several of the contributors here). Though several of those original session panelists confined their remarks to autobiographical observations, the excitement and energy in the room before, during, and after that session demonstrated the import of taking this moment as an opportunity to reflect and, frankly, push more in New Testament studies to grapple with the methods and results of Wire's work, and we immediately assembled a cohort of contributors to a potential volume. Beyond the fabulous colleagues whose work here made it through the twists and turns of these intervening years to arrive in your laps or tablets, then, I want also to acknowledge and thank Holly, Margaret, and Todd, the other panelists, and a couple of colleagues who were not able to continue to contribute here, mostly due to circumstances beyond our control. In short, the impact of *The Corinthian Women Prophets* is even greater than this collection or certainly this set of acknowledgments will be able to name.

Reflecting on *The Corinthian Women Prophets* reminds many of us that there is still so much more work to do, to understand the past differently and make a different present, so that there might still be an *after*, after all. The patient and persistent contributors to this collection know this all too well, and their work—here and elsewhere—open key vistas for scholars, students, and other interested readers and users of these materials. It has been my humbling honor and pleasure to work with and learn from all of them, and to present their essays in one place to concentrate our attention in exciting and challenging ways. Though the volume is dedicated to each of them, Shelly Matthews merits my own special mention, given her unflagging support and sage perspective, both professionally and personally, on this project among so many others. This simply would not have happened without her. We all owe a considerable thanks to Denise Kimber Buell, who offered indispensible insight and direction in several phases of this collection's development, even once she officially cycled off of the Semeia Studies editorial board. It is remarkable how often our feminist peers, mentors, and friends go above and beyond to support other feminist scholars—we count ourselves fortunate to be in that number. Readers solicited by this editorial board and Steed Davidson provided key feedback that improved both the parts and the whole, even as the responsibilities for any shortcomings or perhaps just foibles are those of the author and ultimately myself as the editor. As an editor on this project, I also need to thank Katherine Shaner and Kelsi Morrison-Atkins, for their well-placed words and insightful advice in key penultimate moments. In disorienting, distressing, and debilitating times like these, it is no small relief to collaborate, in renewed gratitude, with the entire team at SBL Press, including Bob Buller, Lindsay Lingo, Heather McMurray, and Nicole Tilford.

The final acknowledgments and dedication, though, belong to all of the contributors to this conversation, those whose essays grace these pages and those we hope will be (further) drawn into engaging after *The Corinthian Women Prophets* and its understated, yet ingenious, and ultimately inimitable author, who summons those women prophets and those still to come.

Abbreviations

2 Macc	2 Maccabees
4 Macc	4 Maccabees
AARAS	American Academy of Religion Academy Series
AB	Anchor Bible
AcBib	Academia Biblica
Agora	*Agora: Journal for metafysisk spekulasjon*
AJA	American Journal of Archaeology
Alleg. Interp.	Philo, *Allegorical Interpretation*
ANTC	Abingdon New Testament Commentaries
ar	Codex Ardmachanus
b	Codex Budapestiensis
BCS	The Bible and Cultural Studies
BCT	*The Bible & Critical Theory*
BibInt	Biblical Interpretation Series
BibInt	*Biblical Interpretation*
BibW	Bible World
BlTh	*Black Theology*
BNTC	Black's New Testament Commentaries
BPC	Biblical Performance Criticism
BRPBI	*Brill Research Perspectives in Biblical Interpretation*
CA	Crossing Aesthetics
ch(s).	chapter(s)
ClQ	*Classical Quarterly*
CO	Camera Obscura
ConBNT	Coniectanea Neotestamentica
Conj. praec.	Plutarch, *Conjugalia Pracepta*
Contr.	Seneca, *Controversiae*
CSSHS	Chicago Series on Sexuality, History, and Society
D 06	Codex Bezae Claromontanus
Dem.	Plutarch, *Demosthenes*

Dial. meretr.	Lucian, *Dialogi meretricii*
Diatr.	Epictetus, *Diatribai*
Doctr. chr.	Augustine, *De doctrina christiana*
E 07	Codex Basilensis
E 08	Codex Laudianus
Ecl.	Stobaeus, *Eclogae*
ECL	Early Christianity and Its Literature
Ep.	*Epistulae*
Eph.	Xenophon of Ephesus, *Ephesiaca*
Exord.	Demosthenes, *Exordia*
F	Codex Fuldensis
F 010	Codex Augiensis
Fug.	Lucian, *Fugitivi*
G 012	Codex Boernianus
Geog.	Strabo, *Geographica*
Germ.	Tacitus, *Germania*
GPBS	Global Perspectives on Biblical Scholarship
GRBS	*Greek, Roman, and Byzantine Studies*
HCS	Hellenistic Culture and Society
HDR	Harvard Dissertations in Religion
Hist.	Herodotus, *Historiae*, or Thucydides, *Historiae*
HR	*History of Religions*
HThKNT	Herders Theologischer Kommentar zum Neuen Testament
HTR	*Harvard Theological Review*
HTS	Harvard Theological Studies
HUT	Hermeneutische Untersuchungen zur Theologie
IAPATS	Intersections: Asian and Pacific American Transcultural Studies
Ign. *Pol.*	Ignatius, *To Polycarp*
Insurrections	Insurrections: Critical Studies in Religion, Politics, and Culture
Ios.	Philo, *De Iosepho*
JBL	*Journal of Biblical Literature*
JBTC	*Journal of Biblical Textual Criticism*
JECS	*Journal of Early Christian Studies*
JFSR	*Journal of Feminist Studies in Religion*
JHistSex	*Journal of the History of Sexuality*
JSNT	*Journal for the Study of the New Testament*

JSNTSup	Journal for the Study of the New Testament Supplement Series
JTS	*Journal of Theological Studies*
Jupp. trag.	Lucian, *Juppiter tragoedus*
KEK	Kritisch-exegetischer Kommentar über das Neue Testament
LCBI	Literary Currents in Biblical Interpretation
LD	*Lectio Difficilior*
LEC	Library of Early Christianity
LNTS	The Library of New Testament Studies
LXX	Septuagint
Metam.	Apuleius, *Metamorphoses*
MFLBMC	Mary Flexner Lectures of Bryn Mawr College
NA^{26}	*Novum Testamentum Graece*, Nestle-Aland, 26th ed.
NA^{28}	*Novum Testamentum Graece*, Nestle-Aland, 28th ed.
Neot	*Neotestamentica*
NICOT	New International Commentary on the Old Testament
NIGTC	New International Greek Testament Commentary
NKJV	New King James Version
NovTSup	Supplements to Novum Testamentum
NRSV	New Revised Standard Version
NTS	*New Testament Studies*
OBT	Overtures to Biblical Theology
OL	Old Latin
Opif.	Philo, *De opificio mundi*
Or.	Dio Chrysostom, Aelius Aristides
ORF	Oxford Readings in Feminism
PCC	Paul in Critical Contexts
PCP	Perspectives in Continental Philosophy
Pol.	Aristotle, *Politica*
PR	*Philosophy and Rhetoric*
Praec. ger. rei publ.	Plutarch, *Pracepta gerendae rei publicae*
pref.	preface
PTMS	Pittsburgh Theological Monograph Series
R	Codex Reginensis
Rep	*Representations*
RRA	Rhetoric of Religious Antiquity
Satyr.	Petronius, *Satyricon*

SBLDS	Society of Biblical Literature Dissertation Series
SBLSBS	Society of Biblical Literature Sources for Biblical Study
SC	Sexual Cultures
SCJ	Studies in Christianity and Judaism
SEAJT	*South East Asia Journal of Theology*
SemeiaSt	Semeia Studies
Signs	*Signs: Journal of Women in Culture and Society*
SocText	Social Text
SP	Sacra Pagina
SRC	*Scholarly and Research Communication*
Strom.	Clement of Alexandria, *Stromateis*
Suppl.	Euripides, *Supplices*
Syr. d.	Lucian, *De syria dea*
ThTo	*Theology Today*
TTC	Transdisciplinary Theological Colloquia
USQR	*Union Seminary Quarterly Review*
vg^{ms}	Latin Vulgate
WisC	Wisdom Commentaries
WP	*Women and Performance*
WUNT	Wissenschaftliche Untersuchungen zum Neuen Testament
ZNW	*Zeitschrift für die neutestamentliche Wissenschaft und die Kunde der älteren Kirche*

Still After:
Reintroducing the
Corinthian Women Prophets at Thirty

Joseph A. Marchal

Landmark works not only break new ground but also serve as points of orientation for years to come. Thirty years after its first publication, Antoinette Clark Wire's (1990) *The Corinthian Women Prophets* undoubtedly fits this description. The contributors to this volume demonstrate its impact on New Testament studies in at least two different ways. First, these essays critically assess and reimagine what did and can still happen *subsequent to* Paul's First Letter to the Corinthians as well as *since* Wire's book. Second, these essays pursue further historical and theoretical possibilities, often *in search of* marginalized people and innovative approaches. We are still after the Corinthian women prophets.

The anniversary of the publication of Wire's *Corinthian Women Prophets* may be the occasion for our reflections, but it is not the main purpose of this collection. Rather, this book is an opportunity to present the state of the field for the interrelated topics treated or since influenced by *The Corinthian Women Prophets*, as they shape the present *and future* of the interpretation of Paul's letters, history of assemblies (*ekklēsiai*), and rhetorical criticism, as well as feminist and other politically and ethically attuned approaches. The second decade of the twenty-first century has already proven to be a reflective time for scholars working within these subfields. Feminist and womanist scholars are increasingly interested in relating their work across the generations, rhetorical critics have begun (re)tracing their genealogies, and Pauline scholars continue to struggle to frame these epistles and their interpretations in light of imperial, racial, and religious differences. When starting over with the past, both proximate and distant—over the past three decades or further back two millennia—when looking for alternative pasts of the biblical and the biblical interpreter, in imagining alternative futures of these pasts or for our presents, it is hard to know where to begin. After Antoinette Clark Wire's *Corinthian Women Prophets*, there is still so much to say, both about the impact her work has had and might still have and about the opportunities missed in the scholarly reception of Wire's work.

Looking Back, After

Two collections, Amy Richlin's (2014) *Arguments with Silence* and Ross Shepard Kraemer's (2011) *Unreliable Witnesses*, provide ways to contextualize a retrospective look at what has come after *The Corinthian Women Prophets*. Richlin not only gathers some of the most important essays she wrote on the history of Roman women; she also revisits and recontextualizes each of them in their setting and in the scholarly conversation since then, often updating rather than simply reproducing the originals. Richlin does not mince words about the clear difficulties of historiography, particularly when concerned with women in the ancient Roman setting. Richlin's (2014, 27) shorthand "no women in the index" calls attention to both the persisting absence of ancient women as a topic and to the persisting absence of women scholars in the index (footnotes and body of an argument). Encountering so much silence from ancient women can be dispiriting (2, 16). That silence is also multiplied by the absence of women's scholarly work (often, but not always, on ancient women) in the discipline (16).

Strategies for Finding Ancient Women

Though it might be difficult to search for obscured women in ancient history, Richlin demonstrates why it is far from impossible. In fact, she details at least ten different strategies for looking for women:

1. "Use a wide range of evidence, from low to high" (Richlin 2014, 11).
2. In considering varied audiences, "look for ways in which different people talked back" (11).
3. Recognize how history writers write their own times.
4. Upon encountering ambiguity, "write two possible solutions" (11).

5. In looking for women, "when they are fragmentary, read fragmentation. Get off the beaten path to look for them" (11).
6. Do not be afraid to "use old tools that … stay useful" (11).
7. "Think about the co-implications of gender, class, and ethnicity," particularly given the enslaving systems of antiquity (11).
8. Approach systems "like religion as necessarily involving all kinds of people, including women" (11).
9. "Make time to broaden your skill base" (12).
10. "Don't take no for an answer. Argue with silence" (12).

I see these strategies reflected in some of the most compelling work on biblical texts and traditions. Indeed, feminists in biblical studies have themselves helped to create and contribute to these strategies, as Richlin (2014, 21, 23, 31, 305–7, 309, 314) repeatedly acknowledges. Richlin draws on the methods and the results of scholars such as Elisabeth Schüssler Fiorenza (1983) and Bernadette Brooten (1982) to highlight other ways of finding ancient women. From Schüssler Fiorenza, in particular, she derives a "combined model" that addresses both women's oppression and agency. Over time, Schüssler Fiorenza (1999, 48–53; 2001, 165–90) developed several hermeneutical strategies along these lines, focused on both suspicion and remembrance. Richlin (2014, 305) seems almost optimistic when she describes this approach: "A combined model would take into account the male nature of the sources while keeping a firm grip on the women hidden behind them."

I do not know whether Richlin has ever read *The Corinthian Women Prophets*, but if she did, she would see one exemplary way to work out this combination: to grapple with a problematic text, but read through its rhetoric to the other people behind the letter and within a longer exchange. This takes a certain kind of close reading of the letter, as an argument, but also specifically an argument shaped to convince an audience that included prophesying women.

Indeed, Wire's approach to reconstructing the Corinthian women prophets through the rhetoric of the Pauline letter independently deploys many of the strategies on Richlin's list. The evidence for their perspective may only be fragmentary, but Wire read that fragmentation and bolstered it by broadening her skills. Wire wanted to know more about the audience for this letter and to contest their presumed silence. In her own introduction, she explains: "The question is whether we can know anything about the Corinthian community beyond the writer's viewpoint. Groups such as the women prophets who come in for Paul's criticism would seem most likely to elude our grasp" (Wire 1990, 1). This (presumed) silence posed an interpretive challenge; as Wire puts it: "This impasse diverted me into the study of rhetoric" (1).

The methodology Wire adapted and developed still provokes, just as her intellectual adaptability inspires. Wire went beyond her translational work on the Nag Hammadi Library (1977; 1988) and turned away from parables and miracle stories (1978; 1981; 1983; 1986) to approach the Corinthian women prophets. This ongoing adaptability is also evident in Wire's later projects, focusing increasingly on the significance of orality and folklore for rethinking ancient storytellers (2002) and the gospels as composed in communal performance (2011). A passionate focus can only be maintained if one stays curious and flexible enough to follow where that curiosity leads in content and interpretive approach.[1]

Rhetoric and Ancient Realities

As Richlin did, Kraemer (2011, 31) takes the occasion to reflect on three decades of feminist scholarship on ancient Mediterranean women and assess the difficulties of our sources for them, the unreliability of our witnesses. Kraemer (1992) admits increased skepticism about the possibilities of historiography than in her previous work due to a number of studies that highlight the ideological function of our ancient sources. For example, Elizabeth Clark (1998) is pessimistic about the historical recovery of ancient women, arguing that texts primarily reflect males talking about females. Likewise, Kate Cooper (1996, 62) insists that a range of early Christian texts that depict women cannot be seen as useful evidence of women, also characterizing them primarily as literary devices in contests between men.[2] Kraemer (2011, 265) strikes a despairing note in her con-

---

1. For a more detailed listing of Wire's publications (up to 2002), see Hearon 2004, 245–48.

2. Often echoing the careful critique made by Shelly Matthews (2002), Kraemer (2011, 130–33) highlights that Cooper's approach is built on her assumption that the authorial intention of texts such as Acts of Paul and Thecla is accessible, particularly to her so that she could judge which ancient audiences read it correctly. For Cooper to reject the women who see Thecla as a precedent for their baptizing and teaching activities as a misreading, she must deny one clear, historically attested function of the Thecla story: "a history of women's alternative readings for their own purposes and interests" (Kraemer 2011, 131)! However, Cooper (2014, especially 1–39) is signifi-

clusion: "What women actually did, and how they themselves construed these practices, is all but unavailable to us."

If Kraemer seems to have succumbed under the weight of this kind of rhetoric-versus-reality argument, Wire's work and legacy offer a strong alternative. Wire (1990, 4) stresses that reconstruction can only proceed by attending to the audience, talking back, before, and after the delivery of a written text; indeed, she suggests in her introduction that "those in close disagreement with Paul should be the ones most accessible through his rhetoric." This approach does not duplicate the perspective of privileged texts as accurate social and historical descriptions, nor does it dismiss the force of the gender ideologies in ancient texts, nor does it despair in the face of the difficulties that both factors present, but it does suggest other ways to read behind and beyond them by acknowledging how they functioned rhetorically.

Rhetorical analysis, as Wire pursues it, does offer a means for historical reconstruction, even of the lives of those who themselves are silent in textual sources. A rhetor, a person trying to persuade others, cannot ignore or argue past their point of view, as Wire (1990, 3) explains: "In no detail can a persuader afford to ignore those who are to be persuaded." Rather, Wire shows how the audience must be gauged carefully: "The more intent the speaker is to persuade, the less he or she can afford to misjudge the audience. An accurate reading of the audience is integral to the self-interest of the persuader, all the more so when part of the audience stands in opposition" (4). Writers such as Paul and Justin have to proceed in ways plausible to their audiences. Certainly, this does not mean that we can simply read a historical situation as directly corresponding to the visions they call up. If one is curious about the people on the other side of the argument, such as ancient women, Wire delineates how one will need to factor for them within the rhetorical situation: "Everything spoken as description or analysis is first of all an address to the intended readers" (9). Here, Wire's approach resonates strongly with a wider set of feminist biblical interpreters who stress that texts are not primarily descriptive of an ancient reality but reflect attempts to be prescriptive of a reality they are seeking to construct (see especially Schüssler Fiorenza 1999). Wire's (1990, 3) focus on the address

---

cantly less skeptical about commenting on women's lives from ancient sources, such as 1 Corinthians, in her more popular work.

or adaptation to the audience, though, shapes a method for reading the arguments of texts such as 1 Corinthians closely and in a particular way. "Because everything spoken must be shaped for them, the measure of the audience as the speaker knows it can be read in the arguments that are chosen."

Wire proposes a way to know something about the women behind texts without dismissing the disposition and direction of these problematic sources. Indeed, it is in precisely attending to these details in materials such as Paul's letters that one learns about audiences, as Wire (1990, 9) especially stresses: "On whatever points Paul's persuasion is insistent and intense, showing he is not merely confirming their agreement, but struggling for their assent, one can assume some different and opposite point of view in Corinth from the one Paul is stating."

The rhetorical techniques Wire develops in *The Corinthian Women Prophets* could resolve some of the uncertainties of Kraemer's *Unreliable Witnesses*, and the resulting picture of these prophets would add texture to Kraemer's (2011, 39–40, 147–50, 249–253, 265–68) curiosity about celibate women. Wire's (see, e.g., 1990, 181–83) rhetorical analysis, for example, links the arguments about celibacy (in 1 Cor 7) and those on prophecy (in 1 Cor 11 and 14) to reflect further on how ancient celibate women would have construed their prayer, prophecy, and other embodied activities.

Where's Wire?

A volume dedicated to the impact of Wire's *Corinthian Women Prophets* also needs to acknowledge that this impact is less than it deserves to be. The absence of substantial engagement with its innovations and insights in some corners of biblical scholarship is part of a larger phenomenon, resonating with Richlin's phrase "no women in the index." Work on (and often by) women, especially featuring feminist approaches, is often siloed and marginalized, and not considered instructive about supposedly general topics (Parks 2019, 51). Sara Parks has labeled the relative absence or circumscribed use of feminist scholarship as the Brooten phenomenon, referring to "the way in which women's scholarship, and scholarship on women, doesn't cross the bridge into what is considered to be 'real' (i.e. male-centered) scholarship" (47). The question, Where is Wire? is one that needs to be asked for a surprising amount of work on women, on the Corinthians, and on rhetorical approaches. Wire's rhetorical procedure helps with problems of historiography, particularly around reconstructing women's roles and rethinking our scholarly approaches to texts such as Paul's First Letter to the Corinthians.

Given the importance of her turn to rhetoric to solve these problems, one might expect some significant traction for Wire's approach in the development of rhetorical criticism within New Testament studies. Where is Wire in rhetorical criticism? One barometer of the place of *The Corinthian Women Prophets* can be Troy Martin's (2014) collection *Genealogies of New Testament Rhetorical Criticism*. To be sure, the collection does not ignore feminist contributions to rhetorical criticism, given how Schüssler Fiorenza is included as one of the five potential pioneers of New Testament rhetorical criticism (see Lanci 2014). Even so, Wire and her landmark project are mentioned almost only in passing. Wire's work is treated as an important example of unconventional approaches highlighted by one of these pioneers, Wilhelm Wuellner (1995, 178; see Hester and Hester 2014, 112). Neither Wire nor Wuellner was willing to settle for more typical modes of analysis, and both refused to rely exclusively on classical sources of rhetoric in their consideration of biblical argumentation.

Unlike Wuellner, Wire completed a concentrated book-length treatment of a crucial text in New Testament studies. *The Corinthian Women Prophets* provides an immensely important example of a creative and constructive rhetorical methodology in practice. This is all but unacknowledged by most rhetorical critics. Todd Penner and Davina Lopez (2014, 264–65) seem aware that Wire was "written out of the genealogy," but they also only note this in passing, as their essay gives way to (apparently) more substantial, Eurocentric/pale malestream interlocutors and examples, moving from Nietzsche, through Foucault, to Burton Mack. Wire's work demonstrates that rhetorical approaches can and indeed should do much more than identify and classify the forms one can find in a rhetorical expression.[3]

Since the 1990s, much of rhetorical analysis has drifted in increasingly formalist directions, making it more often amenable to conservative, even apologist, purposes than the kinds of critical and creative projects represented by Wire or Wuellner, and any of those inspired by them. A cohort of scholars working on socio-rhetorical interpretation have blended aspects of social science and cognitive science with their observations

---

3. Another student of Wire (and Wuellner), Amador (1999, 48–57), warns rhetorical critics that this impulse toward taxonomizing and cataloguing makes rhetorical criticism bland and mechanistic.

about forms in order to pose and focus on rhetorolects (see, e.g., Robbins, von Thaden, and Bruehler 2016). In their next-order kind of formalism, they describe a constellation of *topoi* that can be catalogued into six early Christian rhetorolects (or perhaps we should just call them genres?): wisdom, prophetic, apocalyptic, precreation, miracle, and priestly. Such an approach reinforces and naturalizes these categories, when a project such as *The Corinthian Women Prophets* demonstrates how dynamic and porous these are, given the ways wisdom and apocalyptic can interact and blend to account for prophetic activity. Further, this approach seems to operate mostly to justify and endorse the functioning of these genres as working, rather than inquiring into their effects and how various groups would interact with them. This type of rhetorical criticism is, in the words of David Hester Amador (1999, 31), "a criticism which often avoids judgment or critique concerning the text's rhetorical power or performance. In other words, biblical rhetorical interpretation becomes a criticism that is often arrested before it fulfills its *critical* task." This drift likely accounts for why Martin's (2014) collection overlooks Wire's work and, in turn, demonstrates the importance of rethinking the trajectories of rhetorical criticism, even critique, as they intersect with, or *as*, politically and ethically attuned work.

Wire's project and the various angles taken on 1 Corinthians and other parts of the Pauline tradition in this volume present a distinctively richer and more dynamic take on biblical argumentation than often presented in narrower sorts of rhetorical approaches or appeals to social theory or social description. For instance, one prominent collection of essays that aims to reproduce the most important essays on the community at Corinth features no work from Wire (Adams and Horrell 2004). But this collection discusses her work and its results at several turns. This is more than we can say for a later volume focused on redescribing the Corinthians, which mentions Wire only once, in passing, deep within a footnote (Cameron and Miller 2011, 2 n. 5), along with Schüssler Fiorenza and Elizabeth Castelli (1991). For a scholarly collection ostensibly focused on the relations between Paul and the recipients of 1 Corinthians, it is stunning to find one of Richlin's silences: no women in the subject index. What else but a Wire version of the Brooten phenomenon could explain why works purporting to reconstruct the community at Corinth or redescribe the recipients or rethink the genealogies of rhetorical criticism, as these works promise, do not extensively engage Wire's work? Predominant pale malestream tendencies persist in many corners of biblical interpretation, and this gendered work is apparently still not considered relevant enough for this (apparently) general work.

Seeing where and how Wire's project is and is not taken up in feminist work also proves intriguing. Unfortunately, we also still need to ask, Where is Wire? in feminist hermeneutics as well as projects on ancient Mediterranean women. Wire and *The Corinthian Women Prophets* are nowhere to be found in a recent (and lengthy) overview of "Reading the Bible as a Feminist" (Koosed 2017). Koosed's concluding section, focused on feminist interpretations and uses of the creation stories, likely would have benefited from how Wire reconstructs the influence and reinterpretation of creation among the Corinthian women prophets. Wire is also absent from the first publications in a new feminist commentary series, the Wisdom Commentaries. There are scholarly women in the indexes of the 1 Thessalonians volume by Florence Morgan Gillman (2016) and 2 Thessalonians by Mary Ann Beavis and HyeRan Kim-Cragg (2016), but Wire is not among them. Wire's work even does not appear in the editor's introduction to the series, despite its survey of important examples of feminist biblical interpretation and methods, including rhetorical criticism and performance criticism (Reid 2016, xxvi–xxvii).[4]

Wire's methodology for 1 Corinthians could be helpfully applied to analyses of 1 Thessalonians, as she looks for how the rhetorics of 1 Corinthians are relevant for and adapted to the audience that included women, even when they are not explicitly mentioned.[5] There are no "women's passages" in 1 Corinthians; the entire letter is shaped to convince an audience, an audience that included women, likely in rather prominent roles. Gillman (2016, 8–9) likewise seeks the overlooked women in a letter that says "almost nothing" about women.[6] Some of the enthusiasm interpreters show toward the metaphors of children and nursing in 1 Thess 2 could be tempered by Wire's (1990, 41–47) treatment of the same images in 1 Cor 3, a context where Paul deploys these gendered terms to manage how the

---

4. This irony is only compounded when one recognizes Wire (2019) was preparing the (now-published) commentary on 2 Corinthians for this series. Indeed, other recent work, including Fox 2019, also focuses on 2 Corinthians, demonstrating how generative it could be to apply Wire's approach and results to the analysis of other Pauline letters.

5. For one example of reading for these invisible women, see Johnson-DeBaufre 2010.

6. See especially the strong case for not imagining women in the audience by Fatum 1993.

Corinthians experienced communal life differently than he wanted. This perspective on the terms could help illuminate the problems of conflict and difference with 1 Thessalonians. Additionally, the resonances between Paul's arguments for sexual self-control in 1 Thess 4 and 1 Cor 5–7 could suggest one explanation of the situation in the Thessalonian community: the women there were also withdrawing from sex and marriage (with men), exacerbating the men's need to acquire their own vessels. On any of these points of interest or import, further acquaintance with Wire's results and methods could bolster Gillman's efforts to provide a feminist commentary on another Pauline letter.

By contrast, Cynthia Briggs Kittredge and Claire Miller Colombo (2017) demonstrate the value of Wire's work beyond the study of 1 Corinthians and ancient Corinth in their commentary on Colossians. They find Wire's work helpful for approaching the hymn in Col 1:15–20 and the struggles behind the letter, even if it is deutero-Pauline. Just as Wire traces out competing visions of a life in community after baptism between Paul and the Corinthian women prophets, so Kittredge and Colombo (2017, 152) find competing visions in a baptismal theology of the hymns. Despite the household code and the persistent dynamics of othering at work in the letter, Wire's work is adaptable—the Corinthian women prophets underscore how we can read the letters for more sympathetic views on those who disagree with Paul. Kittredge and Colombo (2017, 173) see a similarity to how Wire reconstructed the women's theological position with their own task:

> She argues that women prophets in Corinth interpret their baptism as allowing them to participate in the resurrection and to withdraw from sexual relations in marriage. In our discussion, we extend Wire's argument to reconstruct a possible historical situation behind Colossians and argue that the baptismal self-understanding of women in the Colossian community was close to that of the women prophets in Corinth with whom Paul disputed. For example, both groups of women understood the resurrection to be a present reality that gave them freedom from the oppression of rulers and powers.

A similar procedure toward the rhetoric of these letters indicates places where the results of Wire's project can provide an illuminating comparison and extension. Wire's (2019) own commentary on 2 Corinthians will undoubtedly demonstrate the continued utility of this approach to other epistles and other assembly communities, as do the essays on 2 Corinthians by Arminta Fox and 1 Timothy by Anna Miller in this collection (see also Miller 2015; Fox 2019).

We could use more of these potential analogies or extensions, or at least similar approaches within the companion to Colossians in the commentary on Philippians (Tamez 2017). However, this kind of feminist rhetorical work—using reconstruction, resistance, or reading against the grain—does not appear (nor does Kittredge 1998, whose work along these lines with Philippians is indispensable). Tamez (2017, 3–35) reads the letter predominantly in the light of Paul's imprisonment; the topic dominates her introduction to the letter, with the women recipients receiving barely a page of discussion within it (19–20). A feminist approach more curious about these recipients (such as D'Angelo 1990; Kittredge 1998; 2003; or Marchal 2006; 2008) would likely ask a different set of questions, akin to those pursued by Wire. Tamez briefly considers how an injunction to humility would have reinforced the status quo for women and/or among enslaved people (noting Williams 2004), but instead chooses to project women as the problem in the community for a countercultural Paul.[7]

Wire's approach and results could be compelling sources of inspiration even for explicitly theological reading projects, such as the one pursued by Frances Taylor Gench (2015). Gench is sympathetic to the Corinthian women's challenges to gendered conventions and appeals to Wire in highlighting their claim for a new basis of honor through their baptism as a significant theological statement (65). Gench tries to stress multiple voices within communal debates and is animated about the women's prayer and prophecy (70, 78). Yet, Gench repeatedly frets about how the Corinthian women would have flouted conventions of propriety and appreciates Paul's (apparently) main concern about decency and order in the community (63–64, 75, 103). She remains puzzled about why these women do not share these views of modesty and respectability and why they acted in this way, when further engagement with Wire's study would have provided clear suggestions (as she acknowledges about the views after baptism). In reading Paul closely, Gench recognizes two different approaches to creation in 11:7–9 and 11:11–12, attributing both a "patriarchal" and an "egalitarian" approach to Paul (50–51). Unfortunately, this proposes Paul as the source of "two possible solutions" (as Richlin 2014, 11, suggests),

---

7. The reception and use of this hymn would have been further complicated by engagement with Briggs's (1989) classic essay (also missing in this commentary), as well as more recent work (such as Shaner 2017).

rather than tracing (as Wire 1990 did) how Paul is deploying not one of his theological commitments but the latter rhetorical strategy to appeal to the Corinthian women prophets while still aiming to limit their participation.

This circumscribed use of Wire also persists in scholarship on ancient women. Indeed, Kraemer (2011, 250) refers to Wire just once in a brief consideration of how prophecy is gendered, but her efforts could have been complemented and even expanded by greater interaction with the results and the approaches of *The Corinthian Women Prophets*. Not only would Kraemer (2011, 251; see also Økland's essay in this collection) have reasons to doubt her presumption that 1 Cor 14:33–36 is an interpolation by a later author and be able to fill out her picture of the celibate women, but she could have elaborated on some of her precise perspectives on the problems of gender and history. In her opening methodological reflections, she proposes: "Alternative reading strategies, although not denying that authors have intentions and purposes, refuse to privilege authorial intentions and purposes. Instead, they attend to other things: to seeing the ways in which texts function regardless of authorial intention" (Kraemer 2011, 9). Kraemer refuses to reduce meaning to matters of intentionality and thus turns to a modified poststructuralism. She aims to strike a balance, recognizing but not remaining with the point of view of a text, but she could have pursued the perspective of the audience with the approach Wire develops. At times, Kraemer draws close to this angle, as when she reconsiders Justin Martyr's account of a Roman matron who sought to lead a new life of celibacy (and proceeds in close correspondence to the arguments in 1 Cor 7:12–16). The rhetoricity of Justin's account does not immediately preclude anything of historical use for our purposes, particularly because "he expects his readers to find it plausible, appealing to a social dynamic that they will recognize and affirm" (Kraemer 2011, 54).

Kraemer's observations move toward Wire's principle of adaptation to the audience, but there are no such efforts in other places. For instance, like Wire and Schüssler Fiorenza, Susan Hylen (2019, 15–16) also focuses on the rhetorical aims of the texts she surveys. Yet, unlike these feminist scholars, the analysis remains at this level, doing little to read against the grain of these texts or to read the arguments for the audiences they aim to reach and persuade. Hylen's technique is to discern the sources' rhetorical goals and demonstrate how much they are consonant with Roman conventions. Yet, it becomes harder to explain the motivations of both Paul and the Corinthian women prophets if all of this is so common and conventional. Writing and delivering letters took some effort in the

Roman imperial context so, if everyone's activity was simply conforming to common expectations, what was the necessity for the letter? Hylen's work shares, with works such as Martin (1995), a studied inattention or just lack of curiosity about the women in the Corinthian assembly or their own interests or rationales for doing things such as prophesying.

These gaps could be addressed, even in part, by following Wire's (1990, 62–66) suggestions that the Corinthian women's status would have been low on most indicators and mixed on only one (free or enslaved). Their relatively lower status would have affected their evaluation of a variety of embodied activities (celibacy, prayer, and prophecy among them), and begins to account for how Paul and the Corinthian women prophets develop different visions of life in the assembly community (as a gain or a loss, see 62–69). Their visions cannot be seen as primarily consonant, and the women's lower status would provide a different historical texture to questions about women's roles in and out of marriage and prophesying uncovered or withdrawing from sex and marriage (with men).[8] This lack of interest, even occlusion, is stark, given the importance of women's roles for explaining 1 Cor 11 or the importance of 1 Cor 11 for accounting for women's roles, and the manifest benefits of the careful rhetorical analysis of the letter performed in light of these women by Wire (1990) that preceded these works, first by several years and now by several decades.

Evasions and Projections

Other scholars' limited and at times fraught interactions with *The Corinthian Women Prophets* reflect, then, some of the broader dynamics at work in biblical interpretation, among feminists and beyond them. Indeed, certain patterns of evasion or projection occur when one's approach chooses to identify first with Paul's perspective and does not try to account for what one might learn about the women prophets or gain from considering Wire's approach to them and the letter. The circumscribed or conflicted use of Wire's project among a number of these interpreters might have more to do with the fact that, as Schüssler Fiorenza (2000, 44) has observed, most interpreters of Paul tend to identify primarily (or even exclusively) with him: "The rhetoric of Pauline interpreters continues not only to identify themselves with Paul but also to see Paul as identical

---

8. For further reflections on the potential motivations (of both scholars and of prophetic females in Corinth), see Matthews 2015, as well as her essay in this collection.

with 'his' communities, postulating that Paul was the powerful creator and unquestioned leader of the communities to whom he writes." These tendencies of identification, between the interpreter and Paul as well as between Paul and the assembly communities, obstruct our abilities to conceptualize and discuss the other voices in these communities, including women: "identifying Paul's discourses with those of the communities to whom he writes and thereby suppressing and eradicating the historical voices and multiplex visions that differ from Paul's" (48). Not only do we lose the potential perspectives of women and or among the enslaved and marginalized, and thus some of the nuance and complexity of these ancient assemblies, but the tendency of these operations also encourages interpreters to pass over or evade the violent rhetorics and politics of othering in the letters (45, 50).

The rhetorical analyses Wire performs in the body of the study are important for showing how 1 Corinthians is building on a series of arguments in each section—explaining the moves that appear to be in tension (for some) as actually fitting into an overarching plan for addressing the prophetic women there. Further, the approach itself to the letter, as an example of rhetoric, should qualify tendencies toward identification with Paul. Wire (1990, 10) notes that within some (Christian) theological traditions, "every study begins and ends with the assumption that Paul's view is normative," and, thus, "our interpreters remain bound by their heritage in Protestant Orthodoxy to cast these opponents negatively in order to affirm Paul." Yet, as Wire highlights, this is not what Paul would have expected and is not the kind of occasion that sparked the writing of Paul's letters. The function of the letter is to persuade or convince. This should alter the default and often unexamined assumption of interpreters who tend to presume that Paul was *already* authoritative (already Saint Paul) and his arguments always already accepted—then or now. Such an assumption seems to misunderstand how these letters function. As Wire argues in her introduction: "Because an argument Paul makes cannot be rejected as unconvincing, it also cannot convince. In this way the authority we attribute to Paul prevents him from persuading us" (10). Wire convincingly explains that such an assumption is actually a disservice to Paul and the manifest effort he expended to persuade through these letters (9–11). This presumption ignores what the letters are and what its author appears to have intended to do in and through them. Wire highlights: "The letters do not claim to be authoritative in their own right or this argument would be redundant" (10). Paul's arguments do not assume agreement or his own unquestionable authority in advance; on the contrary, Wire shows how "Paul expects controversy—provokes it in fact" (11).

This politics of identification often leads to various evasions and projections in the treatment of biblical texts and traditions, particularly as scholars increasingly seek to develop more intersectional approaches and address multiple, interlocking modes of power. Brigitte Kahl (2010) has commendably proposed recontextualizing Paul's struggle against the law as a challenge to Roman imperial law rather than against some (ostensible) Jewish legalism. Yet, this bold thesis reflects some clear limits because of Kahl's primary identification with the figure of Paul. For instance, she opens her work by highlighting how it will help reimagine Paul, and when she describes those scholars with whom she disagrees (in the single reference to Wire in the entire work), she labels them as "Paul-critical" (3–5, 305–6). Yet, Kahl's project would have been better served to try to read for perspectives besides Paul's in the Galatian communities. Instead, when Kahl (15, 247) encounters Paul's most polemical, overtly hostile, and just plain angry letter, she chooses to solve this problem by constructing an opponent that (justifiably) provokes Paul's more authentically anti-imperial stance. Kahl preserves Paul's perspective that these shadowy others are perversely focused on flesh, when these differences in bodily strategies could just be reflecting varieties of negotiating resistance to reigning gender and sexual scripts in an embattled context. In trying to promote an apparently inclusive, progressive, and freedom-loving Paul, she avoids the letter's fraught argumentation about gender and sexuality and displaces the problem onto the (constructed) opposition. This avoidance is nearly complete when it comes to thinking further about Galatian women, rather than Paul. Indeed, despite Kahl's capacious and detailed index there is no entry for women in *Galatians Re-imagined*.

Like Kahl, Kathy Ehrensperger (2004, 188) is both concerned about the utility of our approaches to Paul's letters for contemporary issues and primarily identified with Paul, claiming "the apostle as a source of inspiration and a model for a feminist perspective." Ehrensperger (2007, 193–96) occasionally admits but then minimizes Paul's arguments in support of gendered hierarchies and slavery as "limited challenges," while prioritizing and stressing what she sees as more important parts of these letters. The only way Paul could work as a feminist inspiration and model, then, is if one could isolate and separate the truly important aspects from the rest of his letters. Ehrensperger hopes that Paul can be a paragon of mutuality, enlisted on behalf of women now, since he presents himself as working for the good of the marginalized and the weak in his letter to the Romans. However, this image only holds if one focuses on Rom 14–15 in particular ways (Ehrensperger 2004, 181–94) and avoids the existence and interrelation of texts about women and/or sexuality, including Rom 1:18–2:11 and 16:1–16. Ehrensperger can only claim that Paul generates "a theology of mutuality in the context of relationships of people who are different" (194), with an occasional reference to Rom 1:12, if she ignores the neighboring and much longer rhetoric of violent judgment, in which a set of others who reflect intertwined gender, sexual, racial, and religious difference will be punished and executed in 1:18–32, and a massive study of the women targeted by this rhetoric (Brooten 1996). At one point Ehrensperger (2007, 127–31) even tries to separate Paul's rhetoric of fatherhood in 1 Cor 4 from the dynamics of gender and sexuality. Not only does this involve bracketing the deployment of a similar stereotype of the violently condemned gender, sexual, racial, and religious other (in 1 Cor 5–6; see Ivarsson 2007), but it requires Ehrensperger to ignore Paul's claims to divine power and the threat of impending violence over his children (4:20–21). This bracketing is consistent with Ehrensperger's efforts to evade the troubling arguments for (additional and interrelated) gendered hierarchies in 1 Cor 11 and 14, as already noted.

Such efforts to isolate one aspect as distinctively redeeming about the figure of Paul, bequeathing a positive ethic to women now, ignore so many of the arguments of the person posed as a paragon. These interpretive moves look increasingly like an evasion or cover for the perpetuation of violent and oppressive structures, and demonstrate a surprising yet profound lack of interest or concern about women and others targeted with such arguments. A strategy that tries to separate snippets of mutuality or limited but benevolent power ignores key lessons derived from *The Corinthian Women Prophets* and demonstrates the continued value of Wire's work. Not surprisingly, then, Ehrensperger (2007, 187) notes Wire only once in a brief footnote. This omission (or intentional evasion?) is striking, particularly given Ehrensperger's (2004, 197) startling, inaccurate claim that "although Pauline studies from a feminist perspective are increasing, there still exists no book-length feminist interpretation of a Pauline letter," more than two decades after *The Corinthian Women Prophets*. This tendency to identify with Paul looks increasingly like a concerted commitment, with an accompanying set of evasions and problems for biblical interpreters.

These efforts to separate aspects and project onto others are slightly more convoluted versions of a previously popular strategy for evading or excusing aspects of Paul's letters by arguing that the offending passages are interpolations (see Walker 1975; 2001; Odell-Scott 1991). This strategy of evasion takes a slightly different form when some (at least feminist-allied) readers argue that Paul is quoting other people, with whom he disagrees, in passages such as 1 Cor 11:2–16 (one of those texts that Ehrensperger avoids and minimizes as a limited challenge). As with Kahl, these interpreters (such as Kim 2008; Peppiatt 2015; Bird 2015) require an awful opponent who espouses patriarchal and even misogynist attitudes if they are going to account for what is in 1 Cor 11:2–16 or 14:33–36. The interpretations of the first passage tend to turn on verse 11, which describes some kind of interdependence between man and woman (Bird 2015, 109; Peppiatt 2015, 102; Odell-Scott 1991, 179), rather than the hierarchy described in verses 3–9 (apparently the words of others). However, if any of these scholars had considered the rhetorical analysis of Wire (1990, 128; but see also 116–34), it would be easier to note that this verse "concedes less than it appears," particularly since it reinforces a specific kind of sexual differentiation.

If one identifies at all with a figure who creates or repeats arguments such as those found in 1 Corinthians, it is no wonder that interpreters have to construct (or project) an opposition of domineering men to evade or justify Paul, once more without concern for the women and (or among) the others targeted by such arguments. This disposition persists even when interpreters recognize at least some of the arguments Wire provides for considering texts such as 14:33–36 as original (considered at greater length in Økland's essay).[9] Peppiatt and Kim insist that these verses are also quotations of (other) oppressive males, as they fail to take into Wire's account for how the preceding arguments build up to this section. Thus, even when scholars such as Kim are aware of Wire's (1990, 229–32) compact yet convincing appendixes, acknowledging the arguments made against the interpolation of 14:34–35 in one breath, in the next they seem blithely unaware of or incurious about the appendix on apologies for Paul (204–5), another long-debated, widely practiced, yet problematic approach to dealing with interpretive difficulties.

---

9. Bird's (2015, 109–11) study, however, continues describing the passage as an interpolation.

Indeed, in many ways these observations about practices of identification and evasion, leading to claims about interpolation or opposition, are a rerun of critical conversations about Paul and politics at the turn of the millennium. The various contributions to Richard Horsley's (1997) *Paul and Empire* and then *Paul and Politics* (2000a) collections reflect rather similar shortcomings and critiques. In order to construct a vision of Paul as an anti-imperial force, interpreters such as Horsley (1998) and Neil Elliott (1994; but see also 2008) isolate some of these same passages and minimize the relevance of wider patterns that disrupt their image of Paul as an apocalyptic critic of the Roman imperial system. As a result, several feminist scholars, including Schüssler Fiorenza (2000), Kittredge (2000), Sheila Briggs (2000), and Wire herself (2000) highlight the evasions and simplifications of the emerging empire-critical approach, pointing to the silences around any complications of or capitulations to imperialism and its intersecting treatment of women, gender, slavery, and/or sexuality.[10]

Kittredge (2000) is the most pointed in underscoring the scandal of ignoring Wire's work (among others), and the corresponding incompletion and inadequacy of historical, rhetorical, or political visions that fail to grapple with this work. Kittredge stresses how feminist interpreters treating gender as a central category had *already* provided important qualifications to such views, qualifications that had been ignored in the enthusiasm for an anti-imperial apostle (103–4). She notes that "the challenge posed by Wire and other interpreters should be taken more thoroughly into account by those who read Paul in light of Roman imperial ideology" (104). Attention to gendered relations within Paul's arguments significantly complicates the more ambivalent place and legacy of the letters, as "Paul uses imperial language to both subvert and reinscribe the imperial system" (105). As with later approaches to those problematic passages treated as interpolations or limited challenges (above), empire-critical readers who ignore or evade feminist approaches cast them as just anomalies or sad ironies to the main point or overarching position of the letters (105). In tracing these problems, Kittredge (2000) foregrounds Wire (1990) in several ways, opening and closing with references to the book, and bluntly calling back to it by titling the essay "Corinthian Women Prophets and Paul's Argumentation in 1 Corinthians."

---

10. For a longer discussion of this history of engagements or occlusions, see Marchal 2008.

What Kittredge and these feminist interpreters point out, then, is that colleagues interested in contesting imperialism, or reconsidering Paul in such a light, did not even need to wait until this series of challenges and responses. Thus, interpreters inclined to identify with Paul did not need to notice *Paul and Politics* (Kittredge 2000) or the appendixes tucked into the back of *The Corinthian Women Prophets* for assistance in rethinking and reframing their approaches.

Wire's approach underscores the manifest advantages of beginning differently, particularly given the significant gaps generated by these recurrent tendencies toward identification—across a range of interpreters, among and beyond those considered here. The contributions of this collection suggest ways to be following after the Corinthian women prophets without these kinds of evasions or interpolations. Kittredge (2000, 108) moves toward this kind of conclusion in her exemplary essay:

> The contributions of those scholars who have focused on gender as a central category in 1 Corinthians make the situation of Paul in the Roman imperial context more complicated than simply Paul as radical, his opponents misguided, and his conservative attitudes about gender relations an ironic capitulation to imperial language or a mistaken impression caused by later interpolators. Their work points to further work that needs to be done on the interrelationship between gender hierarchy and imperial system in the ancient world.

While summing up several of the problems considered in this section, I also believe Kittredge was prophetic in asserting that works such as Wire's *Corinthian Women Prophets* point to further work along exciting, unexpected, intersectional, and reflexive trajectories, as evidenced by a range of approaches, analogies, and afterlives, reflected within and beyond what we have collected in *After the Corinthian Women Prophets*.

Prophetic Possibilities: Analogies and Afterlives?

What might be this further work? Where might Wire and *The Corinthian Women Prophets* go or do in an alternative present and future? While I gladly admit that I cannot imagine my own work without them, I believe a reconsideration of both the methods and the results of *The Corinthian Women Prophets* could inform and reshape virtually every area of interest in the odd, even arbitrary zone called Pauline studies.

Empire-critical work, for instance, would have to qualify its overwhelming and often enthusiastic tendency to identify Paul and his letters as anti-imperial in content and effect if it took the arguments of this work more seriously. First of all, simply thinking of women and other recipients of these letters alters not only the interpretive angle on, but also the political resonance of, Paul's intracommunal argumentation. Among other points worth reconsidering in the light of Wire's (1990, 65–71) careful reflections on these rhetorics, Paul perceives membership in these alternative assemblies as involving a loss in status, while others, such as the prophetic women of Corinth, saw their activities as reflecting a relative gain or rise. This would be especially the case if the recipients of the letters came from more marginalized people, rather than the elite who constituted or collaborated with both local and larger imperial forces. Wire's analysis demonstrates the problems with aligning the wisdom claims of the Corinthian women with elitism, an alignment Horsley (2000b; see also Wire 2000) has long favored, including in his arguments for an anti-imperial Paul. Indeed, Paul's arguments more closely correspond to the perspective of these elites when he mocks and minimizes these (albeit slight) gains in a period of imperial anxiety and instability.

The wavering lines of Jewish-gentile difference as reflected in these letters would also look rather differently if we considered the perspective and position of the Corinthian women prophets (and people like them) rather than focusing persistently, even perniciously, on those of Paul. However admirable it is to try to relocate Paul as an ancient (if idiosyncratic) Jew (see, for instance, Eisenbaum 2009; Nanos and Zetterholm 2015), treating Paul as the main arbiter for this loaded site of religious and racial difference, particularly as a Jewish apostle to the non-Jewish nations, reinforces the Western Protestant preference for Paul and its own, ostensibly corresponding but often problematic priorities (for both scholarship and society). These scholars present important complications of Paul's mission to these non-Jews as part of a new, minoritized Jewish communal subgroup (a Christ-oriented kind), within Judaisms, even as these assembly members remain non-Jews. While this approach challenges assumptions about conversion to this movement or group, it also calls for rethinking the potential meaning or motivation for gentiles joining or assembling in this way. Thus, it remains important to think further about the perspective and position of these people and not just Paul's particular perspective on them, particularly if one is trying to rethink and redescribe the ways people were negotiating in, around, and over these lines, or perhaps better, within these sometimes gray zones of affiliation and identification.[11] These Corinthians would seem especially intriguing, even illuminating, considering the ways they used wisdom, prophecy, and apocalyptic as modes of living and organizing in these Jewish subgroups as non-Jews, modes with powerful and historic resonances in Jewish communities and traditions. Would the Corinthian women prophets be a better option than Paul for exploring how these assembly members made sense of this new identity, for how to be non-Jews within a new, possibly unconventional or even countercultural Jewish subgroup? Such a focus could also alter the race-critical reception of Paul's letters, especially given the way Jewish-gentile difference has functioned as one marker of how to think about racial and ethnic difference in contemporary communities.

Such reflections could also, in turn, change more recent scholarly conversations about apocalyptic in Pauline studies (e.g., Gaventa 2013; Davis and Harink 2012). Wire long ago warned against ignoring what these prophetic women might have to say or show about apocalyptic and overplaying any difference between interests in wisdom, apocalyptic, and prophecy (see also Wright and Wills 2005). Wire (1990, 60) cautions: "It is better not to separate the Corinthians from the apocalyptic milieu more radically than Paul does, but instead to delineate how a wisdom-oriented apocalyptic scenario may have been conceived in Corinth." Many of the practices of these women, reflected in the letter, were likely also reflections of what time they thought it was, like and unlike Paul's apocalyptic scenario.[12] Of course, to notice these alternative ideas and practices, one has to be interested in people besides Paul. Scholarship on these topics may not have advanced as far or as widely as it could because work on those people addressed explicitly and implicitly by these letters has not developed as much as one would expect. In this way Wire's focus and the reception of *The Corinthian Women Prophets* end up demonstrating the overwhelming politics of identification in Pauline studies, or, stated another way, the semiautomatic theological sympathy for Paul over any other.

Other ways are possible; still other people besides Paul are worth our time and effort. Wire's work can be one guide for how to pursue them, both within and beyond the context of Corinth, as works by scholars such

---

11. For detailed reflections on the boundaries between Jews and gentiles, and the multiple ways gentiles could cross those boundaries, see Cohen 1999, especially 140–74.

12. For further reflections on this topic, see Marchal 2018.

as Kittredge (e.g., 2000; Kittredge and Colombo 2017) have already demonstrated. Wire's work can be taken up to new purposes, and looking for the Corinthian women prophets can help us see practices besides prophecy with greater nuance. Caroline Johnson Hodge's (2010, 19) approach to mixed marriage is much improved by attending to the arguments within 1 Cor 7:12–16 for the ways they yield multiple readings. Johnson Hodge builds most clearly on Wire's work on this chapter in her reconceptualization of the responses of wives in the Corinthian community to such attempts at persuasion, and the possibility that they may have been the people who prompted Paul's arguments. Indeed, Wire and Johnson Hodge (2010, 22) show some of the ways that a so-called mixed household would not have been a problem to these women, less perturbed by Pauline perspectives on purity, pollution, boundaries, and their gender and sexual behavior. This reading of a tricky portion of the letter is compelling.[13]

Still other ways are possible, for instance, if one mixes insights from Wire with careful and critical engagement of material culture. Laura Nasrallah repeatedly does so, often using ideas and approaches of Wire and other feminist scholars for thinking about those on the other side of Paul's arguments. For Nasrallah (2014; 2019), these others include not only women but also enslaved and freed people in Corinth. Nasrallah (2014, 55) builds on Wire to look for how the audience of 1 Corinthians would have heard its claims about slavery and manumission. This approach helps Nasrallah (2014, 62; 2019, 63) to think beyond Paul's intention and toward how people would have imagined themselves when they were cast as a thing and a commodity.[14] Nasrallah (2019, 172) also revisits Wire's reconstruction of a realized eschatology through baptism in a poignant rethinking of the politics of grief. Given both the grand-scale violence of colonization and its lingering, more quotidian effects (as reflected in higher rates of mortality, including for children), the letters indicate some of the

---

13. This reading contrasts with the way Johnson Hodge's (2007) major work on Paul's ethnic reasoning mostly traces how Paul deploys patrilineal descent in his approach to gentiles and their baptism, without recontextualization. Sadly, there are no entries for either Wire or women in this index, even as Wire showed how at least some women would have had a different sense of baptism.

14. Studies such as Marshall 2017 (43–71) also demonstrate how Wire's innovative work would have further applications in light of broader cultural perceptions, including within archaeological remains, even as it does not push past the perspective of Paul, as Nasrallah and others do.

ways the Corinthians negotiated alliances with the dead in the assembly. Indeed, such a reading is Nasrallah's (2019, 176) effort to summon a transhistorical affiliation with those who are minoritized, against the way Paul tried to constrain their practices. Such a haunting approach highlights both the affective resonances and potentially posthumanist directions flowing out of Wire's efforts to reach back and reconstruct the Corinthian women prophets. The latter is considered at greater length in both Cavan Concannon's essay and Wire's response in this collection, providing striking supplements to Denise Kimber Buell's (2009; 2010; 2014; 2017; 2019) persistent reflections on the haunting heritages of biblical studies and the lingering afterlives and effects of slavery, anti-Semitism, and colonialism. In retrospect, it is notable how much Wire's *Corinthian Women Prophets*, like other works of feminist historical reconstruction, is both affectively loaded and haunted. Her evocative goal is to restore a lost debate, "one that can reach its full stereophonic sound only when the silenced voices within and around it are recovered" (Wire 1990, 11). Such projects are searches for nearly lost specters, as Wire concludes: "But I do hear voices in the distance coming closer" (196).

These voices come closer, or we are better able to approach them, when we follow Wire's approach to the rhetoricity of all of our sources, as Nasrallah, Katherine Shaner, and Concannon do. Shaner (2018, xiv) proceeds by way of analogy with feminist approaches to women in order to deal with similar problems for the materials on and about ancient slavery. As Wire's approach stresses, one cannot read texts as descriptions of people's realities but as prescriptive attempts to persuade, mostly reflecting slaveholding perspectives (Shaner 2018, xiii–xiv). Shaner adds to this by foregrounding the rhetorical qualities of texts and other archaeological materials: "Such rhetorical constructions are not limited to textual sources. Visual images, architecture, city planning, and other kinds of archaeological materials all attempt to persuade and construct certain understandings of who women and enslaved persons are and how they should function in socio-civic spaces" (xvi). This approach, then, provides a better picture of enslaved participants in these communities, as neither simply oppressed nor liberated. Shaner reads against the grain of a variety of materials from Ephesus and their regular attempts to subordinate people, and resituates them within sites of debate and struggle for people who took both enslaved and leading roles in civic and religious groups. Concannon's (2014, 11–13) work, in this collection and elsewhere, proceeds by way of a similar analogy to the specters of women prophets. He turns our attention back to the

Corinthian recipients of Paul's letters, not on the women specifically but on how the Corinthians negotiated ethnicity in their context. In his use of feminist and postcolonial approaches to decenter Paul, Concannon follows the example of Wire, as well as Schüssler Fiorenza and Kittredge. He proposes: "By showing how Paul's rhetoric of ethnicity is one among many in Corinth, we might open up space to reimagine the Corinthian audiences that heard and interpreted Paul's writings" (Concannon 2014, 7). Through these works we see how Corinth continues to haunt interpreters after the Corinthian women prophets.

Such specters point toward multiple absent presences in these ancient assemblies and in our approaches to them. Mitzi Smith's (forthcoming) work on the letter stresses one such absence in Wire's project: the silence around freedwomen in Corinth. Certainly, Wire's (1990, 62–71) reconstruction includes reflections on slavery and enslaved people, most especially in her section on the social status of the women prophets. Of the six factors she considers in tracing their status, she notes that they would have been low on all of them and mixed only when it comes to free versus slave (65). Wire imagines that enslaved women would be among the prophets and admits that freed people complicate our accounting of free or enslaved people (e.g., 64, 65, 67, 69, 86, 181). Wire wonders about the difficulties an enslaved woman would face in attempting to withdraw from sex (181) and contrasts Paul's social status with that of an enslaved, gentile, married woman (67, 86). Yet, beyond a broad recognition of the ambiguous possibilities of freed people, Wire never specifically considers how the manumitted status of a woman would affect their practices and interactions (71). Smith introduces a womanist perspective to this absence in order to reimagine Chloe among enslaved and freed people.

Fittingly, Smith brings womanism and the Corinthian women prophets into closer interaction here and now, since womanist biblical interpretation also emerged around the same time that Wire was completing this project. Several recent overviews (Junior 2015; Smith 2015; Byron and Lovelace 2016) point to key works by Renita Weems (1988) and Clarice Martin (1990; 1991; and occasionally Grant 1989) as providing the first and founding examples of womanist biblical hermeneutics. This concurrence might be coincidental, but after thirty years it is safe to say that their convergence is long overdue. This delay may be due to some of the silences of *The Corinthian Women Prophets*, but a current period of expansion could help to create a critical mass for womanists and allies to assess and further synchronize our approaches to these epistles and their interpretations. Certainly, the turn to reconsider the rhetorics and impacts of race, ethnicity, and slavery within Pauline epistles and interpretations (with some assistance from Wire) demonstrates the need to attend more closely and carefully to the intersections of these dynamics with gender, sexuality, and embodiment, a series of intersections that womanists have particularly foregrounded for decades, starting from the perspective of Black women (see especially Junior 2015; Smith 2015; Byron and Lovelace 2016). Projects by Mitzi Smith, Shanell Smith, and Angela Parker, such as the ones I treat here, point to just a few of the directions these turns could take interpreters and users after the Corinthian women prophets.

In fact, Shanell Smith (2019) uses these prophetic women as one of her main examples in her womanist analysis of female agency in New Testament texts. In her approach, agency does not describe some idealized condition for an unfettered and perfectly free individual, as womanists experience and critically reflect on agency despite opposition and oppression. Smith's confident and continuous assertion that women have always been present and active resonates with (other) feminist historical and rhetorical approaches. In reflecting on her own experiences as an African American woman, she notes that "a rule is not created until it is needed"—the creation of prescriptions or regulations for women are a specific kind of evidence for women's activities (161). Shanell Smith's observation and argument echo the way Wire (1990, 4) reads the rhetorics of 1 Corinthians and her own assertion that "those in clear disagreement with Paul should be the ones most accessible through his rhetoric." Smith (2019, 161) builds on previous feminist work on the use of the baptismal formula found in Gal 3:28 (including Wire 1990; Schüssler Fiorenza 1983) in describing how women and enslaved people likely experienced a rise in status within these communities—a factor Wire stresses to discuss the differences in status and thus perspective between Paul and the Corinthian women. For Shanell Smith (2019, 163), women's prophetic activities are illuminating examples of women who did: "I will focus on women who *did* for the betterment of themselves or others despite those who told them otherwise."

Smith renames each of the texts she reconsiders given the negative ways in which they have been used, often to support a politics of respectability. The Corinthian women prophets become "God-speaking Women with Whipping Hair" (S. Smith 2019, 166). With other recent feminist approaches to 1 Cor 11 (such as Matthews 2015; Marchal 2014), Smith focuses on Paul's argument about women's hair (in 11:5) and the potential statement the women were making by unveiling. With Shelly Matthews

(2015), Smith (2019, 166) notes how these prophetic women troubled multiple social hierarchies including gender but also status or class. She does so by moving and connecting, with Wire, the arguments about women's speaking to the earlier arguments about marriage and celibacy. Smith shows yet again how 11:2–16 is neither an isolated irony nor a limited challenge. The various negative effects for the women prophets who would have been forced to marry to prevent men's sexual sins calls up similar associations for Black women's hair, their social roles, and male desire (S. Smith 2019, 167–68). Women continue to be cast as distractions or problems,[15] but Smith underscores that the Black body can be more than this, as a site of struggle and resistance. The analogy Smith stresses reflects how Black women can do whatever they want with their hair: "We can learn from the Corinthian women prophets, who obviously determined on their own to let their hair down and pray and prophesy regardless of what others were saying" (168). Smith encourages womanist (and allied) interpreters to read between the lines in order to resist the gendered and sexualized stereotypes within the prescriptive arguments of male writers.[16] "Paul tried to extinguish the fire in the Corinthian women's desire to worship with unbound hair, but he failed in execution because the women's resolution was to 'whip it like they just don't care'" (172).

Smith's (2019, 173) reading is both inspired and inspiring, even as I should not underplay how this womanist description of agency reflects ambivalence, of "women who do." The women did not just prophesy; they talked back, echoing other womanist reclamations of sass (M. Smith 2018) as well as Shanell Smith's (2014) previous work on the woman Babylon. In the latter, Shanell Smith proposes to read Revelation with a postcolonial womanist hermeneutics of ambi*veil*ence (50–72). Smith's neologism blends insights from Homi Bhabha's (1994) conceptualization of colonial ambivalence with the veil image in W. E. B. DuBois's (1986) description of African Americans' double consciousness to develop a specifically

---

15. For a related set of reflections, on veils and lap cloths in relation to Black church(es) and veiling passages (mostly in Hebrew Bible, with brief reflections on 2 Cor 3:13–16), see Russaw 2018.

16. For further reflection on such stereotypes of Black people and sexual politics surrounding Black bodies, see Collins 2005. Smith's linked reflections on the prophet called Jezebel, "The Competing Female Prophet in Revelation," as well as persistent concerns around the politics of respectability, suggest the potential of further engagement with Lomax 2018.

womanist lens.¹⁷ It is striking that no biblical interpreter has repositioned Paul's attempt to prescribe women's head covering in prayer and prophecy through DuBois's analysis of this veiling. Smith (2014, 58–61) underscores how this image is used to think through divided consciousness as both an effect on and strategy for Black folks. On the one hand, this seeing oneself through the eyes of the (oppressive) other is a forced veiling, an added layer or rift within self-consciousness, which Black people must overcome. On the other hand, veiled speech can also be a practice of self-protection, sorrowful expression, and even subversion (see DuBois 1986, 185–86; Morrison 1987). A range of interpreters, including myself (Marchal 2014; 2018), Wire (1990, 116–34, 220–22), and Smith (2019), have read the Corinthian women as speaking through their unveiling, but we have yet to read this moment in light of either of these potential resonances. These readings come close to the former sense, but typically without the import of overcoming or breaking through a specifically racialized double consciousness. Even further, the latter sense suggests ways that the Corinthian women could have spoken through reveiling, temporarily responding to prescriptions with a range of strategic aims, even as a veiled way of talking back. Indeed, as Muslim interpreters of veiling practices have long underscored, the Western fixation on women's clothing practices and especially on unveiling not only obscures a variety of sartorial and political strategies women might take but also (re)produces colonial and Orientalizing constructions of Europe and its gendered, sexualized, racialized, and religious others (Yeğenoğlu 1998, 39–67; Ahmed 1992, 144–68; Barlas 2002, 53–58, 158–66). This confluence raises disturbing questions about why many of us in the Global North continue to mark or otherwise argue for the progress of gender or sexual minorities by focusing on a passage on women's head covering practices such as 1 Cor 11:1–16 (see Tofighi 2017).

Smith (e.g., 2014, 1–4, 8–12, 66–67) helpfully embeds the veil within ambi*veil*ence to emphasize the potential of victimization and participation within empires, resistance and complicity both within biblical texts and among biblical interpreters. This also suggests more ambi*veil*ent readings of the Corinthian women prophets, beyond their persistence and resistance—the potential that they participated in the assemblies in a

---

17. Because Bhabha's apparatus has been (partially) adapted for several, if rather limited, attempts at empire-critical readings of Paul's letters (see, e.g., Stanley 2011), I focus above on how Smith's use of DuBois could provoke a more compelling set of strategies for interpretation.

number of ways, uncovered or potentially covered, differently from Paul but still akin to Kittredge's (2000, 105) characterization of his rhetorics as ways "to both subvert and reinscribe the imperial system." Recent work by Parker (2020) and Mitzi Smith (forthcoming) could be seen as something akin to ambi*veil*ent readings of 1 Corinthians.[18] Parker (2020), for instance, engages in a complex assessment of Paul's arguments about both his afflictions and authority (for a related engagement of Pauline body rhetoric, in Galatians, see Parker 2018). Though Paul's shameful display (in 1 Cor 4:6–21) reflects a feminized and minoritized body, given his Jewish ethnoracial identity, he uses these arguments to urge the Corinthian women prophets to sacrifice themselves for the sexual and marital advantage of males in the Corinthian assembly community. As Parker (2020, 78) explains it: "Paul reinstitutes a hierarchy that shames the women and places the blame of their men's morality squarely on women's shoulders." Because she remains persistently interested in how the Corinthian women prophets would have received any of the arguments she surveys from the letter, Parker astutely recognizes how Wire's reconstruction of the women's prayer and prophecy (explicitly in 1 Cor 11 and 14) is also connected to their withdrawal from sex (as stressed in 1 Cor 7). No wonder Parker (2020, 84 n. 17) shares the sentiment expressed in this introduction: "I am still shocked at recent scholarship that dismisses Wire or does not engage with her work at all."

Mitzi Smith proposes that the Chloe who appears in the opening chapter of the letter is a freedwoman, both leading in the community and still subject to the letter's stigmatizing. By situating Chloe as a freedwoman who owned enslaved people, Smith traces some of the complexities of the Roman imperial system of slavery and manumission. These strategies, though, hardly exhaust the possibilities for womanist approaches to these epistles and their interpretations. Mitzi Smith's book (forthcoming) imagines more about the experiences of the ancient Chloe in Corinth by using Aunt Chloe, a freed African slave, and other Black women named Chloe in the literature and legends of the antebellum American South (see Harper 1891). This strategy underscores how womanist interpretive practices have roots beyond conventional feminist and academic lineages, as the history of Black women preachers and users of biblical texts and traditions dem-

---

18. Mitzi Smith (2019) has also built on her engagement with Wire and recontextualization of Chloe in another recent essay, focused on 1 Cor 13.

onstrates (especially stressed in Junior 2015, 39–53). Indeed, elsewhere Smith (2011) examines how the spiritual autobiographies of Zilpha Elaw and Old Elizabeth legitimized their itinerant preaching in this era specifically through their interpretations of Galatians and Acts. These Black women appropriated Paul in directions besides the reinforcement of women's silence and American slavery. Like the Corinthian women prophets, they appealed to the baptismal formula preserved in Gal 3:28; yet, unlike them, these women preachers redeployed Pauline call narratives for themselves (M. Smith 2011, 298–308). Smith (308) posits: "Black female preachers used 'biblical reversal,' grounded in biblical radicalism, to turn ideas of socio-political inequality and male authority on its head."

Womanist interpretations require a further reckoning with more factors that would affect the Corinthian women prophets and our approaches after them. Of course, because slavery is a part of our past that is not yet past, womanists also reflect on incarceration and white supremacy's ongoing role in policing. One of the concluding notes of Shanell Smith's 2019 essay focuses on Black women's consistent striving against such injustices, while Mitzi Smith's (2018, 28–45) consideration of sass and talk back reads the Markan story of the Syrophoenician woman in light of the detention and death of Sandra Bland. This work, alongside a previous essay by contributor Arminta Fox (2017), could resituate the Corinthian women in similarly vulnerable positions, like Junia and Andronicus (Rom 16:7) or Prisca and Aquila (1 Cor 16:19; Rom 16:3–5). The latter pair was apparently known to the Corinthians, so focusing on them restores some further lost angles on this assembly community and decenters approaches to imprisonment centered exclusively on Paul (such as Tamez 2017). Margaret Aymer (2016) reads Rhoda (in Acts 12) darkly and ambi*veil*ently, as an enslaved girl, forced to migrate, vulnerable to sexual abuse, and speaking, yet dismissed. Aymer's (282) approach to Rhoda as both speaking and silenced, since she disappears from the text of Acts, could be one way to reconfigure our views of texts involving women's prophetic speech, as well as our cyclical debates about whether women's textual (in)visibility corresponds to their historical presence or absence. This approach certainly tempers some of our enthusiasm for the activity or agency of women prophets, while attending to some or all of the conditions Aymer outlines for Rhoda would multiply the factors for tracing and placing participants in these assemblies. Stacy Davis's (2016) careful consideration of the politics of singleness for a reading of Numbers 30 could profitably reframe approaches to the sexual practices of the Corinthians, some of whom were avoiding marriage, but without reinforcing either persistent stereotypes or calls for respectability (exercising their pull on Black bodies and feminist biblical interpreters such as Gench 2015).

When womanist work helps us to foreground matters of sexual respectability, propriety, and normativity in these epistles and interpretations, it also indicates the manifest potential of queer approaches to these materials. I have repeatedly made a case much like this for the relevance of 1 Corinthians and Wire's work, in particular, for queer biblical hermeneutics (as I do in this collection and Marchal 2011; 2014; 2018; 2020) but have hardly done so in a vacuum. Gillian Townsley (2017) produced the first and fabulous book-length queer treatment, not simply on 1 Corinthians but specifically on the various interpretations of 1 Cor 11:2–16. Townsley (2017, 22–23) highlights the importance of Wire's analysis for her developing queer hermeneutical approach; yet, unlike Wire and other feminist interpreters, Townsley worries not that the women have been silenced but that the Corinthian men have become invisible (50). Likely the most compelling portions of her project is to try to trace alternative, subdominant views of gender among the Corinthians and, then, to displace evangelical and frankly abusive interpretations by increasingly focusing on the daring potential of disidentifying with bodies cast as monstrous and disgusting. While I am not yet convinced that the primary rhetorical concern of this passage is with the Corinthian men, Townsley's project encourages us to consider a range of figures scholars typically avoid, a project strikingly consonant with Wire's efforts thirty years ago.

At several points in this introduction I consider the role of analogies, and many queer commentaries also proceed by way of analogy, if not always exact identification. When gay-affirmative interpreters turn to Paul's letters, they often try to apply Paul's argument against circumcision for (male) gentiles in Galatians to counter claims that homosexuals must change the way they are to count as Christians (see Siker 1994; Bohache 2000; Cheng 2006). From my perspective a better route is taken by Holly Hearon's (2006) entry on the Corinthian correspondence in *The Queer Bible Commentary*. Hearon multiplies the potential modes of analogy by explicitly attending to multiple voices, reflecting on the tensions within both the Corinthian and more recent LGBTIQ communities. Hearon's commentary works so well because it explicitly learned key lessons from feminist interpretations of these letters (such as Wire 1990), avoiding the pitfalls of identification and evasion to read against the grain of Paul's perspective.

The influence of these feminist insights and techniques in a number of essays appears in a recent queer collection, *Bodies on the Verge* (Marchal 2019), most especially in a playfully outrageous and incisive essay by Lindsey Guy (2019).[19] Guy repurposes the picture Wire drew of the Corinthian women prophets to think of how they might have responded to or embodied accusations of childishness or unprofitability in an intentionally antagonistic way. Like Hearon and other queer and feminist interpreters, Guy decenters Paul's perspective and reads against the grain of the letter, particularly the ways Paul casts the proper path for disrupting expectations of both sexuality and temporality. Guy notes the specifically apocalyptic temporality of Paul's arguments but is more interested in rethinking the Corinthian recipients as examples of failure and queer nonbelonging in the contractions of an imminent crisis. Still, Guy (2019, 64) is not interested in valorizing the Corinthian women prophets but in moving "toward queer antagonism, characterized by a skepticism toward the desirability of authority, leadership, or intelligibility altogether." These prophets then could have refused demands of progress, responsibility, productivity, maturity, and civilization. This queer reading facilitates an interrelated critique of heteronormativity and capitalism, against sexual and/as economic production. Childishness is not simply a Pauline accusation against these recipients but can be (and perhaps was) transformed "as a queer virtue" (Guy 2019, 72), their embrace of childishness and failure reflecting their different orientation to time. Instead of insisting on the legitimacy of their prophesying, as some feminist readings such as Wire's do, Guy is intrigued by the possibilities of resisting productivity and purpose as key to authority (76). Guy thus switches up the ways the letter casts prophesying without interpretation as unintelligible and fruitless (1 Cor 14:6–14).

Guy's approach, then, notes not only the gendered, sexualized, and economic aspects of this correspondence and the ancient community but joins a number of interpreters in reconsidering their racialized dynamics (especially of childishness and immaturity). Her attention to the rhetorics of civility and barbarism (as in 1 Cor 14:11; see Guy 2019, 79) resonates with recent work by Ekaputra Tupamahu (2018). Like Guy, Tupamahu builds on Wire's analysis of the letter as Paul's attempt to construct a certain communal order against apparent chaos (233). Tupamahu specifically focuses on the characteriza-

---

19. Other essays that interact with Wire toward queer ends (though to a lesser degree than Guy 2019) include Hartman 2019; Luckritz Marquis 2019; Twomey 2019.

tion of speaking in tongues but redirects the claims about unintelligibility to reconstruct a multilingual setting for the Corinthian assembly community. He resists the predominant politics of identification in order to trace and resist the letter's consonance with ancient discourses around barbarians as ethnoracial others marked by a linguistic difference (2018, 238). Paul's insistence on translation of these tongues is just another mode of silencing within "a discourse of othering against minority language speakers" (240). Yet, these tongues may signal a more capacious and diverse assembly of voices in the community within this racial-ethnic site of struggle.

Tupamahu and Guy, then, may help us to fill out some of the ways that members of the Corinthian assembly community (among others) negotiated their ethnoracial status within imperial-colonial dynamics. Their approaches could supplement Aymer's (2014, 54) initial yet still multifactored discussion of the different migrant strategies taken within New Testament texts, perhaps even tempering her claims that none of them advocated assimilation to imperial-colonial worldviews. Aymer helpfully locates these texts within a diasporic space where authors moved in uneasy tensions between host and homeland cultures (see also Agosto 2018 on migration). She proposes accommodation as the predominant migrant strategy within these texts, typified by Paul's letters among others, but the work of Wire, Guy, and Tupamahu raises further questions about how one might locate recipients of these texts, such as the Corinthian women prophets, as adopting different forms of liminality, separation, or even accommodation (Aymer 2014, 57–61). Similar supplements are also necessary for Tat-siong Benny Liew's (2008, especially 87–97) convincing way of accounting for Paul's projections onto gendered and sexualized others as a product of his own colonized consciousness. The Corinthian women prophets are among the targets of Paul's arguments "duplicating and displacing colonial abjection onto people who are also in different ways already subjected" (95). Yet, it still remains to consider how these targets themselves would have negotiated a similar colonized context, not as Jewish subjects but among other subject peoples.

Affects and Alternatives After

All of these reflect the still prophetic possibilities of an alternative past, present, and future. As I note on and off through this introduction, this range of approaches to the Corinthian women prophets underscores how affectively loaded our "after" is, was, and likely will be. To be sure, it is not hard to imagine the Corinthian assembly community as a vibrant, even raucous setting shaped by plenty of people including but besides Paul (see Kotrosits 2011, for instance).[20] More broadly, anger and outrage have long animated efforts at making women's history, as Richlin (2014) highlights in pointed and detailed fashion, particularly in terms of our epistemologies, results, and relational conclusions.[21] For some these call up dispiriting silences or potentially overwrought skepticisms. Others are anxious about or resistant to the codes of respectability, perhaps because they feel the pull of apostolic identification or have faced shaming. Sad ironies multiply the effects and affects of tyrannical texts. When looking after these women, we encounter both unreliable witnesses and passionate pursuits. Thus, evasions and projections can be met by dwelling on grief and other haunting absences for longer than a beat (Nasrallah 2019; Buell 2009; 2014). In Guy's hands the absurd ecstasy of the Corinthians refuses the appeals of both paranoia and cruel optimism (Sedgwick 2003; Berlant 2011). They afford opportunities for alternative (dis)identifications with those deemed monstrous or disgusting (see Townsley 2017, as well as Marchal 2020). Abjection affects colonized and racialized subjects in different ways, but women's hair-whipping and back-talking (with S. Smith 2019) signal still other approaches, aims, and alternatives. The contributions to this collection not only exemplify many of these key trajectories in contemporary biblical interpretation but also extend the reach—both of these trajectories and of Wire's landmark project. These lead us back into 1 Corinthians and beyond.

Thus, Shelly Matthews brings a thoughtfully intersectional feminist angle on the reception of scholarship on the voice and agency of wo/men,[22] especially in light of stark repetitions of silencing among both bib-

---

20. While I am briefly noting the affective investments of the work surveyed here, including the already affectively loaded language used within their approaches, I do not attempt to introduce the development of affect-oriented readings within biblical interpretation. For two excellent resources on affect theory and the Bible, see especially Kotrosits 2016; Black and Koosed 2019.

21. See further discussion above, but note especially Richlin's (2014, 292, 296) description of the "wrong because depressing" argument about women's historiography.

22. The neologisms wo/man and wo/men were coined by Elisabeth Schüssler Fiorenza (1999, ix) for the purpose of expanding and complicating the multiplicity of people included under the sign, including nondominant males, and women whose identities are informed by intersections of class, race, sexuality, citizenship, and other identifying markers. It is meant to highlight that there are differences among and

lical interpreters and broader publics. The woman whose head was shaven (in 1 Cor 11:5) is resituated within both the potential utopianism of the past (as reflected in 11:2–16; Gal 3:28) and contemporary interrogations of respectability around gender, status, sexuality, and ethnicity. Jorunn Økland tackles the seemingly traditional domain of textual criticism in order to trace a paratextual approach to the receptions of Wire's own careful refutations of the interpolation theories for another fraught passage, 1 Cor 14:34–35. Økland demonstrates how a turn to the history of transmission with manuscript studies, among broader material approaches, was both anticipated by Wire and could, in turn, expand the audience for feminist biblical criticism.

Concannon seeks out the spectral presence of some Corinthians, entangled within a network with the women prophets, by adapting posthumanist approaches. Such an approach attends to the ways Paul's claims about what might happen if an *ekklēsia* member slept with a prostitute (in 1 Cor 6:12–20) ascribe agencies to nonhuman entities, with relational and corporate effects on both individuals and collectives (of nonunified selves). My own essay connects such rhetorical approaches to feminist and queer perspectives on the affective and archival possibilities of ephemera, such as the fleeting references in these letters or even the letters themselves. In such light the untouching slogan, among other slogans quoted in 1 Corinthians, resonates with butch practices of untouchability and links the arguments between 7:1–40 and 11:2–16.

Pushing beyond 1 Corinthians, then, Arminta Fox develops a decentering and decolonizing feminist approach toward 2 Corinthians (particularly chs. 10–13), applying and expanding on Wire's picture of the Corinthian community. This letter still reflects on debates and differing views and practices among the Corinthians, and between Paul and the prophetic women, the latter resisting the former's claims around communal authority, gendered identity, and sexual deviance or promiscuity. Anna Miller, then, moves the discussion from 1 Corinthians to 1 Timothy, while contesting pictures that relegate women's political activities to domains marked as private. Both letters' efforts to gender speech and space in limiting ways signal another way to think about multiple publics, in which women's participation, authority, and speech in the *ekklēsia* are persistently

---

between women (they cannot be accurately defined in a monolithic or essentializing way), while underscoring that gendered terms are also used to define nonelite or subaltern males as (akin to) women.

marked by discernment and debate. In her closing response, Wire follows this range of new directions before focusing further on 2 Corinthians in light of the challenges of posthumanist critique. As all of these essays do, Wire reconsiders notions of agency and materiality and the shifts in Paul's arguments beyond subordination, conceding something akin to a rhizomatic interdependency of a multitude of actants, hinting toward the precarious possibilities of our present.

These, then, are prophetic possibilities. The essays in this collection evoke and interact with the many dynamic analogies, absences, and afterlives traced in this introduction, and they are but a few of the ways in which we are, still, after the Corinthian women prophets.

Works Cited

Adams, Edward, and David G. Horrell, eds. 2004. *Christianity at Corinth: The Quest for the Pauline Church*. Louisville: Westminster John Knox.

Agosto, Efraín. 2018. "Islands, Borders, and Migration: Reading Paul in Light of the Crisis in Puerto Rico." Pages 149–70 in *Latinxs, the Bible and Migration*. Edited by Efraín Agosto and Jacqueline Hidalgo. New York: Palgrave.

Ahmed, Leila. 1992. *Women and Gender in Islam: Historical Roots of a Modern Debate*. New Haven: Yale University Press.

Amador, J. David Hester. 1999. *Academic Constraints in Rhetorical Criticism of the New Testament: An Introduction to a Rhetoric of Power*. Sheffield: Sheffield Academic.

Aymer, Margaret. 2014. "Rootlessness and Community in Contexts of Diaspora." Pages 47–62 in *Fortress Commentary on the Bible: New Testament*. Edited by Margaret Aymer, Cynthia Briggs Kittredge, and David A. Sánchez. Minneapolis: Fortress.

———. 2016. "Outrageous, Audacious, Courageous, Willful: Reading the Enslaved Girl of Acts 12." Pages 265–89 in *Womanist Interpretations of the Bible: Expanding the Discourse*. Edited by Gay L. Byron and Vanessa Lovelace. SemeiaSt 85. Atlanta: SBL Press.

Barlas, Asma. 2002. *"Believing Women" in Islam: Unreading Patriarchal Interpretations of the Qur'an*. Austin: University of Texas Press.

Beavis, Mary Ann, and HyeRan Kim-Cragg. 2016. *2 Thessalonians*. WisC 52. Collegeville, MN: Liturgical Press.

Berlant, Lauren. 2011. *Cruel Optimism*. Durham, NC: Duke University Press.

Bhabha, Homi. 1994. *The Location of Culture*. New York: Routledge.
Bird, Jennifer Grace. 2015. *Permission Granted: Take the Bible into Your Own Hands*. Louisville: Westminster John Knox.
Black, Fiona C., and Jennifer L. Koosed, eds. 2019. *Reading with Feeling: Affect Theory and the Bible*. SemeiaSt 95. Atlanta: SBL Press.
Bohache, Thomas. 2000. "'To Cut or Not to Cut': Is Compulsory Heterosexuality a Prerequisite for Christianity?" Pages 227–39 in *Take Back the Word: A Queer Reading of the Bible*. Edited by Robert E. Goss and Mona West. Cleveland: Pilgrim.
Briggs, Sheila. 1989. "Can an Enslaved God Liberate? Hermeneutical Reflections on Philippians 2:6–11." *Semeia* 47:137–53.
———. 2000. "Paul on Bondage and Freedom in Imperial Roman Society." Pages 110–23 in *Paul and Politics: Ekklesia, Israel, Imperium, Interpretation; Essays in Honor of Krister Stendahl*. Edited by Richard A. Horsley. Harrisburg, PA: Trinity Press International.
Brooten, Bernadette J. 1982. *Women Leaders in the Ancient Synagogue: Inscriptional Evidence and Background Issues*. Chico, CA: Scholars Press.
———. 1996. *Love between Women: Early Christian Responses to Female Homoeroticism*. CSSHS. Chicago: University of Chicago Press.
Buell, Denise Kimber. 2009. "God's Own People: Specters of Race, Ethnicity, and Gender in Early Christian Studies." Pages 159–90 in *Prejudice and Christian Beginnings: Investigating Race, Gender, and Ethnicity in Early Christian Studies*. Edited by Elisabeth Schüssler Fiorenza and Laura Nasrallah. Minneapolis: Fortress.
———. 2010. "Cyborg Memories: An Impure History of Jesus." *BibInt* 18.4–5:313–41.
———. 2014. "Hauntology Meets Post-humanism: Some Payoffs for Biblical Studies." Pages 29–56 in *The Bible and Posthumanism*. Edited by Jennifer L. Koosed. SemeiaSt 74. Atlanta: Society of Biblical Literature.
———. 2017. "Embodied Temporalities: Gender, Ethnicity, and Other Transformations." Pages 454–76 in *The Bible and Feminism: Remapping the Field*. Edited by Yvonne Sherwood with the assistance of Anna Fisk. Oxford: Oxford University Press.
———. 2019. "Posthumanism." Pages 197–218 in *The Oxford Handbook of Gender and Sexuality in the New Testament*. Edited by Benjamin Dunning. Oxford: Oxford University Press.
Byron, Gay L., and Vanessa Lovelace, eds. 2016. *Womanist Interpretations of the Bible: Expanding the Discourse*. SemeiaSt 85. Atlanta: SBL Press.

Cameron, Ron, and Merrill P. Miller, eds. 2011. *Redescribing Paul and the Corinthians*. ECL 5. Atlanta: Society of Biblical Literature.
Castelli, Elizabeth A. 1991. *Imitating Paul: A Discourse of Power*. LCBI. Louisville: Westminster John Knox.
Cheng, Patrick S. 2006. "Galatians." Pages 624–29 in *The Queer Bible Commentary*. Edited by Deryn Guest, Robert E. Goss, Mona West, and Thomas Bohache. London: SCM.
Clark, Elizabeth A. 1998. "Holy Women, Holy Words: Early Christian Women, Social History, and the Linguistic Turn." *JECS* 6.3:413–30.
Cohen, Shaye J. D. 1999. *The Beginnings of Jewishness: Boundaries, Varieties, Uncertainties*. HCS 31. Berkeley: University of California Press.
Collins, Patricia Hill. 2005. *Black Sexual Politics: African Americans, Gender, and the New Racism*. New York: Routledge.
Concannon, Cavan W. 2014. *"When You Were Gentiles": Specters of Ethnicity in Roman Corinth and Paul's Corinthian Correspondence*. Synkrisis. New Haven: Yale University Press.
Cooper, Kate. 1996. *The Virgin and the Bride: Idealized Womanhood in Late Antiquity*. Cambridge: Harvard University Press.
———. 2014. *Band of Angels: The Forgotten World of Early Christian Women*. New York: Overlook.
D'Angelo, Mary Rose. 1990. "Women Partners in the New Testament." *JFSR* 6:65–86.
Davis, Joshua B., and Douglas Harink, eds. 2012. *Apocalyptic and the Future of Theology: With and beyond J. Louis Martyn*. Eugene, OR: Cascade.
Davis, Stacy. 2016. "The Invisible Women: Numbers 30 and the Politics of Singleness in African Communities." Pages 22–47 in *Womanist Interpretations of the Bible: Expanding the Discourse*. Edited by Gay L. Byron and Vanessa Lovelace. SemeiaSt 85. Atlanta: SBL Press.
Du Bois, W. E. B. 1986. *The Souls of Black Folk*. New York: Library of America.
Ehrensperger, Kathy. 2004. *That We May Be Mutually Encouraged: Feminism and the New Perspective in Pauline Studies*. New York: T&T Clark.
———. 2007. *Paul and the Dynamics of Power: Communication and Interaction in the Early Christ-Movement*. LNTS 325. London: T&T Clark.
Eisenbaum, Pamela. 2009. *Paul Was Not a Christian: The Original Message of a Misunderstood Apostle*. New York: HarperOne.
Elliott, Neil. 1994. *Liberating Paul: The Justice of God and the Politics of the Apostle*. Maryknoll, NY: Orbis.

———. 2008. *The Arrogance of Nations: Reading Romans in the Shadow of Empire*. PCC. Minneapolis: Fortress.

Fatum, Lone. 1993. "1 Thessalonians." Pages 250–62 in *Searching the Scriptures: A Feminist Commentary*. Edited by Elisabeth Schüssler Fiorenza with Ann Brock and Shelly Matthews. New York: Crossroad.

Fox, Arminta. 2017. "Decentering Paul, Contextualizing Crimes: Reading in Light of the Imprisoned." *JFSR* 33.2:37–54.

———. 2019. *Paul Decentered: Reading 2 Corinthians with the Corinthian Women*. PCC. Minneapolis: Lexington/Fortress Academic.

Gaventa, Beverly Roberts, ed. 2013. *Apocalyptic Paul: Cosmos and Anthropos in Romans 5–8*. Waco, TX: Baylor University Press.

Gench, Frances Taylor. 2015. *Encountering God in Tyrannical Texts: Reflections on Paul, Women, and the Authority of Scripture*. Louisville: Westminster John Knox.

Gillman, Florence M. 2016. *1 Thessalonians*. WisC 52. Collegeville, MN: Liturgical Press.

Grant, Jacquelyn. 1989. *White Women's Christ and Black Women's Jesus: Feminist Christology and Womanist Response*. Atlanta: Scholars Press.

Guy, Lindsey. 2019. "Wasting Time at the End of the World: Queer Failure, Unproductivity, and Unintelligibility in 1 Corinthians." Pages 63–82 in *Bodies on the Verge: Queering Pauline Epistles*. Edited by Joseph A. Marchal. SemeiaSt 93. Atlanta: SBL Press.

Harper, Frances E. Watkins. 1891. *Sketches of Southern Life*. Philadelphia: Ferguson.

Hartman, Midori E. 2019. "A Little Porneia Leavens the Whole: Queer(ing) Limits of Community in 1 Corinthians 5." Pages 143–63 in *Bodies on the Verge: Queering Pauline Epistles*. Edited by Joseph A. Marchal. SemeiaSt 93. Atlanta: SBL Press.

Hearon, Holly E, ed. 2004. *Distant Voices Drawing Near: Essays in Honor of Antoinette Clark Wire*. Collegeville, MN: Liturgical Press.

———. 2006. "1 and 2 Corinthians." Pages 606–23 in *The Queer Bible Commentary*. Edited by Deryn Guest, Robert E. Goss, Mona West, and Thomas Bohache. London: SCM.

Hester, James D., and J. David Hester. 2014. "The Contribution of Wilhelm Wuellner to New Testament Rhetorical Criticism." Pages 93–126 in *Genealogies of New Testament Rhetorical Criticism*. Edited by Troy W. Martin. Minneapolis: Fortress.

Horsley, Richard A., ed. 1997. *Paul and Empire: Religion and Power in Roman Imperial Society*. Harrisburg, PA: Trinity Press International.

———. 1998. *1 Corinthians*. ANTC. Nashville: Abingdon.

———, ed. 2000a. *Paul and Politics: Ekklesia, Israel, Imperium, Interpretation; Essays in Honor of Krister Stendahl*. Harrisburg, PA: Trinity Press International.

———. 2000b. "Rhetoric and Empire—and 1 Corinthians." Pages 72–102 in *Paul and Politics: Ekklesia, Israel, Imperium, Interpretation; Essays in Honor of Krister Stendahl*. Edited by Richard A. Horsley. Harrisburg, PA: Trinity Press International.

Hylen, Susan E. 2019. *Women in the New Testament World*. New York: Oxford University Press.

Ivarsson, Fredrik. 2007. "Vice Lists and Deviant Masculinity: The Rhetorical Function of 1 Corinthians 5:10–11 and 6:9–10." Pages 163–84 in *Mapping Gender in Ancient Religious Discourses*. Edited by Todd Penner and Caroline Vander Stichele. BibInt 84. Leiden: Brill.

Johnson-DeBaufre, Melanie. 2010. "'Gazing upon the Invisible': Archaeology, Historiography, and the Elusive Wo/men of 1 Thessalonians." Pages 73–108 in *From Roman to Early Christian Thessalonike: Studies in Religion and Archaeology*. Edited by Laura Nasrallah, Charalambos Bakirtzis, and Steven J. Friesen. Cambridge: Harvard University Press.

Johnson Hodge, Caroline. 2007. *If Sons, Then Heirs: A Study of Kinship and Ethnicity in the Letters of Paul*. New York: Oxford University Press.

———. 2010. "Married to an Unbeliever: Households, Hierarchies, and Holiness in 1 Corinthians 7:12–16." *HTR* 103:1–25.

Junior, Nyasha. 2015. *An Introduction to Womanist Biblical Interpretation*. Louisville: Westminster John Knox.

Kahl, Brigitte. 2010. *Galatians Re-imagined: Reading with the Eyes of the Vanquished*. PCC. Minneapolis: Fortress.

Kim, Yung Suk. 2008. *Christ's Body in Corinth: The Politics of a Metaphor*. PCC. Minneapolis: Fortress.

Kittredge, Cynthia Briggs. 1998. *Community and Authority: The Rhetoric of Obedience in the Pauline Tradition*. HTS 45. Harrisburg, PA: Trinity Press International.

———. 2000. "Corinthian Women Prophets and Paul's Argumentation in 1 Corinthians." Pages 103–9 in *Paul and Politics: Ekklesia, Israel, Imperium, Interpretation; Essays in Honor of Krister Stendahl*. Edited by Richard A. Horsley. Harrisburg, PA: Trinity Press International.

———. 2003. "Rethinking Authorship in the Letters of Paul: Elisabeth Schüssler Fiorenza's Model of Pauline Theology." Pages 318–33 in *Walk in the Ways of Wisdom: Essays in Honor of Elisabeth Schüssler*

Fiorenza. Edited by Shelly Matthews, Cynthia Briggs Kittredge, and Melanie Johnson-DeBaufre. Harrisburg, PA: Trinity Press International.

Kittredge, Cynthia Briggs, and Claire Miller Colombo. 2017. *Colossians*. WisC 51. Collegeville, MN: Liturgical Press.

Koosed, Jennifer L. 2017. "Reading the Bible as a Feminist." *BRPBI* 2.2:1–75.

Kotrosits, Maia. 2011. "The Rhetoric of Intimate Spaces: Affect and Performance in the Corinthian Correspondence." *USQR* 62:134–51.

———. 2016. "How Things Feel: Biblical Studies, Affect, and the (Im)Personal." *BRPBI* 1:1–53.

Kraemer, Ross Shepard. 1992. *Her Share of the Blessings: Women's Religions among Pagans, Jews, and Christians in the Greco-Roman World*. New York: Oxford University Press.

———. 2011. *Unreliable Witnesses: Religion, Gender, and History in the Greco-Roman Mediterranean*. New York: Oxford University Press.

Lanci, John R. 2014. "Elisabeth Schüssler Fiorenza and the Rhetoric and Ethic of Inquiry." Pages 133–63 in *Genealogies of New Testament Rhetorical Criticism*. Edited by Troy W. Martin. Minneapolis. Fortress.

Liew, Tat-Siong Benny. 2008. *What Is Asian American Biblical Hermeneutics? Reading the New Testament*. IAPATS. Honolulu: University of Hawaii Press.

Lomax, Tamura. 2018. *Jezebel Unhinged: Loosing the Black Female Body in Religion and Culture*. Durham, NC: Duke University Press.

Luckritz Marquis, Timothy. 2019. "Dionysus, Disidentifications, and Wandering Pauline Epiphanies." Pages 191–207 in *Bodies on the Verge: Queering Pauline Epistles*. Edited by Joseph A. Marchal. SemeiaSt 93. Atlanta: SBL Press.

Marchal, Joseph A. 2006. *Hierarchy, Unity, and Imitation: A Feminist Rhetorical Analysis of Power Dynamics in Paul's Letter to the Philippians*. AcBib 24. Atlanta: Society of Biblical Literature.

———. 2008. *The Politics of Heaven: Women, Gender, and Empire in the Study of Paul*. PCC. Minneapolis: Fortress.

———. 2011. "The Corinthian Women Prophets and Trans Activism: Rethinking Canonical Gender Claims." Pages 223–46 in *Bible Trouble: Queer Reading at the Boundaries of Biblical Scholarship*. Edited by Teresa J. Hornsby and Ken Stone. SemeiaSt 67. Atlanta: Society of Biblical Literature.

———. 2014. "Female Masculinity in Corinth?: Bodily Citations and the Drag of History." *Neot* 48:93–113.

———. 2018. "How Soon Is (This Apocalypse) Now?: Queer Velocities after a Corinthian Already and a Pauline Not Yet." Pages 45–67 in *Sexual Disorientations: Queer Temporalities, Affects, Theologies*. TTC. Edited by Kent L. Brintnall, Joseph A. Marchal, and Stephen D. Moore. New York: Fordham University Press.

———, ed. 2019. *Bodies on the Verge: Queering Pauline Epistles*. SemeiaSt 93. Atlanta: SBL Press.

———. 2020. *Appalling Bodies: Queer Figures before and after Paul's Letters*. New York: Oxford University Press.

Marshall, Jill E. 2017. *Women Praying and Prophesying in Corinth: Gender and Inspired Speech in First Corinthians*. WUNT 2/448. Tübingen: Mohr Siebeck.

Martin, Clarice J. 1990. "Womanist Interpretations of the New Testament: The Quest for Holistic and Inclusive Translation and Interpretation." *JFSR* 6.2:41–61.

———. 1991. "The *Haustafeln* (Household Codes) in African American Biblical Interpretation." Pages 206–31 in *Stony the Road We Trod: African American Biblical Interpretation*. Edited by Cain Hope Felder. Minneapolis: Fortress.

Martin, Dale B. 1995. *The Corinthian Body*. New Haven: Yale University Press.

Martin, Troy W., ed. 2014. *Genealogies of New Testament Rhetorical Criticism*. Minneapolis: Fortress.

Matthews, Shelly. 2002. "Thinking of Thecla: Issues in Feminist Historiography." *JFSR* 17.2:39–55.

———. 2015. "A Feminist Analysis of the Veiling Passage (1 Corinthians 11:2–16): Who Really Cares That Paul Was Not a Gender Egalitarian after All?" *LD* 2.

Miller, Anna C. 2015. *Corinthian Democracy: Democratic Discourse in 1 Corinthians*. PTMS 220. Eugene, OR: Pickwick.

Morrison, Toni. 1987. "The Site of Memory." Pages 101–24 in *Inventing the Truth: The Art and Craft of Memoir*. Edited by William Zinsser. Boston: Houghton Mifflin.

Nanos, Mark D., and Magnus Zetterholm, eds. 2015. *Paul within Judaism: Restoring the First-Century Context to the Apostle*. Minneapolis: Fortress.

Nasrallah, Laura Salah. 2014. "'You Were Bought with a Price': Freedpersons and Things in 1 Corinthians." Pages 54–73 in *Corinth in Contrast: Studies in Inequality*. Edited by Steven J. Friesen, Sarah A. James, and Daniel N. Schowaler. NovTSup 155. Leiden: Brill.

———. 2019. *Archaeology and the Letters of Paul*. New York: Oxford University Press.

Odell-Scott, David W. 1991. *A Post-patriarchal Christology*. AARAS 78. Atlanta: Scholars Press.

Parker, Angela N. 2018. "One Womanist's View of Racial Reconciliation in Galatians." *JFSR* 34.2:23–40.

———. 2020. "Feminized-Minoritized Paul? A Womanist Reading of Paul's Body in the Corinthian Context." Pages 71–87 in *Minoritized Women Reading Race and Ethnicity: Intersectional Approaches to Constructed Identity and Early Christian Texts*. Edited by Mitzi J. Smith and Jin Young Choi. Lanham, MD: Lexington.

Parks, Sara. 2019. "'The Brooten Phenomenon': Moving Women from the Margins in Second Temple and New Testament Scholarship." *BCT* 15:46–64.

Penner, Todd, and Davina C. Lopez. 2014. "Of Mappings and Men (and Women): Reflections on Rhetorical Genealogies." Pages 245–69 in *Genealogies of New Testament Rhetorical Criticism*. Edited by Troy W. Martin. Minneapolis. Fortress.

Peppiatt, Lucy. 2015. *Women and Worship at Corinth: Paul's Rhetorical Arguments in 1 Corinthians*. Eugene, OR: Cascade.

Reid, Barbara E. 2016. "Editor's Introduction to Wisdom Commentary: 'She Is a Breath of the Power of God' (Wis 7:25)." Pages xv–xxxiii in *1 Thessalonians; 2 Thessalonians*. By Florence M. Gillman; Mary Ann Beavis and HyeRan Kim-Cragg. WisC 52. Collegeville, MN: Liturgical Press.

Richlin, Amy. 2014. *Arguments with Silence: Writing the History of Roman Women*. Ann Arbor: University of Michigan Press.

Robbins, Vernon K., Robert H. von Thaden Jr., and Bart B. Bruehler, eds. 2016. *Foundations for Sociorhetorical Exploration: A Rhetoric of Religious Antiquity Reader*. RRA 4. Atlanta: SBL Press.

Russaw, Kimberly D. 2018. "Veils and Lap Cloths: The Great Cover Up of Bynum and the Bible in Black Churches." *BlTh* 16:248–62.

Schüssler Fiorenza, Elisabeth. 1983. *In Memory of Her: A Feminist Theological Reconstruction of Christian Origins*. New York: Crossroad.

———. 1999. *Rhetoric and Ethic: The Politics of Biblical Studies*. Minneapolis: Fortress.

———. 2000. "Paul and the Politics of Interpretation." Pages 40–57 in *Paul and Politics: Ekklesia, Israel, Imperium, Interpretation; Essays in Honor of Krister Stendahl*. Edited by Richard A. Horsley. Harrisburg, PA: Trinity Press International.

———. 2001. *Wisdom Ways: Introducing Feminist Biblical Interpretation*. Maryknoll, NY: Orbis.

Sedgwick, Eve Kosofsky. 2003. *Touching Feeling: Affect, Pedagogy, Performativity*. Series Q. Durham, NC: Duke University Press.

Shaner, Katherine A. 2017. "Seeing Rape and Robbery: *Harpagmos* and the Philippians Christ Hymn (Phil. 2:5–11)." *BibInt* 25:342–63.

———. 2018. *Enslaved Leadership in Early Christianity*. New York: Oxford University Press.

Siker, Jeffrey S. 1994. "Homosexual Christians, the Bible, and Gentile Inclusion: Confessions of a Repenting Heterosexist." Pages 179–94 in *Homosexuality in the Church: Both Sides of the Debate*. Edited by Jeffrey S. Siker. Louisville: Westminster John Knox.

Smith, Mitzi J. 2011. "'Unbossed and Unbought': Zilpha Elaw and Old Elizabeth and a Political Discourse of Origins." *BlTh* 9:287–311.

———. 2015. "Introduction." Pages 1–13 in *I Found God in Me: A Womanist Biblical Hermeneutics Reader*. Edited by Mitzi J. Smith. Eugene, OR: Cascade.

———. 2018. *Womanist Sass and Talk Back: Social (In)Justice, Intersectionality, and Biblical Interpretation*. Eugene, OR: Cascade.

———. 2019. "'Love Never Fails': Rereading 1 Corinthians 13 with a Womanist Hermeneutic of Love's Struggle." Pages 230–46 in *Theologies of Failure*. Edited by Roberto Sirvent and Duncan B. Reyburn. Eugene, OR: Cascade.

———. Forthcoming. *Chloe and Her People: A Womanist Reading of 1 Corinthians*. Eugene, OR: Cascade.

Smith, Shanell T. 2014. *The Woman Babylon and the Marks of Empire: Reading Revelation with a Postcolonial Womanist Hermeneutics of Ambiveilence*. Minneapolis: Fortress.

———. 2019. "'She Did That!': Female Agency in New Testament Texts—A Womanist Response." Pages 157–75 in *The Oxford Handbook of New Testament, Gender, and Sexuality*. Edited by Benjamin H. Dunning. New York: Oxford University Press.

Stanley, Christopher D., ed. 2011. *The Colonized Apostle: Paul through Postcolonial Eyes*. PCC. Minneapolis: Fortress.

Tamez, Elsa. 2017. *Philippians*. WisC 51. Collegeville, MN: Liturgical Press.

Tofighi, Fatima. 2017. "Unveiling the European Woman." Pages 477–92 in *The Bible and Feminism: Remapping the Field*. Edited by Yvonne Sherwood with Anna Fisk. London: Oxford University Press.

Townsley, Gillian. 2017. *The Straight Mind in Corinth: Queer Readings across 1 Corinthians 11:2–16*. SemeiaSt 88. Atlanta: SBL Press.

Tupamahu, Ekaputra. 2018. "Language Politics and the Constitution of Racialized Subjects in the Corinthian Church." *JSNT* 41:223–45.

Twomey, Jay. 2019. "Stranger in a Stranger World: Queering Paul with Michel Faber's *The Book of Strange New Things*." Pages 267–88 in *Bodies on the Verge: Queering Pauline Epistles*. Edited by Joseph A. Marchal. SemeiaSt 93. Atlanta: SBL Press.

Walker, William O., Jr. 1975. "1 Corinthians 11:2–16 and Paul's Views Regarding Women." *JBL* 94:94–100.

———. 2001. *Interpolations in the Pauline Letters*. JSNTSup 213. London: Sheffield Academic.

Weems, Renita J. 1988. *Just a Sister Away: A Womanist Vision of Women's Relationships in the Bible*. San Diego: LuraMedia.

Williams, Demetrius K. 2004. "Philippians." Pages 482–89 in *The Global Bible Commentary*. Edited by Daniel Patte. Nashville: Abingdon.

Wire, Antoinette Clark. 1977. "Introduction: Allogenes XI/3." Pages 490–91 in *The Nag Hammadi Library in English*. Edited by James M. Robinson. Philadelphia: Fortress.

———. 1978. "Structure of the Gospel Miracle Stories and Their Tellers." *Semeia* 11:83–113.

———. 1981. "The Miracle Story as the Whole Story." *SEAJT* 22:29–37.

———. 1983. *The Parable Is a Mirror*. Atlanta: Office of Women, General Assembly Mission Board, Presbyterian Church (USA).

———. 1986. "Ancient Miracle Stories and Women's Social World." *Forum* 2:77–84.

———. 1988. "Introduction: Allogenes XI/3; Revised and Extended." *The Nag Hammadi Library in English*. 2nd ed. Edited by James M. Robinson. Philadelphia: Fortress.

———. 1990. *The Corinthian Women Prophets: A Reconstruction through Paul's Rhetoric*. Minneapolis: Fortress.

———. 2000. "Response: The Politics of the Assembly in Corinth." Pages 124–29 in *Paul and Politics: Ekklesia, Israel, Imperium, Interpretation;*

Essays in Honor of Krister Stendahl. Edited by Richard A. Horsley. Harrisburg, PA: Trinity Press International.

———. 2002. *Holy Lives, Holy Deaths: A Close Hearing of Early Jewish Storytellers.* Leiden: Brill.

———. 2011. *The Case for Mark Composed in Performance.* BPC 3. Eugene, OR: Cascade.

———. 2019. *2 Corinthians.* WisC 48. Collegeville, MN: Liturgical Press.

Wright, Benjamin G., III, and Lawrence M. Wills, eds. 2005. *Conflicted Boundaries in Wisdom and Apocalypticism.* Atlanta: Society of Biblical Literature.

Wuellner, Wilhelm. 1995. "Rhetorical Criticism." Pages 149–86 in *The Postmodern Bible: The Bible and Culture Collective.* Edited by Elizabeth A. Castelli et al. New Haven: Yale University Press.

Yeğenoğlu, Meyda. 1998. *Colonial Fantasies: Towards a Feminist Reading of Orientalism.* Cambridge: Cambridge University Press.

Hearing Wo/men Prophets:
Intersections, Silences, Publics

Shelly Matthews

Antoinette Clark Wire's *Corinthian Women Prophets* has made possible a significant turn in the way we imagine the in-Christ assemblies of ancient Corinth, and by analogy, of all such assemblies scattered across the cities of the ancient Mediterranean world. This essay aims to honor Wire's contribution first by highlighting argumentative strands of her scholarship that are particularly salient—even if not fully understood and sometimes misread in its reception over the past thirty years. Second, it then offers an analysis of two major strands of her argument that bear reclaiming and repeating, in view of the resistance to them in mainstream scholarship: first, the proposal that ancient women in the Corinthian assembly had agency and voice, and second, the argument that these women were inspired by egalitarian ideals to struggle against hierarchies that privileged one social grouping over another. Finally, I reflect on shifts in scholarly discourse that have required reframing the historical situation in Corinth. Here I note that scholarship over the past thirty years especially in the fields of gender criticism, queer theory, and intersectional theory has expanded and complicated women as a category. Thus, I propose that it may be more apt to characterize the social agents of interest to us as the Corinthian *wo/men* prophets, with the slash indicating an expanded notion of the kinds of people included under the sign, across a fluid gender continuum, marked by race and class as well as gender.[1]

---

1. The neologisms *wo/man* and *wo/men* were coined by Elisabeth Schüssler Fiorenza (1999, ix) for the purpose of expanding and complicating the multiplicity of people included under the sign, including nondominant men, and women whose identities are informed by intersections of class, race, sexuality, citizenship, and other identifying markers.

Reviewing the Argument

Wire's *Corinthian Women Prophets* shifts the center of focus in the study of the Corinthian correspondence away from Paul, who is traditionally understood as having the *only* voice in the Corinthian assembly (and the divinely inspired, fully authoritative, canonized voice of sacred Scripture at that!), to others who deliberated with him in that ancient assembly. This is not to say that numerous Pauline scholars have not taken up the project of reconstructing the viewpoints of Paul's opponents, imagining what Corinthians did and said to provoke Paul's letter. For example, the once-popular view that Paul's opponents in Corinth were gnostics, or proto-gnostics engaging in libertine practices, has been recently revived by Jay Smith (2008). But Wire's reconstruction of those with whom Paul deliberates is to be distinguished from traditional Pauline scholarship for the following reasons:

First, building on the axiom adopted from Chaïm Perelman and Lucie Olbrechts-Tyteca's new rhetoric, that Paul's rhetoric aims to persuade, Wire takes as a given that Paul's rhetoric contains significant clues about the view of his interlocutors and subjects that rhetoric to a fine-grain analysis. Her working premise is that we find more in Paul's letters than the musings of one individual, since in order for any attempt at persuasion to be successful, speakers must shape their arguments to include at least some common ground with the audience addressed. This means that a persuasive argument presents more than merely one side of an argument, "because to argue is to gauge your audience as accurately as you can at every point, to use their language, to work from where they are in order to move them toward where you want them to be" (Wire 1990, 3).

Wire deftly identifies points of agreement between Paul and the Corinthian women prophets along with points of conflict, analyzing both the content of Paul's arguments and the *kinds* of arguments Paul makes and does not make. For instance, after unspooling a number of instances in which Paul argues "from community benefit," she notes:

> It is remarkable that Paul nowhere uses the argument from the common good explicitly to defend or restrict women.... Women's head covering is not said to benefit the church nor their bare heads to harm the church.... It may not have been credible to argue directly that the restricting or silencing of women was a benefit to the community. (Wire 1990, 19)

With respect to Paul's infamous hierarchical ordering of heads in 1 Cor 11:3 ("But I want you to know that of every man the head is Christ, and the head of woman is man, and the head of Christ is God" [Wire's translation]), she classifies this as an argument "from definition," noting that "defining seldom happens where meanings are not contested, and competing definitions are at least implied" (Wire 1990, 23). Such insights lead to credible historical reconstructions of the Corinthian women prophets as respected members of the in-Christ assemblies, with advocates and viewpoints that Paul himself must recognize as potent.

Second, Wire reconstructs the voices and actions of those with whom Paul argues sympathetically, as meriting a hearing from readers today. This is a significant shift from traditional scholarship where Paul's arguments are accepted as oracular truths, and his rhetorical attempts to denigrate and/or dismiss his opponents are accepted at face value. Reading Paul's insults and dismissals straightforwardly in the traditional way has led to negative conclusions that his audience is libertine (for example, Paul's concession and then qualification of the Corinthian slogan in 1 Cor 10:23, "All things are lawful," is read to make the case that the Corinthians have no ethics or morals) or enthusiast (for example, Paul's taunt in 1 Cor 4:8, "Already you have all you want! Already you have become rich!" [NRSV] leads to deriding the Corinthians for a misguided and excessive embrace of a realized eschatology). Wire instead suggests that such arguments by Paul owe to his attempt to corral into obedience and submission an assembly whose self-understanding is not libertine or enthusiast but rather confident and strong. She argues that the Corinthian women prophets embrace and celebrate their strength for positive theological reasons, noting that "they do not see the strong human being as a threat to God's glory by usurping God's wisdom." Instead, and in contrast to Paul, "They see the weak person as the threat to God's glory by rejecting God's gifts of wisdom and authority" (Wire 1990, 114–15).

Because New Testament scholars are often influenced by ancient associations of the city of Corinth with denizens of prostitutes and sexual flagrancy,[2] and because Paul's arguments concerning sexual immorality are often read to suggest that most every (free, male) Corinthian indulged in sexual relations with prostitutes and in-laws (cf. 1 Cor 5:1; 6:15), it is important to highlight

---

2. See, for instance, Strabo, *Geog.* 8.6.20, for the claim that the temple of Aphrodite owned more than one thousand temple prostitutes/enslaved people.

Wire's counterproposal concerning the commitment to sexual renunciation among the Corinthian women prophets. Pointing to the strong correlation in the ancient world between prophecy and celibacy, and the many kinds of women apparently committed to celibacy in Corinth (see 1 Cor 7 for Paul's directives pertaining to celibacy among women who are married, divorced, widowed, and engaged virgins), she argues that the Corinthian women defying social custom by refusing sexual relations must have constituted "a movement of considerable proportions, involving some kind of general calling" (Wire 1990, 81). From this vantage point, she regards Paul's references to sexual immorality in 1 Cor 5 and 6 not as indications of widespread misconduct among a sex-crazed assembly but rather as an attempt to shock his hearers, a strategy in support of his overarching concern to persuade the celibate women prophets to make themselves available for sexual union, whether with husbands whom they have deprived of conjugal relations or wish to divorce, or with fiancés they wish not to marry.

A key aspect of her sympathetic reconstruction of the Corinthian women prophets with whom Paul deliberates is her argument that the life experience of these women differs dramatically from Paul with respect to social status. Wire agrees with many scholars that Paul experiences his entry into the in-Christ community as a voluntary debasement, one in which he has cut himself off from his Pharisaic heritage and denied himself various privileges owing to his male gender and social standing as a free person. Paul's arguments privileging the foolishness of the cross and the "voluntary plunge of the divine" are understood in this scholarship as reflective of his own experience of self-emptying and status disavowal. Wire then proposes the original insight that the Corinthian women prophets would have experienced their entry into the in-Christ community differently from Paul, because of the value that would have been granted to them in response to their newly acquired spiritual gifts of prophecy and wisdom. As Wire (1990, 65) characterizes this shift:

> The women prophets' rank ... could be interpreted in terms of a new household, a new inheritance, even a new *cursus honorum* within the community. To the Corinthian housewife at the hearth, or slave at the churn, it would appear that the whole city were now coming to the door to see and hear, whether at her home or that of other women.

The social experience of starting quite low on a scale of social status and rising to a relatively higher standing leads them, differently from Paul, to articulate religious understandings that do not privilege debasement but rather elevation. Shifting from an emphasis on crucifixion to resurrection, their elevation is articulated as the experience of Christ's rising in them.[3]

This insight—that the conflicting theologies of Paul and the Corinthian women prophets owe to their different social experiences—leads to a broader understanding of the reasons for clashes between them. It allows us to reconstruct Paul's audience as complex human beings rather than as negative foils for Paul's own views, human beings with legitimate theological views, who lack neither a moral compass nor honorable intentions.[4]

Finally, to state the obvious, Wire focuses not on the Corinthian in-Christ assembly as a whole but on one segment of the assembly, the Corinthian women prophets.[5] With this focus on women's agency, struggle, and voice, Wire situates her work squarely within feminist biblical scholarship on two key fronts. First, it is in line with the project of historical reconstruction and retrieval articulated so forcefully in the watershed work of Elisabeth Schüssler Fiorenza (1983), *In Memory of Her*, in her proposal that it is both possible and methodologically sound to reconstruct the early Jesus movement with women at the center. Second, it moves in the direction of much feminist biblical scholarship, away from the single, charismatic, heroic male typically positioned at the center of scholarly narrative, and toward communities and movements, understood to be engaged in dialogical, cooperative struggle to articulate and live into the *basileia* of G-d.[6]

---

3. Wire, drawing on scholarship on the social world of Paul from the 1980s, adopts the view that Paul's social standing is "relatively high." More recent work on the question of poverty in the Pauline churches has challenged that assessment. See, e.g., Friesen 2004; Meggitt 1998.

4. See Wire (1990, 71) for the implications of these findings more broadly for the study of religion.

5. While Wire (1990, 9) is sometimes misread as assuming that Paul's audience consists *solely* of the Corinthian women prophets, she acknowledges that she is focusing on only one part of Paul's audience and invites further scholarship devoted to reconstructing other parts of this audience.

6. For inroads into scholarship that decenters Paul, see, e.g., Schüssler Fiorenza 2000; Johnson-DeBaufre and Nasrallah 2011; Kittredge 2003; Marchal 2015. See also arguments framing Paul as a "plural subject" or "collective author" in Tamez 1993, 48–49; Schottroff 1995, 207.

Women's Voice and Agency, in the Public Square and the Guild

On this thirtieth anniversary of its publication, we take the opportunity to underscore and reflect on the radical nature of Wire's proposal that women in the in-Christ assemblies of Corinth had voice and agency, and the strong headwinds both she and those of us who take up her work face in pressing for recognition of this fact. As classicist Mary Beard (2017) notes, attempts to exclude women from speaking in public are at least as old as Homer and deeply embedded in Western culture. To argue as Wire does that women did speak, prophesy, pray, and lead assemblies in prayer, or, as Anna Miller (2015) does, that Corinthian women were active discerning participants who understood themselves to be empowered to judge those who spoke as leaders, runs counter to the forceful prohibition of such voice and agency in 1 Cor 14:33b–36, and the infamous companion prohibition of women's speaking and teaching authority in 1 Tim 2:11–15. Under the weight of Western culture that takes women's public silence for granted, such biblical prohibitions are assumed to reflect that historical silence. Rather than being read as *prescriptions* for women's silence (and thus as historical indications of women's speech that authorities attempted to stifle), these passages are commonly read as *descriptions* of a situation already in place, a widespread situation of mute and passive women.

These headwinds in Western culture beating down on attempts to grant women social agency are directed not just at historical reconstructions of women in the ancient world but also at women leaders, including women biblical scholars, in our own time. In 2018, the second year of the US Republican presidential administration of Donald Trump, we learned that his cabinet regularly engages in Bible study and that in this first cabinet-level Bible study in the United States in more than one hundred years, no woman is allowed to lead. As BBC journalist Owen Amos (2018) reports, the conservative Christian organizer of the study, Ralph Drollinger, justifies this exclusion by explaining, "There is a prohibition of female leadership in marriage and female leadership in the church. And those are clear in scripture."

That women's speech concerning the Bible is prohibited in the highest echelons of political leadership of the most powerful Western democracy in the world in the early twenty-first century may surprise a more progressive audience of Bible readers and biblical scholars. But there is an analogous impulse to silence women's speech in the mainstream or malestream scholarly guild as well. The important edited volume on the Corinthian correspondence, *Redescribing Paul and the Corinthians*, published by the Society of Biblical Literature twenty years after *Corinthian Women Prophets* contains no entry on Wire's work in its bibliography (Cameron and Miller 2011). In this scholarly forum on Corinthians, Wire does not "teach or have authority over any man," but is rendered invisible, indeed, nonexistent. The absence of any acknowledgment of Wire's scholarship in this volume is particularly unsettling when it is considered alongside the otherwise erudite and generative contribution of Stanley Stowers. Stowers's (2011a, 141) hypotheses concerning the social field in which Paul operates in Corinth include the following remark: "I think it likely that the women criticized in in 1 Cor 11 and 14, as well as the tongue-speakers who, in Paul's view, need interpreters to make their speech intelligible, were non-elite resisters and experimenters whose practices were not necessarily Paul's and did not fit Paul's intellectualist mode." While Stowers's hypothesis is built on a different model of understanding the ancient world than Wire employs, still it might have been reinforced and supplemented by Wire's published work on this precise issue, work that reaches strikingly similar conclusions and precedes his own by several years. But as it stands, it reads as his own original insight, with no precedent in the scholarship of a woman in the guild, within a volume in which women's voices scarcely register.

Thus, thirty years later, it seems important to recognize that the interpretive shift Wire's book makes possible is not a shift that is inevitable or obvious. In order to safeguard the principles that women were historical agents in the ancient Corinthian assemblies and continue to have insight into public intellectual and/or spiritual matters in the present, we do well to recognize that such assertions defy common sense in patriarchal contexts. Rather than taking women's authoritative speech for granted, both in the present and in historical reconstruction, we do well to be vigilant about the resistance to such speech, both within the Christian Right and in the mainstream scholarly community.[7]

---

7. Notable interventions in feminist biblical scholarship confronting the Christian Right directly include Scholz 2011; Schüssler Fiorenza 2016, 75–93; Townsley 2017. For womanist intersectional analysis of the racist and sexist context of biblical interpretation, see M. Smith 2018. For a recent critical engagement with Wire's work, see Marshall 2017; S. Smith 2019.

Reconstructing History as Resistance and Struggle: The Significance of Galatians 3:28 in Corinth and Beyond

As with many feminist and other theoliberative approaches to Pauline literature, Wire focuses on Gal 3:28, widely understood as a pre-Pauline baptismal formula and as a source of inspiration for struggles against divisive social hierarchies within in-Christ assemblies.[8] Before turning to the interpretive payoff of such a reading of Gal 3:28, I summarize scholarship on the connection of this formula to Hellenistic Jewish interpretations of the Genesis creation accounts.

A strand of Platonically inflected Jewish interpretation of the Genesis creation stories, expressed in elaborate form in the writings of Paul's contemporary Philo of Alexandria, held that the creation accounts in Gen 1 and Gen 2 were of radically different natures. The spiritual human created according to Gen 1 was understood to be an ideal form, without material substance, not marked by the male-or-female gender binary and possessing immortality. The fleshly humans of Gen 2, in contrast, were understood to be formed from a palpable substance—the clay of the earth, gendered as either male or female, and constrained by mortality.[9]

We have evidence of early Jesus believers familiar with this interpretation of Gen 1 and 2, who speculated that in the messianic era people currently plagued by the material limitations of their earthly bodies, hierarchical gender distinctions, and death (the creatures of Gen 2) might be restored to the pristine state of the spiritual and androgynous *anthrōpos* created in Gen 1. Paul himself offers up his own speculation over the Messiah's role in restoring humanity to its ideal state with reference to creation motifs from Genesis in 1 Cor 15:49: "Just as we have borne the image of the man of dust [Gen 2], we will also bear the image of the man of heaven [Gen 1]" (NRSV). As I have argued previously, the insistence in some textual traditions of Eph 5:30 that the church is the body of Christ's *flesh and bone* represents a preference for the hierarchical gendered division of Gen 2, over against the nongendered spiritual creature of Gen 1, as a model for church order (Matthews 2017a).

---

8. For a foundational argument that Gal 3:28 reflects a pre-Pauline formula, see Betz 1979, 181–85.

9. See especially Philo, *Opif.* 134; *Alleg. Interp.* 1.31–32, along with the foundational studies of MacDonald 1987; Meeks 1974.

Not all of our ancient extant sources reflecting on Gen 1 and this myth of the primal androgyne read the story as having sociopolitical consequences.[10] But I argue both that the pre-Pauline baptismal formula cited in Gal 3:28 drew on the idea of humans restored to the primal spiritual state in the messianic era and that this formula had a leveling effect on social relations within Christ communities.[11] The formula, prefaced by an introductory reminder of baptism, reads:

> As many of you as were baptized into Christ have clothed yourselves with Christ.
> There is no longer Jew or Greek,
> there is no longer slave or free
> there is no longer male and female
> for all of you are one in Christ Jesus. (Gal 3:27–28 NRSV)

The influence of the creation according to Gen 1:27 on the proclamation of Gal 3:28c is seen both in the use of "male and female" rather than "man and woman," and in that the "neither nor" pattern of 3:28ab is disrupted by the use of the conjunction *and* at 3:28c.[12] Though Paul repeats a version of this formula, absent the gendered pair, in 1 Cor 12:13 ("For in one spirit we were all baptized into one body, whether Jews or Greeks, whether slaves or free, and were all given one spirit to drink"), it is evident that the question of the consequences of baptism into Christ with respect to the proclamation "no male and female" yet informs the arguments of this letter. This is clear from chapter 7, which addresses the Jew-Greek and slave-free pairings only briefly (vv. 18–24), while expanding at considerable length about proper relations between male and female (vv. 1–16, 25–40).

That proper interpretation of the Genesis creation stories with respect to gender relations in the messianic era preoccupies Paul and his Corinthian interlocutors is also evident from the arguments concerning the

---

10. MacDonald (1987) provides useful analysis of a span of readings of the "no male and female" saying, including, e.g., Clement of Alexandria's (*Strom.* 3.13.93) allegorizing male and female as vices to be overcome.

11. For a recent summary of the scholarship on Gal 3:28 and its implications for reading Pauline literature with respect to issues of spirit, flesh, and egalitarianism, see Matthews 2017a.

12. Gen 1:27 LXX: "And God created the human being; according to the image of God he made them; male and female he made them" (unless otherwise indicated, all translations are mine). See also Wire 1990, 124.

veiling of women who pray and prophesy in the assembly in 1 Cor 11:2–16. Put simply, the question at hand in this pericope seems to have been which creation story—Gen 1 or 2—governs the social roles of men and women in the assembly. Or, to ask another way, Do the gender hierarchies signified by veiling give way in some eschatological future, or are they abolished already for those baptized into Christ?[13] Paul's resort to the story of the Gen 2 creation of Adam *before* Eve in LXX and subsequent extracanonical elaborations as a justification for a hierarchy of man over woman in this passage (see especially vv. 7–10, 12) makes clear that he wishes for the Corinthian *ekklēsia* to be governed by the hierarchies established in this story. The Corinthian women prophets and their allies, in contrast, through resisting the argument for the veiling of women in the assembly, appear to insist that the restoration of creation to its primeval state, complete with the abolishment of gender distinction (no male and female), is the result of their baptism into Christ.[14]

Wire herself does not read 1 Cor 11:2–16 as an indication that the Corinthian women prophets understood baptism into Christ as a *restoration* of the primal androgynous state of Gen 1, according to the messianic speculation outlined above, stressing instead their experience of God's *new* creation. Yet, her interpretation of this passage converges with my arguments here at crucial points, particularly in her observation that the Corinthian women prophets would have read the baptismal formula as having social consequences, in the form of social leveling. She writes: "'Not male and female' was understood to mean overcoming in Christ a division cutting across the whole of society, which privileged one group at the expense of another.... It is an announcement of God's new act to create in Christ, God's image, a new reality lacking the privilege of male over female" (Wire 1990, 126). And further:

---

13. For one argument that the hierarchy instituted in the second creation story and its extrabiblical elaborations figures starkly in Paul's reasoning in 11:2–16, see BeDuhn 1999. Along with scholars holding arguments as disparate as Martin (1995, 229–49) and Wire (1990), BeDuhn concurs that Paul's disagreement with the Corinthian women over veiling centers on this question of timing.

14. In the ancient imagination the abolishment of the gender distinction may have been conceived in terms of an *androcentric* androgyny. See, e.g., Gilhus 1983; Castelli 1991. But, as argued in Matthews 2015, androcentric androgyny and egalitarian impulses are not necessarily mutually exclusive concepts.

> Rejecting all social privilege and social disadvantage, [the Corinthian women prophets] take on a single common identity in Christ and practice gifts of prayer and prophecy without regard to gender. The fact that Paul thinks it is necessary to redefine their identity in order to get the women prophets to cover their heads suggests that they have set aside a traditional covering because they are a new creation in God's image. (126)

Wire's arguments that the Corinthian women prophets embraced Gal 3:28 as a baptismal formula with social consequences aligns her scholarship with that of numerous feminists and others interested in ideological and theoliberative criticism of early Christian texts who make links between ancient and modern struggles for liberation. In her historical reconstruction, at least some of those baptized in Christ were captivated by ideas of justice, egalitarian impulses, and the reordering of power in this world, and wished to express these impulses through praying and prophesying unveiled in the assembly. As companion views we may cite again the groundbreaking arguments pertaining to this baptismal formula by Schüssler Fiorenza,[15] the arguments by Sheila Briggs (2004, 175–76) that we might apprehend the ghostly traces of such liberative impulses within the androcentric canon, or Richard Horsley's (2005, 394) proposal that we understand the Corinthian *ekklēsia* as "an international anti-imperial movement of communities … constituting an alternative society of justice, co-operation and mutuality." Though he assumes a posture of epistemic neutrality rather than a liberation stance, we may note that even Stowers's historical work on the Pauline assemblies likens these communities to philosophical schools engaged in radical social experimentation and countercultural practices. Consider, for instance, Stowers's (2011b, 235–36) observations on the philosopher Zeno's *Politeiea*:

> Zeno's state had no slavery, marriage, or traditional families. Men and women performed the same occupations, wore the same clothes, exercised naked together, and had sex and children in common…. There would be common meals and the glue that held the city together would be rational *erōs* and friendship. The second-century Christian Epiphanes, who tried to institute a community similar to Zeno's, believed that he was following Paul.

---

15. Schüssler Fiorenza's (1983) well-known position that Gal 3:28 is pre-Pauline and central to the antikyriarchal utopian impulse in the Jesus movement has been continually elaborated and refined (see, e.g., Schüssler Fiorenza 1999, 149–73; 2009).

With these scholars, we argue that historical reconstructions that imagine a significant number of early Jesus believers holding to utopian ideals and engaging in egalitarian struggles does better justice to our historical sources than reconstructions denying such ideals and struggles. Furthermore, memorializing those struggles and ideals is a means of honoring those ancient forbearers, while also serving as a source of inspiration for those engaged in modern struggles for justice.[16]

Yet, as with the basic conceptual point that wo/men had agency and voice in the ancient world (and should be granted such today), the argument that at least some ancient people held to utopian visions and engaged in struggles for justice is one that still meets strong opposition, some thirty years after Wire's work. Because the posture of epistemic neutrality is still the dominant posture of biblical scholars in the field, those who disclose their explicit interests in liberation remain at the margins of the discipline. Because scholars who benefit from the status quo have no need to reconstruct history in which challenges to the status quo are registered, it is common to see dismissals of historical reconstructions that trace out struggles for justice, including gender justice, as the product of anachronism or even as feminist fantasy.

It would be anachronistic to imagine that the ancients embraced Enlightenment notions of human rights, or to imagine that ancients could conceptualize utopian societies as perfectly egalitarian spaces. Thus, scholars of the ancient past interested in ancient egalitarian struggles do best to imagine egalitarianism on a continuum, to speak of egalitarian strivings, or utopian impulses, while always acknowledging that such strivings are, inevitably, caught up and constrained by the kyriarchal forces of the social worlds in which they are embedded—both then and now. To my knowledge, no serious feminist scholar engaged in historical reconstruction of early Christian communities makes bolder claims than this. Still, feminist historical reconstruction is often characterized as employing such unsophisticated conceptualizations as a means of refuting it.[17]

The vehemence with which some scholars insist that egalitarian struggles for justice could not have occurred in the ancient world may well be

---

16. On this point, see Hewitt 1995. Consider also Allen Callahan's (2000, 217) pithy observation that "In every historical moment, hegemony allows, overlooks, loses, forsakes, or concedes some free space which emancipatory strategies may exploit."

17. For further discussion of feminist biblical scholarship on ancient egalitarian ideals, and the resistance to such scholarship, see Beavis 2007; Matthews 2015.

fueled by the anxious recognition that to do so is to make value claims about the past and the present. As William Arnal has so eloquently argued in the context of historical Jesus research, such value claims are not in the interest of those who benefit from the status quo. As Arnal (1997, 317, emphasis original) puts it, in his reflections on why feminist and minoritized scholars readily refuse the "cloak of disinterest," while mainstream biblical scholarship typically adopt the posture of objectivity:

> What is ultimately at stake in the *desire* for objectivity [is] a desire to view the object of one's inquiry through the lens of things-as-they-are. The distinction between a fact and a value is itself not based on fact, but on a dichotomy between things as they are and things as one wishes them to be; the removal of so-called "value" from scholarship is really the removal of hope, something which is not central or necessary to the daily ideological work of the privileged. The ultimate value that undergirds the desire to avoid epistemic bias—hence the most basic and hidden epistemic bias of all—is the desire to conserve the world roughly as it is.

In line with others who engage in biblical scholarship while holding to the hope of a world with less suffering, in which divisions privileging one group at the expense of another are overcome, Wire imagines Gal 3:28 as inspiring ancient Corinthians to strive toward that utopian ideal.

From Women to Wo/men:
Troubling Gender Binaries, Recognizing Intersectional Identities, Clarifying the Enslaved's Plight

Above I highlight aspects of Wire's arguments that merit repetition, in view of the strong resistance posed by mainstream biblical scholarship to her important and challenging work. Here I consider shifts in scholarly discourse that have required reframing the historical situation in Corinth since the publication of *The Corinthian Women Prophets*.

Wire's work on women in Corinth from the 1990s assumes the gender binary as an adequate analytical frame for imagining ancient gender identities. Furthermore, while Wire takes some account of enslaved women's perspective in her work, *The Corinthian Women Prophets* did not give expansive attention to the historical situation of enslaved women in ancient Corinth. This is particularly so with respect to Paul's arguments for sexual purity and against *porneia*, given that enslaved people did not have the privilege of refusing the sexual advances of those who held power over them. Scholarship over the past thirty years in the fields of queer theory and intersectionality studies has challenged the adequacy of the gender binary in accounting for human experience of gender and sexuality, and complicated our understandings of how identity is constructed through intersections of gender and sexuality with class, status, ethnicity, and race. Alongside and sometimes intertwined with these approaches, scholarship on ancient slavery in the past thirty years has brought the situation of enslaved people into sharper focus, particularly with respect to their sexual vulnerability.

Since the publication of *The Corinthian Women Prophets*, Paul's reflections on sexual ethics in 1 Cor 5–7, including his assertion of the mutual exclusivity of the body of Christ on the one hand, and the prostitute/*pornē* on the other, along with his rhetorical exhortations to shun *porneia* (1 Cor 6:15–18), have been subject to sustained reflections by scholars recognizing the plight of the enslaved person as an object of sexual use in the ancient world.[18] Thus, Briggs challenged the focus of many Pauline scholars by raising questions about the sexual plight of the enslaved underclasses. She asks:

> If a slave prostitute were able to leave her brothel (and in some cases prostitutes were chained to their brothels), would she have been allowed to join the Christian community? Put in the language of 1 Corinthians 6, could the body of a slave prostitute be "a temple of the Holy Spirit" and could she become "one spirit" with Christ? (Briggs 2000, 115)

Jennifer Glancy (2002, 39–70) has posed a similar question, pressing the issue of whether the sexual use of enslaved people was considered morally neutral in Pauline assemblies or whether such enslaved people would have been prohibited from joining the assemblies on the grounds of sexual impurity.

The category of wo/men has also been complicated in recent scholarship on 1 Cor 11:2–16, Paul's arguments with respect to women veiling while praying or prophesying in the assembly. Here the focus has been

---

18. On 1 Corinthians specifically, see Briggs 2000. On slavery in the Pauline churches, see Glancy 2002, 39–70. For the sexual vulnerability of Onesimus, see Marchal 2011.

on 1 Cor 11:5, where Paul likens the woman who refuses to veil to the *exurēmenē*[19]—a woman whose head has been shaven.

Engaging with the work of Judith Butler (1990) and Jack Halberstam (1998), Joseph Marchal's analysis of the women refusing to veil in Corinth has taken us beyond the question of how the respectable women might have been shocked by Paul's introduction of the *exurēmenē* into his argument, to the question of what the Corinthian women prophets held in common with the figure of the *exurēmenē*. In Marchal's (2014, 101) felicitous phrasing, he asks what it means that these women are "repeating a shaving-esque practice rather than a covering practice." His answer is that in the repetitions and citations of masculinity by those refusing to veil in Corinth we might recognize a sort of "female masculinity"—that is, a reworking of, and thus resistance to, imperially scripted norms of masculinity.

While accepting the arguments of Marchal with respect to gender troubling, in my own analysis of 1 Cor 11:5 I have asked further whether the *exurēmenē* conjured by Paul suggests that Corinthian women prophets subverted not only gender norms but also the closely intertwined identity markers of status and race (Matthews 2017b).[20] A wo/man whose head was shorn or closely cropped was a multivalent signifier in the ancient world. The practice is associated with women who assumed countercultural postures of masculinity, as noted in Marchal (2014);[21] it was also a practice taken on by respectable women in periods of mourning, or on the assumption of particular religious vows.[22] Sometimes women's heads were shaven against their will, as a deliberate and violent act of shaming associated with accusations of adultery.[23] Furthermore, the forcibly shaven head (and sometimes the shaven and *branded* head) was a signifier of the shame

---

19. Because English has no one-word equivalent to the Greek feminine passive participle signifying one whose head has been shaven, I use the Greek term throughout this discussion.

20. It has often been argued that in Greco-Roman slavery, unlike trans-Atlantic slavery, race was not a factor. But more recent scholarship on slavery in antiquity challenges the idea that ancient slavery was devoid of racism. See, e.g., Isaac 2004, 170–94.

21. On this question, see also Lucian, *Dial. meretr.* 5.1–3; and the discussion of Brooten 1996, 51–53.

22. Examples of shaving as part of religious vows include those who practice the rites of Adonis at the Temple to Aphrodite at Byblos (Lucian, *Syr. d.* 6).

23. For example, Tacitus, *Germ.* 19.2; Dio Chrysostom, *Or.* 64.3; cf. Num 5:18.

and degradation of slavery.[24] Since Paul's rhetorical strategy in mentioning the *exurēmenē* is to shame the women prophets into veiling, and since he commands the shaving of those who resist (1 Cor 11:6), we may assume that Paul has these degraded categories of shorn women in view. Especially in these instances in which shaving is employed as a disciplinary tool to shame and debase, we confront a figure of obviously low status, possibly foreign or ethnically other, possibly even outside gender classification.[25]

Though Paul wishes to shock the Corinthian wo/men into veiling by conjuring the *exurēmenē* as the figure they embody in refusing to do so, we might ask whether this rhetorical strategy would have been convincing to them. Might the Corinthian wo/men prophets have regarded this insult as a badge of honor? As proof that by taking up a practice that effectually defined them in the eyes of the world as "one and the same as the *exurēmenē*," they were participating in God's strange reordering of power in the direction of the low and despised, that is to say, in the direction of God's "foolishness" (see 1 Cor 1:18-31)?

But even if one is not convinced that Paul's insult was ineffective, or that the Corinthian women prophets would have gladly embraced the *exurēmenē* into their own midst, it is worthwhile to contemplate why it goes without saying for Paul that the *exurēmenē*, like the prostitute of 1 Cor 6:16, functions as the other to the assembly of the saints. At the least, it should be noted that Paul's rhetoric of exclusion and othering with respect to these two figures stands in tension with his earlier exhortations in 1 Cor 1–4 celebrating the paradoxical divine elevation of those on the lowest end of the social ladder—that is, the refuse, and the "off-scouring" (1 Cor 4:13) of the world.

In short, in this section I introduce Paul's arguments concerning sexual purity and the prostitute/*pornē* in 1 Cor 5–6, along with the figure of the *exurēmenē* of 1 Cor 11:5, to illustrate ways in which the category

---

24. For the use of an enslaved person with shaved and branded head, see Herodotus, *Hist.* 5.35. Other references to shaven heads as the mark of an enslaved person include Apuleius, *Metam.* 9.12; Petronius, *Satyr.*103; Lucian, *Fug.* 27; Xenophon of Ephesus, *Eph.* 5.5.

25. For an argument that within the debased condition of US slavery gender assignments were confounded and even dissolved altogether, see Spillers 1987. This foundational essay by Spillers, a scholar of American literature, could be fruitfully mined for analogues by scholars theorizing gender in the context of ancient practices of extreme degradation, including slavery and crucifixion.

women has been interrogated since the publication of *The Corinthian Women Prophets*. Recognizing gender identity along a continuum rather than according to a simple binary, and recognizing gender as *performative* rather than a biological given, has enabled scholars to complicate reconstructions of the wo/men among Paul's interlocutors, including reconstructions of how they might have resisted his prescriptions concerning gender conformity. Attention to slave status, including recognition of the sexual vulnerability of enslaved people, has enabled reconstructions that emphasize the wide disparity between the implications of Paul's rhetoric for free women and for the enslaved. Attention not only to what might be called the respectable women Paul wishes to veil, but also to the shamed figure of the *exurēmenē* he invokes, heightens our awareness of the kinds of wo/men populating ancient Corinth and thus provides us with richer historical reconstructions of that social world.

Going Public?

To conclude, I reflect on the question of how Wire's scholarship, along with theoliberative scholarship closely aligned with Wire's, might receive a wider audience, including an audience with progressive religious activists and practitioners outside the academy.[26] Many a biblical reader might respond that the chief roadblock standing in the way of a wider appreciation of Wire's work is her act of decentering Paul, a move that inevitably challenges the authority of one of the most influential voices within the New Testament. Anticipating that objection in the introduction to *The Corinthian Women Prophets*, Wire (1990, 10) perspicaciously reminds that since Paul writes to persuade, we do better justice to his arguments if we take them seriously enough to weigh them rather than bow to them without question:

> Paul claims a hearing on the basis of insistent arguments from God's calling, from revelation, from hard work and from modeling Christ. The letters do not claim to be authoritative in their own right or this argument would be redundant. For Paul, such intrinsic authority belongs to

---

26. This question is inspired by Schüssler Fiorenza's (2016, 65–122) recent account of the widespread success of conservative and fundamentalist religious thinking at the level of grassroots activism, and how feminists might counter that discourse with a more liberative and egalitarian religious vision, also in grassroots activist settings.

God alone. Paul's letters' authority depends on free assent to Paul's arguments because they are convincing.

Foregrounding this argument might be an effective strategy for persuading audiences beyond the classroom—whether in confessional settings or in the public square—of the merits of Wire's groundbreaking reading of Paul's First Letter to the Corinthians.

When advocating for the merits of *weighing* Paul's words and recognizing the validity of other voices in Corinth, it might also be effective to first identify points of agreement between Paul and his interlocutors. This brings us, as indicated already above, to passages in Paul's letter that speak directly to the question of the divine reordering of power, whereby those who are most despised and degraded in the world are chosen and elevated through Christ, who is for this audience the "Wisdom of God" (1 Cor 1:25–30). I identify this proclamation as one that is agreeable to both Paul and the wo/men prophets, one that may also be agreeable to those engaged in contemporary liberative practices in marginalized and minoritized communities.[27] From this point of agreement with respect to this first chapter of 1 Corinthians—that divine Wisdom chooses to elevate those most despised in the world—challenges may be raised of Paul himself, about whether he lives up to his own rhetoric of divine reordering and inclusion as his letter progresses. Are not the *pornē* of 1 Cor 6:16 and the *exurēmenē* of 1Cor 11:5 also among those despised by the world, but embraced by the foolishness of God, and if so, who is Paul to condemn them?

Works Cited

Amos, Owen. 2018. BBC News. "Inside the White House Bible Study Group." https://tinyurl.com/SBL06102a. April 8.

Arnal, William E. 1997. "Making and Re-making the Jesus-Sign: Contemporary Markings on the Body of Christ." Pages 308–19 in *Whose Historical Jesus?* Edited by William E. Arnal and Michel Desjardins. SCJ 7. Waterloo, ON: Wilfrid Laurier University Press.

Beard, Mary. 2017. *Women and Power: A Manifesto*. New York: Liveright.

---

27. Though see Wire's (1990, 47–71) own proposal of a complex relationship of both agreement and disagreement between Paul and the prophets on how they experience Christ as this Wisdom.

Beavis, Mary Ann. 2007. "Christian Origins, Egalitarianism, and Utopia." *JFSR* 23:27–49.
BeDuhn, Jason. 1999. "'Because of the Angels': Unveiling Paul's Anthropology in 1 Corinthians 11." *JBL* 118:295–320.
Betz, Hans Dieter. 1979. *Galatians: A Commentary on Paul's Letter to the Churches in Galatia*. Hermeneia. Philadelphia: Fortress.
Briggs, Sheila. 2000. "Paul on Bondage and Freedom in Imperial Roman Society." Pages 110–23 of *Paul and Politics: Ekklēsia, Israel, Imperium, Interpretation*. Edited by Richard A. Horsley. Harrisburg, PA: Trinity Press International.
———. 2004. "Slavery and Gender." Pages 171–92 in *On the Cutting Edge: The Study of Women in Biblical Worlds; Essays in Honor of Elisabeth Schüssler Fiorenza*. Edited by Jane Schaberg, Alice Bach, and Esther Fuchs. New York: Continuum.
Brooten, Bernadette. 1996. *Love between Women: Early Christian Responses to Female Homoeroticism*. CSSHS. Chicago: University of Chicago Press.
Butler, Judith. 1990. *Gender Trouble: Feminism and the Subversion of Identity*. New York: Routledge.
Callahan, Allen D. 2000. "Paul, *Ekklēsia*, and Emancipation in Corinth." Pages 216–23 in *Paul and Politics: Ekklēsia, Israel, Imperium, Interpretation; Essays in Honor of Krister Stendahl*. Edited by Richard A. Horsley. Harrisburg, PA: Trinity Press International.
Cameron, Ron, and Merrill P. Miller, eds. 2011. *Redescribing Paul and the Corinthians*. ECL 5. Atlanta: Society of Biblical Literature.
Castelli, Elizabeth. 1991. "'I Will Make Mary Male': Pieties of the Body and Gender Transformation of Christian Women in Late Antiquity." Pages 29–49 in *Body Guards: The Cultural Politics of Gender Ambiguity*. Edited by Julia Epstein and Kristina Staub. New York: Routledge.
Friesen, Steven J. 2004. "Poverty in Pauline Studies: Beyond the So-Called New Consensus." *JSNT* 26:323–61.
Gilhus, Ingvild Saelid. 1983. "Male and Female Symbolism in the Gnostic *Apocryphon of John*." *Temenos* 19:33–43.
Glancy, Jennifer. 2002. *Slavery in Early Christianity*. Oxford: Oxford University Press.
Halberstam, Jack (Judith). 1998. *Female Masculinity*. Durham, NC: Duke University Press.
Hewitt, Marsha Aileen. 1995. "Memory, Revolution, and Redemption: Walter Benjamin and Elisabeth Schüssler Fiorenza." Pages 14–70 in

Critical Theory of Religion: A Feminist Analysis. Minneapolis: Augsburg Fortress.

Horsley, Richard A. 2005. "Paul's Assembly in Corinth: An Alternative Society." Pages 371–95 in *Urban Religion in Roman Corinth: Interdisciplinary Approaches*. Edited by Daniel N. Schowalter and Steven J. Friesen. HTS 53. Cambridge: Harvard University Press.

Isaac, Benjamin. 2004. *The Invention of Racism in Classical Antiquity*. Princeton: Princeton University Press.

Johnson-DeBaufre, Melanie, and Laura S. Nasrallah. 2011. "Beyond the Heroic Paul: Toward a Feminist and Decolonizing Approach to the Letters of Paul." Pages 161–74 in *The Colonized Apostle: Paul through Postcolonial Eyes*. Edited by Christopher D. Stanley. Minneapolis: Fortress.

Kittredge, Cynthia Briggs. 2003. "Rethinking Authorship in the Letters of Paul: Elisabeth Schüssler Fiorenza's Model of Pauline Theology." Pages 318–33 in *Walk in the Ways of Wisdom: Essays in Honor of Elisabeth Schüssler Fiorenza*. Edited by Shelly Matthews, Cynthia Briggs Kittredge, and Melanie Johnson-DeBaufre. Harrisburg, PA: Trinity Press International.

MacDonald, Dennis R. 1987. *There Is No Male and Female: The Fate of a Dominical Saying in Paul and Gnosticism*. HDR 20. Philadelphia: Fortress.

Marchal, Joseph A. 2011. "The Usefulness of an Onesimus: The Sexual Use of Slaves and Paul's Letter to Philemon." *JBL* 130:749–70.

———. 2014. "Female Masculinity in Corinth? Bodily Citations and the Drag of History." *Neot* 48:93–113.

———, ed. 2015. *The People beside Paul: The Philippian Assembly and History from Below*. ECL 17. Atlanta: SBL Press.

Marshall, Jill E. 2017. *Women Praying and Prophesying in Corinth: Gender and Inspired Speech in First Corinthians*. WUNT 2/448. Tübingen: Mohr Siebeck.

Martin, Dale. 1995. *The Corinthian Body*. New Haven: Yale University Press.

Matthews, Shelly. 2015. "A Feminist Analysis of the Veiling Passage (1 Corinthians 11:2–16): Who Really Cares That Paul Was Not a Gender Egalitarian after All?" *LD* 2.

———. 2017a. "Fleshly Resurrection, Wifely Submission, and the Myth of the Primal Androgyne: The Link between Luke 24:39 and Ephesians 5:30." Pages 101–17 in *Delightful Acts: New Essays on Canonical and*

Non-canonical Acts. Edited by Harold Attridge, Dennis MacDonald, and Claire Rothschild. WUNT. Tübingen: Mohr Siebeck.

———. 2017b. " 'To Be One and the Same with the Woman Whose Head Is Shaven' (1 Cor 11:5b): Resisting the Violence of 1 Corinthians 11:2–16 from the Bottom of the Kyriarchal Pyramid." Pages 31–51 in *Sexual Violence and Sacred Texts*. Edited by Amy Kalmanofsky. Cambridge, MA: FSRBooks.

Meeks, Wayne A. 1974. "The Image of the Androgyne: Some Uses of a Symbol in Earliest Christianity." *HR* 13:165–208.

Meggitt, Justin J. 1998. *Paul, Poverty and Survival*. Edinburgh: T&T Clark.

Miller, Anna. 2015. *Corinthian Democracy: Democratic Discourse in 1 Corinthians*. PTMS 220. Eugene, OR: Pickwick.

Scholz, Susanne. 2011. "The Forbidden Fruit for the New Eve: The Christian Right's Adaptation to the Post Modern Word." Pages 289–315 in *Interreligious Hermeneutics in Pluralistic Europe: Between Texts and People*. Edited by David Cheetham, Ulrich Winkler, Oddbjørn Lirvik, and Judith Gruber. Amsterdam: Rodopi.

Schottroff, Luise. 1995. "Auf dem Weg zu einer feministischen Rekonstruktion der Geschichte des frühen Christentums." Pages 173–248 in *Feministische Exegese: Forschungserträge zur Bibel aus der Perspektive von Frauen*. Edited by Silvia Schroer and Marie-Theres Wacker. Darmstadt: Wissenschaftliche Buchgesellschaft.

Schüssler Fiorenza, Elisabeth. 1983. *In Memory of Her: A Feminist Theological Reconstruction of Christian Origins*. New York: Crossroad.

———. 1999. *Rhetoric and Ethic: The Politics of Biblical Studies*. Minneapolis: Fortress.

———. 2000. "Paul and the Politics of Interpretation." Pages 40–57 in *Paul and Politics: Ekklēsia, Israel, Imperium, Interpretation; Essays in Honor of Krister Stendahl*. Edited by Richard A. Horsley. Harrisburg, PA: Trinity Press International.

———. 2009. "Slave Wo/men and Freedom: Some Methodological Reflections." Pages 123–46 in *Postcolonial Interventions: Essays in Honor of R. S. Sugirtharajah*. Edited by Tat-siong Benny Liew. Sheffield: Sheffield Phoenix.

———. 2016. *Congress of Wo/men: Religion, Gender, and Kyriarchal Power*. Cambridge, MA: FSRBooks.

Smith, Jay E. 2008. "The Roots of a 'Libertine' Slogan in 1 Corinthians 6:18." *JTS* 59:63–95.

Smith, Mitzi J. 2018. *Womanist Sass and Talk Back: Social (In)Justice, Intersectionality, and Biblical Interpretation.* Eugene, OR: Cascade.

Smith, Shanell T. 2019. "'She Did That!': Female Agency in New Testament Texts—A Womanist Response." Pages 157–75 in *The Oxford Handbook of New Testament, Gender, and Sexuality.* Edited by Benjamin H. Dunning. New York: Oxford University Press.

Spillers, Hortense J. 1987. "Mama's Baby, Papa's Maybe: An American Grammar Book." *Diacritics* 17:64–81.ill

Stowers, Stanley K. 2011a. "Kinds of Myths, Meals and Power: Paul and the Corinthians." Pages 105–49 in *Redescribing Paul and the Corinthians.* Edited by Ron Cameron and Merrill P. Miller. ECL 5. Atlanta: Society of Biblical Literature.

———. 2011b. "Does Pauline Christianity Resemble a Hellenistic Philosophy?" Pages 219–43 in *Redescribing Paul and the Corinthians.* Edited by Ron Cameron and Merrill P. Miller. ECL 5. Atlanta: Society of Biblical Literature.

Tamez, Elsa. 1993. *The Amnesty of Grace: Justification by Faith from a Latin American Perspective.* Translated by Sharon H. Ringe. Nashville: Abingdon.

Townsley, Gillian. 2017. *The Straight Mind in Corinth: Queer Readings across 1 Corinthians 11:2–16.* SemeiaSt 88. Atlanta: SBL Press.

Wire, Antoinette Clark. 1990. *The Corinthian Women Prophets: A Reconstruction through Paul's Rhetoric.* Minneapolis: Fortress.

The Celebrity Paratexts: The 1 Corinthians 14 Gloss Theory before and after *The Corinthian Women Prophets*

Jorunn Økland

Introduction: A Reception History in First-Person

The Corinthian Women Prophets by Antoinette Clark Wire is a milestone in feminist criticism of 1 Corinthians and of early Christian texts in general. This is evident from the frequency of quotes, citations, reviews, scholarly discussions and engagements with it. By way of introduction I present my own first encounter with Wire's rhetorical analysis and historically reconstructive claims. What has received less attention among feminist critics, but constitutes its claim to fame among specialists in textual criticism, are the key contributions found in the book's paratextual materials. As an exercise in disciplinary diplomacy, the larger part of this chapter engages with Wire's argument in the paratexts and traces some of their further reception history in New Testament exegesis and textual criticism. I also present some analyses on the scholarly responses to Wire's decision to consider a hypothesized gloss an authentic part of Paul's letter. What is at stake, and why was Wire's argument on gloss theories largely overlooked by mainstream exegetes when the book as a whole was taken seriously? These are central questions I pursue in this essay. I argue that Wire's conclusions regarding 1 Cor 14 and gloss theories are the logical, persuasive outcomes of her sustained rhetorical approach and feminist imagination.

By the end of the first semester's work on my doctoral thesis, *The Corinthian Women Prophets* (Wire 1990) had taken over my research. We still read paper books in the 1990s, and when I got my copy sometime probably in 1992 or 1993, the book was still only out in its first hardback edition. Every page of the copy is full of underlined sections, arrows, comments, protests, question marks.

I was at the time already teaching at university and had received funding from the Norwegian Research Council for a project on women's cultic functions in the Corinthian *ekklēsia* compared with women's functions in other contemporary Corinthian religious cults. The project was meant to contain text-internal analysis of both 1 Cor 11–14 and of a few of the most comparable and relevant other texts on the topic, Christian, Jewish, and pagan. The project would also include a comparison and discussion involving a broader range of materials. Theoretically, the plan was to draw on ancient rhetorical theory supplemented with more modern theories of argumentation, reception as well as gender theory. Inspiration came from my previous work on Paul, Corinth, and rhetorical analysis: like many New Testament scholars at the time, in my thesis (roughly equivalent to an MA thesis), I, too, had found the rediscovery and renewal of ancient rhetoric eye-opening. Further in the background were a first degree in classics and studies in Hellenistic language and culture against the backdrop of a contemporary setting in a multireligious and multicultural city. My main questions were: In what ritual functions are women mentioned in the Corinthian correspondence, and what was Paul's reaction to women exercising such functions?

Encountering *The Corinthian Women Prophets*, I immediately realized that I could safely leave the rhetorical analysis behind, because rhetorical analysis with an eye toward women's cultic functions had already been carried out in a near-perfect way by Wire as part of a larger study of 1 Corinthians *as a whole*. Wire's primary goal was to reconstruct an image of the women prophets in ancient Corinth, their social situation and theology, based on the central role they played in the rhetorical situation of the letter. Her analysis of the argument in 1 Corinthians was based on Chaïm Perelman's rhetorical theories. The basic sociorhetorical question was: To which situated challenge was this letter a response? Although Paul focuses on many other things than women and gender issues in his letters, the letter is *also* addressed to the women prophets. Wire's thesis is that the women prophets are always in his wider field of vision whenever he imagines the Corinthian *ekklēsia* and writes them letters.

In relation to this highly persuasive approach, I could limit my task to trying to relate Wire's findings to the broader basis of material and literary evidence of the Corinthian context that should belong naturally in any study of the Corinthian correspondence. Such a project would firmly ground the Christian women prophets in a broader polytheist or multireligious context that had not yet heard the word *Christianity*, where Paul's terms to describe the new life in Christ were not yet charged in any Christian direction. Since he was the first Christian author, people had no choice but to hear the terms innocently with the meaning they had in society at large, and it took time for terms such as *charis* and *pistis* to be fully charged with a specific Christian content. I decided to go down this route with more in-depth study of the archaeological record and the literary and philosophical texts relating to gender and ancient Corinth particularly, and Roman Greece more generally. This route in turn produced more incisive questions regarding theoretical frameworks useful for exploring the attraction of earliest Christianity for women in a multireligious, multicultural context, which ended in some interpretations that deviated slightly from Wire's. Yet, *The Corinthian Women Prophets* remained a constant reference point, as it has since.

Appendix and Topoi

In addition to consistently pursuing a set of questions within a coherent theoretical framework, another of the key contributions of Wire's book is found in its paratextual material! That is, in an excursus, in the extensive footnotes to that excursus, and, finally, in the appendices at the back of the book following up the excursus even further (Wire 1990, 149–52).

In old Bible manuscripts and modern editions, in literary as in academic works, *paratexts* are all the added fringes of the main text that control or assist one's reading of the text's main argument/content: cover, cover art and illustrations, author's name, title, front matter, back matter, introductions and appendices, fonts and formatting, notes, headers and title headings, critical apparatus in the lower margin, and cross-references in the side margins, among other things. This chapter deals with *The Corinthian Women Prophets*'s paratexts, which again deal with the paratexts in certain ancient manuscripts to the New Testament. Literary theorist Gérard Genette has theorized this rather mundane textual phenomenon. Quoting Philippe Lejeune, Genette (1997, 1–2) admits that the paratext is defining for how the text is received: the paratext is "at the service of a better reception for the text and a more pertinent reading of it."

The paratextual components that I treat in this essay deal with textual criticism, an understudied topic from a feminist perspective. Looking back at the appendices of *The Corinthian Women Prophets* now thirty years later, it is strange how dated most of them look in comparison with the rest of the book. Most of them deal with topics that were dated already in 1990, or at least they had been around for over one hundred years: "Apology for Paul" (appendix 3), the conflict in Corinth (appendix 4), Apollos (appendix 5), and virgins (appendix 9), although virgins are eternally interesting, it seems, together with the next one on wisdom (appendix 6) and also resurrection (appendix 12).

One could wonder why Wire included these appendices, and so many of them. After more than twenty-five years of further experience in Pauline studies, I now suspect she did because these dated questions were what Wire was confronted with every time she presented her work in progress among established colleagues in the 1980s. Back then these seemed like obligatory and standard questions, or to put it in terms of ancient rhetoric: topoi. If one heard a paper on 1 Corinthians, these were the questions one should ask no matter how relevant they were to the topic at hand, no matter how many times they had been answered before, or how interested one was in the answer.

Wire seems not to have wished to be distracted off her own path by the discipline's unofficial lists of standard topoi (of course her meta-understanding of topoi as well as argumentative structures is as well crafted as one would expect from a scholar of rhetoric). So the separate appendices that also include helpful bibliographies were a way of satisfying the discipline's demand that its topoi be addressed, while not letting the topoi lead her off her path. Among the appendices are also topoi established more recently, such as rhetorical criticism (appendix 1), the social location of the Corinthian Christians (appendix 7), women's head covering (appendix 8), and prophecy (appendix 10). Social-scientific criticism, still a relatively new topos, had revived old questions (such as prophecy) in new ways without having exhausted these questions.

Finally, there are a couple of appendices that deal with topics only starting to be taken seriously in the 1980s and in their own right years later: early twentieth-century research on women (appendix 2), an interesting branch of women's and gender studies today, and the intersection of theology, exegesis, and textual criticism found in appendix 11, which deals with 1 Cor 14:34–35.[1]

---

1. From reading the appendices another thing becomes clear: how Wire had not just read recent research literature but really followed these questions back in time and thus avoided transmitting mistakes, as is so common in research.

In the excursus on 1 Cor 14:34–35 and the corresponding appendix 11, Wire opens up a new way of discussing textual criticism and pairing it with canon history, early reception history, and history of interpretation; or, rather, critique of the latter. A generation later, these two paratexts come across as some of the most forward-looking parts of the book. Whereas, at the time, rhetorical criticism and feminist criticism were already current, what has happened since the first publication of *The Corinthian Women Prophets* is that reception history, social/feminist history, and textual criticism have converged and combined with new materialist approaches in unexpected ways. These two paratexts together provide an early example from New Testament studies of this convergence. I return to this topic toward the end of the chapter.

The rest of this chapter engages with Wire's argument in the paratexts and traces some of their further reception history in New Testament exegesis and textual criticism. As mentioned in the introduction, I also present some analyses on the scholarly responses to Wire's decision to consider a hypothesized gloss an authentic part of Paul's letter.

Reception History, Social/Feminist History, and Textual Criticism Converge

In her excursus and appendix, Wire traces the genealogy of an idée reçue regarding the textual criticism of 1 Cor 14 that she demonstrates as being built on false premises: the received idea is that 1 Cor 14 contains an interpolation, a gloss. That scholars do not even agree where the interpolation starts and ends illustrates the problem. One of Wire's (1990, 231–32) many important observations is that the number of verses included in the interpolation theory has gradually been extended through the twentieth century (vv. 34–35, 33b–35, 33b–36 or 33–38), probably since it did not solve any problems to consider only verses 34–35 an interpolation.

The year before the publication of *The Corinthian Women Prophets*, Kurt Aland and Barbara Aland (1989, 298–300) had drawn on the metaphor of the earthquake and the seismograph to illustrate the point that where no significant variation in the transmission of a pericope is found, we can trust the "Tenazität der Überlieferung" and safely conclude that there has been no drastic alteration of the text prior to the earliest documented stage. We can also assume the opposite: that the more drastic alteration a text has gone through at the stages before the earliest documentation, the greater variation in the extant manuscripts. In other words:

if the text's transmission shows no signs of rupture, we can safely assume ruptures did not exist prior to the documented stages either. They draw examples from the Pauline correspondence and reject the various source-critical approaches to the Corinthian correspondence for the lack of support in the documentary evidence from the texts' transmission (Aland and Aland 1995, 291–92).

Following this logic, if our verses had been a piece of text entered into the letter at a stage between Paul's writing and the earliest surviving manuscript, it should be easy to see where the gloss starts and ends. But it is not. As Wire (1990, 149) points out in the excursus, "No surviving manuscript lacks these words or puts them in a third place." This means in practice: not a single one of the Greek witnesses nor the Latin versions has omitted the verses in question, and thus no textual evidence supports the interpolation theory. What there is evidence of is an altering of the text sequence in some manuscripts, so that verses 34–35 are placed after verse 40. That some scholars who favor the gloss theory even suggest that Paul may be the author also of the gloss adds to the confusion (Wire 1990, 230).

I quote the passage at length here to set the stage for a further discussion. Following the quoted passage, I present what textual critics call the external evidence, the attestation of the different variants of the text in early manuscripts and versions—as opposed to internal evidence or criteria, which are more hermeneutically concerned with content: gaps, fissures, inconsistencies, argumentative structure, and so on. I suggest that internal criteria have not been helpful to settle the question of authorship and the relationship between the passage and the rest of the letter:

> 33 God is a God not of disorder but of peace. As in all the churches of the saints, 34 women should be silent in the churches. For they are not permitted to speak, but should be subordinate, as the law also says. 35 If there is anything they desire to know, let them ask their husbands at home. For it is shameful for a woman to speak in church. 36 Or did the word of God originate with you? Or are you the only ones it has reached? (NRSV)

Attestation of disturbances in 1 Cor 14:34–40:

The following Greek manuscripts contain the verses quoted above in a different location or in altered sequence:

- D 06, or Codex Bezae Claromontanus, approximately sixth-century Greek-Latin bilingual; the section 1 Cor 14:34–35 is placed after 1 Cor 14:40[2]
- F 010, or Codex Augiensis, bilingual, dated to the ninth century
- G 012, or Codex Boernianus, bilingual, dated to the ninth century; "study sample"; that F and G follow the variants given in D throughout 1 Corinthians is easily seen by a quick view on the apparatus of critical editions of the New Testament
- the minuscle 88, dating from the twelfth century,[3] and the minuscle 915[4]

All of the above were considered as belonging to the so-called Western text in the previous times when scholars relied more on such genealogical organization of Greek manuscripts than they do today, in a research field revolutionized by digital humanities (see Clivaz, Gregory, and Hamidović 2014).

The following manuscripts of Old Latin and Vulgate versions (the Latin language still represents, naturally, more Western Christianities) document this alternative sequence, or traces of it:

---

2. Wire (1990, 149) also mentions another majuscle, E, allegedly a copy of D 06, but it is not clear that any of the majuscles otherwise known as E (07 and 08, respectively) contain the passage of the Pauline letters in question (E 07 is gospels, E 08 is apparently missing the relevant section of Corpus Paulinum); see the overview "08 (BC 20008)."

3. For this variant, see the thorough discussion in Wire 1990, 151; Payne 1998.

4. My comments here refer to Kloha (2006, 499), the nice overview presented in Peres (2017, esp. n. 8), and the fuller comparison between the two manuscripts in Kloha (2006, 503–9), rather than my firsthand observations and verification of minuscle 915. Kloha (506–8) considers 88 to share ancestry with 915 and concludes: "Not only is there at least one other extant 'non-Western' manuscript that reads 14:34–35 after 14:40, that manuscript is from the same tradition as 88 and shows what the predecessor of 88 read—not an omission of 14:34–35, as Payne argues—but a reading already known in the tradition (506).... What took place in 88 is easily described when we have knowledge of 915. The scribe wrote v. 36 immediately after v. 33, before he realized that the verses were in an unfamiliar position. He added a superscript double slash at the beginning of v. 36, as well as in the margin, to mark the location at which the verses should be placed. He then continued writing until the end of v. 40, where he placed a double slash both in the text and in the margin. After this the scribe wrote vv. 34–35. This is precisely what stood in his examplar, now known through 915. Payne had described this as a possibility before ruling it out."

- ar 61, Codex Ardmachanus, a Vetus Latina manuscript dating from ninth century; this manuscript not only puts verses 34–35 after verse 40; it leaves 1 Cor 14:36–39 completely out
- b 89 (a codex currently in Budapest), a Vetus Latina manuscript dating from the eighth to ninth century
- R, Codex Reginensis, Vulgate manuscript written in the eighth century in the area of Ravenna[5]
- F, Codex Fuldensis, (or Cod Bon 1), a sixth-century Vulgate manuscript,[6] should also be mentioned in this list over irregulars; see below
- Ambrosiaster also has the verses in this order, which only confirms that they were seen as part of 1 Corinthians at its time of writing (365–384)

I do not go into similar detail with all the other manuscripts, which represent the majority of the total attestation of this pericope and which render the verses in the order on which the introduction of verse and number divisions in the late sixteenth century were based. Neither do I discuss extensively the already listed manuscripts attesting the variant sequence, although they do require some more comment below. When *Novum Testamentum Graece*'s twenty-seventh edition was published in 1993, shortly after the appearance of *The Corinthian Women Prophets*, the evidence for the variant sequence presented above was judged too insignificant for the editors to produce a *positive apparatus* on this issue.[7] Wire herself points out that the small number of manuscripts placing the verses at the end of the chapter are Greek-Latin *bilinguals* or Old Latin manuscripts. This does mean that they are one step removed from the original Greek but could of course still in theory represent earlier variants of the text. The Greek manuscripts—with the exception of the twelfth-century minuscle 88 (and probably 915; see above)—follow the sequence we today consider

---

5. Aland and Aland 1989, 197. Kloha (2006, 499) also mentions Vetus Latina manuscripts 75, 77, and 78, as well as Sedulius Scotus.

6. Aland and Aland 1989, 197: "F: Codex Fuldensis (Neues Testament), 547 für Bischof Viktor von Capua geschrieben (und von ihm korrigiert), heute in der Landesbibliothek Fulda." For a full treatment of this codex, see Scherbenske 2013, 175–232.

7. It was present in NA^{26} 1979/1985 and is back in the most recent edition (NA^{28} from 2012), though, perhaps as a result of the discussions I describe in this chapter. It now mentions positively that "*vss* 34/35 *pon. p.* 40" in D, F, G, ar b vg^{ms} and Ambrosiaster.

the numerical position. Wire (1990, 284 n. 18) explicitly states that she was not able to locate any Old Latin texts of the I (first European) type that had verses 34–35 at their numerical position. The Vulgate revision of the Old Latin tradition replaces the verses back to where they are in the Greek manuscripts.

Wire (1990, 229) starts her appendix presentation by summing up the *exegetical* debates of the verses: "They hold that Paul does not say these lines, that he does not mean them, or that the Corinthian women ask for them." In the ensuing reception history, she outlines the three different trajectories of interpretation, in reverse order. First, the one well represented by Heinrich A. W. Meyer (1890) in 1839. He thought exaggerated emancipation tendencies among the Corinthian women meant that they asked for it and finds resonance for such a view among those who justified Paul's comment with reference to the fact that the women displayed orgiastic tendencies. The second trajectory is found among those who thought that the ban on women's speech is genre or situation specific (the view I argue in Økland 2004). Wire lists among others James Moffatt (1938), Werner Kümmel (in Leitzmann and Kümmel 1969), Paul Wendland (1968), and Charles Barrett (1971) as early representatives of this view; more recent are E. Earle Ellis (1978), Christian Wolff (1982), and Elisabeth Schüssler Fiorenza (1983). Wire herself does not find this view persuasive, as she finds "let the women be silent in the assemblies" rather general and unconditional. The third trajectory is one where the passage is taken as a quote followed by a refutation of the quote. Given the excursus earlier in the book, it is natural that Wire deals at greatest length with this text-critical and text-historical trajectory: that Paul did not author 14:34–35, but the redactor of Paul's letters did at a later stage, which explains why the wording here is echoed in the deutero-Pauline 1 Timothy. Alternatively, Paul added the verses himself in the margin at a later stage, which explains why they are inserted in different places in some manuscripts.

Wire may have felt a need to add these pieces of paratext (an excursus and an appendix), in order to deal with a *status quaestionis* in which no exegete could say anything with credibility on 1 Corinthians without having first discussed partition and interpolation theories. The alternate placement of 14:34–35 has been mentioned by scholars since the nineteenth century (Heinrici 1880, 457–58; Weiss 1910, 342), but the more general interpolation and partition theories and hypotheses have been around since the eighteenth century. Hans Dieter Betz (1985, 3) argues that Johannes Semler introduced the possibility in 1776.[8] The interpolation/partition theories were initially based on internal criteria, such as fractures in the argument (as the exegete perceived it): Paul is emotionally involved with his argument and hence does not argue stringently, or the amanuensis does not pay sufficient attention to write down the exact words Paul is dictating, or even the letter is corrupted. Or: 1 Corinthians is seen as a collection of writings, of smaller letter fragments joined together by a later editor. This interpretation of the apparent lack of a clear outline in 1 Corinthians gained pace with Johannes Weiss (1910) in the early twentieth century. According to Walter Schmithals (1969, 84–89), 1 and 2 Corinthians as we know them could in theory be combined, edited versions of up to nine letters.[9] But Hans Conzelmann (1975, 3–4) argued persuasively with some caution against such a theory, that "it becomes convincing, to be sure, only if it can be shown not merely that there are sudden transitions of thought, but that different situations must be presupposed for different parts of the epistle."[10] *The Corinthian Women Prophets* and numerous later investigations into the social and material situation(s) in early Roman Corinth have not been able to prove sufficiently differing situations behind the different parts of 1 and 2 Corinthians to make the partition hypotheses more convincing.

Although the source-critical method has ensured progress in gospels research, it has not been successful when applied to the letters. More than two hundred years of research on the Corinthian correspondence to identify later interpolations and to trace signs of a later redaction have not brought any consensus. The reason is probably exactly the abovementioned dependence on internal criteria when it came to 1 and 2 Corinthians, based on *perceptions* of the letters' overall message and *interpretations* of the argumentative structure—or lack of such. Lacking any compelling presence of manuscripts with diverging sequences or absences of

---

8. More precisely, Semler (1776, 238; see also unpaginated preface, 235, 310) suggests that 2 Corinthians may in fact contain three letters and that especially 2 Cor 9 is a separate letter since it basically repeats in other words what is already said in 2 Cor 8 ("res agitur eadem; ut sere tantum phrases different.... In *eadem Epistola* idem argumentum sere repeti").

9. For a more moderate position, see Conzelmann 1975, 13–15. For an overview, see Betz 1985, 3.

10. Many have continued to treat 1 Corinthians as one letter. For further discussion of the criteria, see Merklein 1984, 153.

verses, the partition theories were from the outset dependent and based on hermeneutic speculation. By comparison, I mentioned above that the manuscript ar 61 actually lacks 14:36–39 completely. Yet, no one has yet suggested that the omitted verses should therefore be considered a later interpolation in all the other manuscripts—in spite of the fact that such a theory would be easier to ground in the manuscript evidence than any gloss theory regarding 33b–36, or even 34–35.

When the interpolation explanation has been used with reference to 1 Cor 14:33–36 since the 1970s onwards, then, it has happened on the basis of some further, specific internal criteria: modern ideas of gender equality and how Paul's views of gender have been defined in relation to them. The discrepancy between what the verses say and a modern view of women as full human beings is problematic in a theological-anthropological perspective, no matter the verses' human origin. But Pauline scholars in particular have tended to think that the verses present less of a problem if they cannot be seen as representing the views of Paul the apostle but a later disciple. This is because it has not been uncommon to assume that Paul wrote under divine inspiration, which gives his words in particular more weight than those of a later, merely human redactor. Even, for example, the NRSV text quoted above has 14:33b–36 in brackets, that is, treats the verses as secondary in accordance with its policy of inclusivity. Raymond Collins (1999, 515) points out that this editorial choice of parantheses or brackets in NRSV and other recent translations of 1 Cor 14:33b–36 "betrays the editors' hesitancy as to the authenticity of the verses." Judging from numerous oral conversations over *The Corinthian Women Prophets* over the years, the most common criticism of the book is that Wire considers all of 14:33b–36 to be authentic.

The Reception History of Wire's Paratexts on 1 Corinthians 14:34–35

An early reception of *The Corinthian Women Prophets* came through a repudiation of exactly the paratexts I am discussing, in the form of an article by Philip Payne (1995), followed up later by a series of publications by the same author (Payne 1998; 2009; 2017), as well as responses to and criticism of his analyses, among which Curt Niccum is the main representative. I focus mostly on the earliest article, because this is where Payne most clearly takes his cue from *The Corinthian Women Prophets* (although not properly acknowledged). Payne builds on Wire's thorough presentation of the manuscript evidence but takes the evidence further in a different direction: from the noted, altered verse sequence in some manuscripts, Payne argues that 14:34–35 is a later interpolation. Payne's arguments do not concern what is still the most widespread interpolation theory, according to which 33b–36 is an interpolation, and for which one of the main arguments is that the *tais ekklēsias tōn hagiōn* ("the churches of the saints") of 33b is post-Pauline terminology (contra Ellis 1981). Verse 33b is considered Pauline even by Payne; he argues the case of verses 34–35. In other words, Payne's external and the still-current internal criteria are fighting different cases.

Payne argues on the basis of two Latin codices in particular, which are important in establishing the text of the Stuttgarter Vulgata:

1. Codex Fuldensis (mentioned above, and see also Scherbenske below), a Latin New Testament pandect codex and an early witness to the Vulgate revision, in the case of Pauline letters mixed with Old Latin readings. This text was copied and corrected in 547 for bishop Victor of Capua—who also contributed to corrections and wrote his own preface; and
2. Codex Reginensis (mentioned above), containing only Pauline writings.

Both of these were already thoroughly discussed in Wire (1990, 285 n. 19).

Payne (1995, 261) includes a facsimile of the relevant page of Codex Fuldensis that contains 14:34–35 in its current place. From the facsimile one can see how the placing of verses 36–40 both in the text and in the margin is confusing. Payne argues that the facsimile shows that Bishop Victor's copyist did not rewrite verses 36–40 in the side margin, as implied by Wire (285 n. 19), but under the text, as "bottom-margin," and Payne attaches great importance to this distinction. Wire (1990, 151) herself also shows awareness of a lower margin, although in a different context. Taken together with a siglum that stands between verses 33 and 34, Payne reads the placement as an indication that the scribe meant to omit verses 34–35—although the scribe actually included the verses in the main text.

There is also a line over the first letter of verse 34 in Codex Fuldensis. The siglum after verse 33 could also mean that verses 36–40 as noted in the margin should be inserted there, that is, before verses 34–35 (as Wire 1990, 285 n. 19, suggests). Through this interpretation of its sigla, the manuscript faithfully renders the two main readings, either 33-34-35-36-37-38-39-40 or 33-36-37-38-39-40-34-35. Wire (1990, 285 n. 19), on her side, suggests that the possible double occurrence of verses 36–40 reveals traces of the conflict between Old and Vulgate Latin versions—also plausible in my view.

Payne (1995, 251) further draws attention to the Greek minuscle 88 from the twelfth century, which also transposes the two verses in question after verse 40. For Payne's discussion of this minuscle, too, he is dependent on Wire's initial presentation, although his rendering of it is not transparent (see criticism by Niccum below). In a later article, he develops his work and thoughts on minuscle 88 further—for understandable reasons: although late and therefore on its own irrelevant as documentation of the earliest stages of 1 Cor 14:33–40, it is still noteworthy that a Greek text witness that is not a Greek-Latin bilingual has this alternative order (Payne 1998).

Payne finally draws attention to some sigla in Codex Vaticanus that he regards as stemming from the codex's original hand and as text-critical sigla. The sigla are most clearly there; the question is who inserted them and what exactly they are meant to indicate. There is no doubt that Codex Vaticanus renders the majority text in the order that was later confirmed by verses and numbers, and that Vaticanus has been edited and amended by several hands. Generally, the sigla are as a main rule added later, which is the reason why Jesse Grenz (2018, 20) argues that if the aim is to identify the earliest layer of Vaticanus's textual divisions, it is necessary to limit the study to the codex's use of space on the page (ektheses, intralinear spacing).

That one later corrector of Codex Vaticanus knew of the alternate verse order of the pericope in question, for example, from the version rendered by D 06, with verses 34–35 being placed after verse 40, is possible. Thus, Payne is correct that the sigla in Vaticanus open up a new window onto the early history of the New Testament text. If we were to follow him in his belief that these particular sigla stem from the codex's original hand and were meant as text-critical sigla, the only logical conclusion is that the scribe showed critical awareness of other variants than those he (most certainly a "he," but see Haines-Eitzen below) in the end chose to reproduce. So, even if Payne were to be right in his assumption, these sigla—without reference and without further, clear information about what exactly they signify—do *not* constitute sufficient basis to establish a different text as more authentic than the one Vaticanus itself reproduces as the more trustworthy. One can more easily argue the opposite: when Codex Vaticanus is regarded as a trustworthy text witness, it is because of the text it has chosen to authorize and because of which variants it has dismissed.¹¹

As the wide field of textual criticism is more and more about grasping the historical development and gradual fixation of a New Testament text—and less and less about establishing its first rough drafts—early versions have increased in importance. In spite of this, when establishing a scientific text (such as *Novum Testamentum Graece* or the United Bible Societies editions), Latin translations are not usually trumping Greek text witnesses and are not on their own considered decisive.¹² This may change in the future, though, as much of textual research is now computer assisted and allows for new quantitative methods.¹³ Still, Payne's text-critical procedure to regard as primary a text sequence possibly indicated by sigla and text in the bottom margin of a late sixth-century translated manuscript (i.e., Fuldensis) will probably remain unpersuasive. So, to bolster a weak argument, Payne (1995, 241, 246, 250) elaborates his praise of Bishop Victor to build up the latter's credibility. This Bishop Victor, who clearly was keen to correct the biblical text, did so also here.

In his extensive discussion of "*Codex Fuldensis* and the Vulgate Revision of the *Corpus Paulinum*," Eric Scherbenske (2013, 175–76) describes Fuldensis as not only one of the earliest datable texts of the Vulgate revision (of the early Latin translations), but also as a codex that offers a glimpse into a variety of early receptions harnessed by Bishop Victor and by him "redeployed under a new hermeneutical aegis governed by Victor's ecumenical inclusivity." He encloses a list of the various and sundry contents of the codex, which is much more than just a testimony to the development of the Vulgate text. Victor's broad ecumenism supplied a new lens for reading the once hermeneutically disparate, sometimes contradictory paratexts (Scherbenske 2013, 176–77). Scherbenske points out that several

---

11. Grenz (2018) leaves his mention and references to Payne's contributions to his n. 48, complete with a few references to Payne's interlocutors.

12. In Augustine's words (*Doctr. chr.* 2.11.16, translated by Scherbenske 2013, 182), "in the beginning of the faith whenever a Greek codex found its way into the hands of anyone and he seemed to have some faculty of his own tongue and the other, he ventured to translate it."

13. See useful websites such as the Center for the Study of New Testament Manuscripts (http://csntm.org/). But see above all Clivaz, Gregory, and Hamidović 2014, especially the two contributions by Clivaz and the one by Houghton (2014). See also Wasserman and Gurry 2017 for a presentation of how these changes affect the methods for establishing the text of the scientific editions.

of the materials he included in his "multiple interpretive layers of editorial production" had heretical origins and included Marcion's edition, materials from both sides of the Pelagian controversies, and *both* Old Latin versions *and* the Vulgate revision (176). This variety, then, Scherbenske analyzes and uses to identify Victor's "*editorial hermeneutics*" especially with regard to Corpus Paulinum, which I do not go further into here since he does not even mention 1 Cor 14:34–35, as there are far larger and more significant changes/issues to deal with. For our purposes it is important to note, first, that Fuldensis is much, much more than just a text witness of the Vulgate revision; it is in many ways an early example of a hypertext. Second, it is also a window into a different approach to canonicity in early Christianity, a question to which I return below.

The reception history of the paratextual material in *The Corinthian Women Prophets* continues with Niccum (1997), who responded to Payne (1995). His contribution is a detailed and devastating refutation of Payne's text-critical arguments and their exploitation of *The Corinthian Women Prophets*'s groundwork. Niccum points out that the first to actually rediscover that it was verses 36–40 that were written in the margin of Fuldensis and not verses 34–35 was Wire (1990, 285 n. 19) herself and not Payne, as Payne (1995, 242) makes it seem.

A third reception worth mentioning is Teunis Van Lopik's (1995) reaction to Payne's reception of *The Corinthian Women Prophets* regarding 1 Cor 14:34–35. In light of what manuscripts and especially sigla Payne has drawn in for support, Van Lopik concludes, "if the occurence of a pericope in different places can be explained as due to liturgical reasons, the variants occasioned by the lectionary system is of no value whatsoever for assessing the 'authenticity' of the variants, that is, for determining its (their) original place and context" (291).

To defend himself against the reactions by Niccum and Van Lopik, Payne produced further articles (see esp. the already-mentioned Payne 1998) corrobating his points but not really bringing in new, less disputable proof. He cannot change the manuscript situation, only argue for hidden but fixed meanings behind the sigla, since his ultimate goal is to find a way to argue on the basis of the Bible that "man and woman" is one in Christ and that we are called to move from hierarchy to equality (Payne 2009; 2017). These may be laudable and ambitious aims for an academic career, and as a feminist I wish he could be right. But in my view these goals lead Payne into rather anachronistic readings of early Christian manuscripts. I therefore argue no further with Payne's recent work in this little reception history.

I give Payne so much space because he has undoubtedly fueled and maintained a discussion that *The Corinthian Women Prophets* restarted—and he has received much scholarly interaction for his publications in this area, perhaps even more than Wire herself received on this point. The trajectory from Wire to Payne demonstrates why textual criticism has to be part of the feminist exegetical project, and what critical questions and insights may get lost in transmission when feminist exegetes withdraw from further discussions of text-critical details.

I round off this presentation of the text-critical paratexts in *The Corinthian Women Prophets* and their early reception in Payne, Van Lopik, Niccum, and others[14] with the quote from Kurt Aland and Barbara Aland's (1995, 291) *Text of the New Testament* that I mentioned at the start of this chapter: "The limitless variety and complexity of the New Testament textual tradition serves the function of a seismograph, because the higher it registers the greater the earthquake, or in the present context the greater the disruption of the New Testament textual tradition."

This in turn, in their view, demonstrates two reliable principles:

> 1. When the text of the New Testament has been tampered with in its transmission, the readings scatter like a flock of chickens attacked by a hawk, or even by a dog, and 2. Every reading ever occurring in the New Testament textual tradition is stubbornly preserved, even if the result is nonsense.... Any interference with the regular process of transmission ... is signaled by a profusion of variants. This leads to a further conclusion which we believe to be both logical and compelling, that where such a profusion of readings does *not* exist the text has not been disturbed but has developed *according to the normal rules*. (Aland and Aland 1995, 291–92)

In the introduction to this chapter I note how the Alands wrote this before *The Corinthian Women Prophets* and Payne's, Niccum's, Van Lopik's and Miller's articles. The Alands represent in its most solid form the strand of textual criticism on which Wire explicitly builds—but which Payne seems to downplay. It has been suggested that the twenty-first century will be the century of the old translations in New Testament textual criticism, as the twentieth century was for the papyri. But methodologically the translations

---

14. Notably J. Edward Miller (2003), who belongs in this reception history but to a lesser extent engages the key priorities of this chapter.

will be used in further ways than merely as evidence of a hypothetical original autograph, something I hinted at above but will finally turn to now.[15]

Further Reception

In the introduction I state that I would not analyze content-based, internal criteria for evaluating the primary or secondary status of 14:34–35. Nonetheless, such criteria or arguments still need to be mentioned as part of a broader meta-discussion.

To briefly recapitulate the internal arguments against the verses' Pauline authorship, they are, first, the verses are not regarded as fitting in the context; second, they may not be in harmony with what Paul really meant, which is taken to be his acceptance of women praying and prophesying in chapter 11 as well as the baptismal formula he quotes in Gal 3:28: "There is not male and female";[16] and third, the plea of church tradition in 11:16 and 14:33 is considered an un-Pauline and later argument. Yet many recognize 11:2–16 as Pauline while holding that 14:33b–35 is deutero-Pauline, because more un-Pauline language use is found in the latter passage.

A main achievement of *The Corinthian Women Prophets*, in my view, was to demonstrate persuasively that 14:34–35 fit well in the argumentative structure of the letter as a whole. The book, as Paul's letter, builds up to these verses' categorical climax. *The Corinthian Women Prophets* implicitly makes clear how the gloss theory emerged to solve a seeming inconsistency in Paul's advice. However, Wire's conclusion did not go down well with what was then perhaps a majority of New Testament scholars, who agreed that it is proven beyond reasonable doubt that Paul did not author verses 33–34–35–36 or any part thereof.

Scholarly assumptions change, however, regarding as well authors/authorship as texts and their interrelationships. Epistemologies change, too, regarding how meaning is produced in texts and regarding which claims it is within the realm of scholars to make concerning ancient texts.

---

15. See also Bart Ehrman's (1994) suggestion of the development from the codices to papyri in the twentieth century, to patristic citations in the late twentieth century, and his reference to the twofold goal of textual criticism: not only to establish the original text but also to write the history of its transmission.

16. How could Gal 3:28 be considered Paul's deeply held opinion any more than 1 Cor 14:33b–36, since it is considered by many of the same Pauline scholars to be a *quote* of the pre-Pauline baptismal formula?

After thirty years, might it be that such changes are making it increasingly harder for the interpolation theories to do their job convincingly? Better understanding of the material processes that are involved in the (re)production of textual content might have worked to make the proposal of *The Corinthian Women Prophets* the more persuasive one. I now turn, first, to the changes in readings; second, to the changes in methods; and third, to changes in the understanding of material processes and what is entailed in the study of the material side of text transmission.

Since the 1990s, final-text readings have become more common. This means that scholars try to make sense of the text as it stands, interpreting its gaps and fissures rather than blaming them on some more or less successful editor. A rhetorical analysis such as Wire's is a final-text analysis. Since it is all about structure, the buildup of arguments, and selection of topoi (inter alia), it would be impossible to apply such analysis to texts one perceives as fragmentary, with large parts missing. The exception is ancient oratory, of course, where the conventions are followed down to the tiniest detail and the reader immediately identifies the section of a standard oration to which a particular fragment belongs. The stretch is slightly longer when rhetorical analysis is applied to letters, and even longer when applied to a slightly nondisciplined orator/letter composer such as Paul. Wire is not, and never was, the only New Testament scholar drawing on rhetorical analysis who prefers to work on the established text unless there is clear text-critical evidence making other readings plausible.[17]

Perhaps one difference between Payne and Wire is according to what Joël Delobel (1994, 102) has described as two major schools in text-critical methodology. Payne would then belong to the radical eclecticist school, for whom manuscripts are suppliers of readings: "A singular reading has equal rights with a broadly attested variant, a reading in a late minuscule or even in a remote version is valued equally with a variant in an ancient papyrus. Full weight is given exclusively to internal criticism," that is, exegetical considerations. Wire, on the other hand, argued along the lines of the local-genealogical school, which studies size, comprehensiveness, or fragmentariness of the documentation for each variant reading. This

---

17. There have been many ways of reconstructing Paul's argument in chapter 14 that have made adequate sense of vv. 33–36. See Barton 1986; Ellis 1981; Eriksson 1998; Mitchell 1992, 281; Niccum 1997; Osburn 1993; Wire 1990, 149–52. Eriksson, Mitchell, and Wire, who make particularly clear sense of the passage, all share a rhetorical perspective and an interest in letter composition.

approach was the basis for the Nestle-Aland editions of the Greek New Testament text, as expressed in Aland and Aland's introduction to the twenty-sixth edition, and (as quoted by Delobel) they see this approach as "the only one which meets the requirements of the New Testament textual tradition."[18] They studied the internal relationships between manuscripts and sorted them into families and interrelated branches. Greek manuscripts are more important than manuscripts containing early versions, and older in principle more important than younger. Wire is fully consistent with this approach when she does not consider siglas inserted at a later stage, whose meaning remains an interpretation, and lets them weigh more heavily than a consistent manuscript tradition including all the verses of 1 Cor 14:33–36 (although the verses can be found in a different order).

Since these discussions in the 1990s, critical questions about interpretation and ideology have come more to the surface also in textual criticism, as part of the move toward more critical reflection on the integration of exegesis and textual criticism, which, as Delobel (1994, 98) points out, were always two sides of the same issue anyway. Yet another methodological development is the interest in variants and single manuscripts and their social-historical setting rather than in the genealogies and families of manuscripts that were so important for the arguments in the paratext under discussion.[19]

In the introduction I indicate that the paratexts on textual criticism in *The Corinthian Women Prophets* provide an early example of how reception history and textual criticism have since converged in unexpected ways. To the list we could add studies in material culture, history of the Book, and exegesis. Better understood today are the implications of the fact that Paul did not write his own letters, his scribe(s) did; and that they were not, as Wire repeatedly pointed out, considered canonical from their inception, and hence not all of them are preserved. When I was teaching textual criticism in the early 1990s, I made sure the students understood

---

18. I.e., Aland and Aland 1979, 43*; cf. Delobel 1994, 103. Delobel points to the extremely vast and complex documentation of the NT text compared with all other texts from antiquity, but suggests that the radical eclectisist approach might still be good for texts that are known to us only from a few, eclectic manuscripts.

19. Without going into detail regarding the extensive publication record of Bart Ehrman (1993), it is clear that he has spearheaded much of this development, from his *Orthodox Corruption of Scripture* onward (see also Haines-Eitzen below).

that what they were interpreting in the exegetical classes was the translation of a reconstructed, hypothetical Greek text whose original does not exist. What they should think about instead was how it happened that we arrived at a concept of the Bible. It has become much more important—and possible (see below)—to study the ideological and material processes through which texts were selected, rejected, amended, and handed down to us through the centuries—so that we can read the (temporary) results in modern Western versions today.

The scholars who came up with partition and gloss theories did not respect any untouchable sacrality of the biblical text. The theories came up as part of a general, historical-critical project. This is especially clear in Semler (I mention this in the beginning of the chapter). Still, in the landscape of academic tribes and territories (see the Tony Becher 1989 book title), scholars specializing in textual criticism and ancient manuscripts have had a reputation for preferring this field because it allowed them to engage historically with the Bible without having to ask critical questions that might have theological or ethical implications; specialists were often aligned with conservative religious communities where such questions are unwelcome. In the opening pages of his *Misquoting Jesus*, Bart Ehrman (2005) describes this phenomenon in more detail (using himself as a typical representative).

I doubt that the drive of the majority of textual critics is still the desire to reconstruct the ipsissima verba of Jesus or the Pauline letters as Paul himself dictated them. A different engagement with manuscripts and their communities can be observed today. In a broader sense it involves reception historians, scholars inspired by the history-of-the-book trend, and social history, among others. As Scherbenske (2013, 7) puts it in the introduction to his book *Canonizing Paul: Ancient Editorial Practice and the Corpus Paulinum*:

> I envision this work as incorporating two trends in recent New Testament text-critical scholarship: the focus on variant readings as a window for reconstructing social history; and the importance of manuscripts themselves as tradents of the text of the New Testament and this history.... A renewed emphasis has been placed on the importance of the individual variant reading as a site wherein interpretations of the text have been transmitted diachronically.

A big change from research in 1990 when *The Corinthian Women Prophets* was first published is that today's research is assisted by the digitalization of ancient manuscripts and the application of methods from digital humanities at large. Based on a personal example given by Umberto Eco (in Eco and Origgi 2003), Claire Clivaz (2012) argues that the internet and the accessibility of digital texts make the notion of the original text disappear. She thus writes off the idea that the new emphasis on variants in New Testament textual criticism has to do with any ideological debate of "postmodern scepticism" versus "the quest for the genuine autographa"; rather, it has to do with changes in the material conditions for the production and reproduction of texts. These changes in turn led to the cultural weakening or even disappearance of the notion of original text that Eco talks about. These changes apply across the humanities that work on ancient texts, not just in biblical scholarship. Although Payne's interest in the later manuscripts and versions with their variants and editorial comments was clearly driven by an urge to establish a text more original than the one given in the Greek manuscripts, his articles could also be said to be an early move in the same direction: a greater interest in variants and the production of manuscripts, which testify to the extremely diverse and interesting growth of early Christianity and the significant role of women as part of it.

But it is tempting to turn his work on its head and ask: What kind of communities would see it in their interest to re-place 14:34–35 to a less pivotal location in the letter? Who would see it in their interest to bear the cost of the production of a new manuscript containing the letter with the verses omitted?

Let us return to Wire's (1990, 230) summary: "1 Corinthians is in circulation across the Mediterranean before Paul's letters are collected, as *1 Clement*, Ignatius, and probably the *Didache*" show. Further, "no copy survives without this passage in some location. This presses the date of the interpolation back and puts in question if we can solve the problem of this text by finding a time band between the unambiguously spiritual days of Paul and the beginning of the letter's circulation when someone proscribed women's speech in the margin." Where Payne leads astray, is only in his anachronistic use of manuscripts from many centuries down the line to argue for the existence of an original that was not even seen by the time of the collection of the letters of Paul. The rest of his evidence can be read in other ways. Payne repeats and rephrases authority-producing statements regarding Bishop Victor to build up the latter's credibility. Bishop Victor, who corrected the Latin biblical text on several occasions, did so also here. Why?

The basic presupposition of such textual intervention is that the text can be corrected: it is not in itself sacrosanct and untouchable. Or—even if the wording is, the paratext is not. Scherbenske (2013, 13) has demonstrated how early scribes could use paratext creatively if they were not satisfied with the text's content: "The blatant hermeneutical tensions between the various paratexts testify to the physical manuscript as a locus of authority, over which many early Christians through editorial practices were trying to gain interpretive control, if not by altering the text, then by furnishing paratexts." So two alternative conclusions that in this light can be drawn from Payne's evidence are

1. either Bishop Victor and his crew held a different view of the canonicity of the Pauline text, wherein the canonicity was located, and what were its implications; or
2. they had some hesitations about the content of the passage in question and used the paratext to modify it.

Clearly, 1 Corinthians was canonical enough to be worthy of transmission, and we must remember that manuscript production and translation required both honed skills and generous funding. But the canonicity was not located in the exact words (this being a translation, and further with Bishop Victor's corrections), unlike with those early scribes who copied Mark's Gospel and, worried that by selecting one ending over the other they might leave out even an *iota* from the word of God, included all three endings of Mark just to be on the safe side. These examples display more than text-critical variants, and thus they reflect different approaches to canonicity and what it means.[20]

Conclusion

In this essay I show *The Corinthian Women Prophets*'s paratexts regarding 1 Cor 14:34–35 have quite a reception history of their own, a history of which most readers and users of the excellent volume may not even be aware. These paratexts have expanded the audience for the book—and hence for feminist biblical criticism more generally. In light of the later development of New Testament scholarship, it is particularly important that the fields of New Testament textual criticism and manuscript studies

---

20. See more on interesting parallels in the formation and establishment even of the Homeric texts in Scherbenske 2013, 16–32; Økland 2018, 49–51.

have been exposed to Wire's ideas. Studies in the New Testament as part of broader material approaches to history of the Book are perhaps the most important growth area in New Testament scholarship at the moment, well assisted by digital humanities, an area with little track record in gender-critical approaches so far.

To the broader collegium of New Testament scholars, the paratexts of *The Corinthian Women Prophets* demonstrated that the interpolation theories regarding 1 Cor 14 vary so much between them that it is a question whether they could even be treated as the same theory. There is no agreement where any possible interpolation starts and where it ends, and why it should be considered an interpolation in the first place. Internal and external criteria point in different directions. In 1990, it was still important to confront any move to edit out texts that might put Paul in an unfavorable light in a modern world where gender equality was still a value and an aim (unlike in the post-postmodern twenty-first century, it seems …). I maintain that the importance of Wire's argument regarding 14:34–35 is lasting, although the presuppositions surrounding the argument have changed. At the pinnacle of the belief in an original Pauline text that could be excavated, established, and exegeted, just before scholars started to lose their faith and enthusiasm regarding an original *auctor* and the original hand, Wire delivered a final, strong defense why interpolation theories tend to deconstruct themselves and why 14:34–35 must have had the same *auctor* as the rest of the letter.

When the quest for the original text gave way for the quest for the history of transmission, the combined text-critical/reception-/social-historical analyses that *The Corinthian Women Prophets* in so many ways paved the way for could start to develop. The field of studying social history through the material processes of transmission of manuscripts has by now exploded. Inspired by David Parker, Scherbenske (2013, 8) notes that "this trend represents a movement away from the *Text* as a disembodied tradition to *texts* as embodied in manuscripts." Textual criticism is no longer about reconstructing an original text but about tracing the historical embodiments and discussions of a text, since "the text has no existence apart from those copies in which it exists" (Parker 1997, 209–10). Wire anticipated some of this in her paratexts, and imagined and projected the historical discussion of what came to be 1 Corinthians back to the stage when the letter was still in the making.

Finally, if I may attempt an imaginary group of women as interlocutors to Bishop Victor, as Wire imagined a group of women prophets as interlocutors to Paul: as so much critical research on gender in early and late ancient Christianities has shown, in the fourth to the sixth centuries, there existed Christian communities where women had retained some of the authority and influence they had had in the earliest days of the movement. This influence remained in spite of being surrounded by what Ehrman (1993; see, briefly, 2015, 7) has labeled "proto-orthodox Christianity," a product of the fourth century. The enduring, imposing presence of the women in the cult is not at all strange, as paganism continued to thrive until the late fourth century and survived well into the sixth century in some locations. This means that women's cultic leadership continued to be part of the cultural koine shaping also the development of Christian groups into the time period even of Bishop Victor. Women's leadership became more difficult as the churches were centralized and aligned with the state, of course.

But even then there were ways. In her follow-up to the groundbreaking *Guardians of Letters* (Haines-Eitzen 2000), Kim Haines-Eitzen (2012, xi) "presses [the] evidence for glimpses of women's roles in the production, reproduction, and dissemination of early Christian literature." She does not have to press hard and thereby demonstrates again that the problem is not always a lack in evidence but a lack in the historical imagination required to interpret it. For imagination is gendered. In this essay I indirectly build an argument for how women come more into view when we stop pressing the variant evidence to prove a hypothetical, undocumented version of 1 Cor 14:34–40 and instead press the variant evidence for what it might yield regarding the times the different manuscripts were produced. What we could reap are glimpses of women's agency in the material processes of production and reproduction of the Pauline texts. Women copyists had no need to prove that Paul was not a misogynist because what he says in 1 Cor 14:33–36 would not be out of step with the gender ideology they knew from their daily life. On the other hand, as Haines-Eitzen (2012, 6) demonstrates, women scribes and transmitters did have an interest in and a possibility of agency in giving women a voice; they might make "some kind of 'proto-feminist' [attempts] at rewriting the silencing of women." Haines-Eitzen goes on to demonstrate that there are multiple textual variants in the transmission of New Testament texts and other early Christian literature that "betray controversy about women, about the body, and its nakedness" (8). In this light, it becomes all the more likely that the fourth- to sixth-century heirs of Wire's Corinthian women prophets may have quietly acted to soften the blow of 1 Cor 14:34–35 by rendering it in a sort of scare quotes—which sigla could also be seen as[21]—creating confusion regarding the verses' correct place and status in the letter. If this speculation is correct,[22] the still-ongoing discussions over the verses are proof that these "'proto-feminist' [attempts] at rewriting the silencing of women" succeeded indeed.

That some churches of this later period with prominent women in their midst had great interest in undermining this categorical teaching ban by an otherwise respected apostle (as churches have today) is not at all surprising. The difference between then and now is that with a different notion of canonicity, as something still in the making, early Christians felt another freedom to make minor amendments, and perhaps especially in the translations. Today we consider the canon more as fixed, and we deal with texts that we find problematic, inconsistent, or otherwise strange through hermeneutical methods. Possibly, Bishop Victor's matrons or female scribes experienced that the verses did not at all fit with who they were in Christ, their picture of the Jesus of the gospels, or with their own spiritual experience and expertise. That Bishop Victor, for these or other reasons, wished to preserve the Old Latin alternative with a different verse order is more probable in my view than that that the whole text tradition up until then (and after) is false (see the Alands' imagery again).

Such an imaginary reading of textual history and manuscript transmission is in line with Wire's own reading of 1 Corinthians. We look for where the women in the Christian groups must have been located. The difference between 1990 and today is that we know much more about the diversity in early Christian performances, ideologies, and authorizations of gender. We know more about female characters, historical or imagined. It is in this light that this alternative construction of Bishop Victor's amendment can be made plausible.

---

21. Haines-Eitzen (2012, 92) does not analyze 1 Cor 14; she only mentions the discussion in passing in a one-page overview. This is regrettable because it would have proven her point. What she finds most interesting in the transmission of this text, and hugely under-discussed, is that Codex Alexandrinus adds that the women should be submissive to "their husbands" (*tois androis*), not to men in general. This addition reduces the scope of the submission considerably.

22. At a later stage I received access to Kloha's (2006, 547; cf. 556) dissertation, which confirms this speculation: "The 'gloss theory' becomes unnecessary when it is recognized that the editorial activity seen in 1 Cor 14 in D F G and the Latin tradition takes place elsewhere in the *Corpus Paulinum* text of those same witnesses.... Several of them ... indicate a particular awareness of the book of Acts and the role of Prisc(ill)a with respect to what happens 'in all the churches.'"

Works Cited

"08 (BC 20008)." New Testament Virtual Manuscript Room. https://tinyurl.com/SBL06102b.

Aland, Kurt, and Barbara Aland. 1979. "Introduction." Pages 39*–72* in *Novum Testamentum Graece*. 26th ed. Stuttgart: Deutsche Bibelgesellschaft.

———. 1989. *Der Text des Neuen Testaments: Einführung in die wissenschaftlichen Ausgaben sowie in Theorie und Praxis der modernen Textkritik*. 2nd ed. Stuttgart: Deutsche Bibelgesellschaft.

———, eds. 1993. *Novum Testamentum Graece*. 27th ed. Stuttgart: Deutsche Bibelgesellschaft.

———. 1995. *The Text of the New Testament: An Introduction to the Critical Editions and to the Theory and Practice of Modern Textual Criticism*. 2nd ed. Translated by Erroll F. Rhodes. Grand Rapids: Eerdmans.

Barrett, Charles Kingsley. 1971. *A Commentary on the First Epistle to the Corinthians*. BNTC. 2nd ed. London: Black.

Barton, Stephen. 1986. "Paul's Sense of Place: An Anthropological Approach to Community Formation in Corinth." *NTS* 32:225–46.

Becher, Tony. 1989. *Academic Tribes and Territories: Intellectual Enquiry and the Culture of Disciplines*. Buckingham: Open University Press.

Betz, Hans Dieter. 1985. *2 Corinthians 8 and 9: A Commentary on Two Administrative Letters of the Apostle Paul*. Edited by George W. MacRae. Hermeneia. Philadelphia: Fortress.

Clivaz, Claire. 2012. "Homer and the New Testament as 'Multitexts' in the Digital Age." *SRC* 3.3:1–15. https://tinyurl.com/SBL06102c.

Clivaz, Claire, Andrew Gregory, and David Hamidović, eds. 2014. *Digital Humanities in Biblical, Early Jewish and Early Christian Studies*. Leiden: Brill.

Collins, Raymond F. 1999. *First Corinthians*. SP 7. Collegeville, MN: Liturgical Press.

Conzelmann, Hans. 1975. *1 Corinthians: A Commentary on the First Epistle to the Corinthians*. Translated by James W. Leitch. Edited by George W. MacRae. Hermeneia. Philadelphia: Fortress.

Delobel, Joël. 1994. "Textual Criticism and Exegesis: Siamese Twins?" Pages 98–117 in *New Testament Textual Criticism, Exegesis, and Early Church History: A Discussion of Methods*. Edited by Barbara Aland and Joël Delobel. Kampen: Kok Pharos.

Eco, Umberto, and Gloria Origgi. 2003. "Auteurs et autorité: Un entretien avec Umberto Eco." Pages 215–30 in *Texte-e: Le texte à l'heure de l'Internet*. Edited by Gloria Origgi and Noga Arikha. Paris: Bpi/Centre Pompidou.

Ehrman, Bart D. 1993. *The Orthodox Corruption of Scripture: The Effect of Early Christological Controversies on the Text of the New Testament*. New York: Oxford University Press.

———. 1994. "The Use and Significance of Patristic Evidence for NT Textual Criticism." Pages 118–35 in *New Testament Textual Criticism, Exegesis, and Early Church History: A Discussion of Methods*. Edited by Barbara Aland and Joel Delobel. Kampen: Kok Pharos.

———. 2005. *Misquoting Jesus: The Story behind Who Changed the Bible and Why*. San Francisco: HarperSanFrancisco.

———. 2015. *The New Testament: A Historical Introduction to the Early Christian Writings*. New York: Oxford University Press.

Ellis, E. Earle. 1978. *Prophecy and Hermeneutic in Early Christianity: New Testament Essays*. Tübingen: Mohr.

———. 1981. "The Silenced Wives of Corinth (1 Cor 14:34–5)." Pages 213–220 in *NT Textual Criticism, Its Significance for Exegesis: Essays in Honour of Bruce M. Metzger*. Edited by Eldon Jay Epp and Gordon D. Fee. Oxford: Clarendon.

Eriksson, Anders. 1998. *Traditions as Rhetorical Proof: Pauline Argumentation in 1 Corinthians*. ConBNT 29. Stockholm: Almqvist & Wiksell.

Genette, Gérard. 1997. *Paratexts: Thresholds of Interpretation*. Translated by Jane E. Lewin. Cambridge: Cambridge University Press.

Grenz, Jesse R. 2018. "Textual Divisions in Codex Vaticanus: A Layered Approach to the Delimiters in B (03)." *JBTC* 23:1–22. https://tinyurl.com/SBL06102d.

Haines-Eitzen, Kim. 2000. *Guardians of Letters: Literacy, Power, and the Transmitters of Early Christian Literature*. New York: Oxford University Press.

———. 2012. *The Gendered Palimpsest: Women, Writing, and Representation in Early Christianity*. New York: Oxford University Press.

Heinrici, C. F. Georg. 1880. *Das erste Sendschreiben des Apostel Paulus an die Korinthier*. Berlin: Hertz.

Houghton, Hugh A. G. 2014. "The Electronic Scriptorium: Markup for New Testament Manuscripts in Digital Humanities in Biblical, Early Jewish and Early Christian Studies." Pages 31–60 in *Digital Humanities in Biblical, Early Jewish and Early Christian Studies.* Edited by Claire Clivaz, Andrew Gregory, and David Hamidović. Leiden: Brill.

Kloha, Jeffrey John. 2006. "A Textual Commentary on Paul's First Epistle to the Corinthians." Vol. 2. PhD diss., University of Leeds.

Leitzmann, Hans, extended by Werner G. Kümmel. 1969. *An die Korinther I and II.* 5th rev. ed. Tübingen: Mohr.

Merklein, Helmut. 1984. "Die Einheitlichkeit des ersten Korintherbriefes." *ZNW* 75:153–83.

Meyer, Heinrich A. W. 1890. *Critical and Exegetical Handbook to the Epistles to the Corinthians.* New York: Funk & Wagnalls.

Miller, J. Edward. 2003. "Some Observations on the Text-Critical Function of the Umlauts in Vaticanus, with Special Attention to 1 Corinthians 14.34–35." *JSNT* 26:217–36.

Mitchell, Margaret M. 1992. *Paul and the Rhetoric of Reconciliation: An Exegetical Investigation of the Language and Composition of 1 Corinthians.* Louisville: Westminster John Knox.

Moffatt, James. 1938. *The First Epistle of Paul to the Corinthians.* London: Hodder & Stoughton.

Niccum, Curt. 1997. "The Voice of the Manuscripts on the Silence of Women: The External Evidence for 1 Cor. 14.34–5." *NTS* 43:242–55.

Økland, Jorunn. 2004. *Women in Their Place: Paul and the Corinthian Discourse of Gender and Sanctuary Space.* JSNTSup 269. London: T&T Clark.

———. 2018. "Odysseer: Om bådflyktninger, fremmedkrigere og dem reisen forvandler til det ugjenkjennelige." *Agora* 4:33–51.

Osburn, Carroll D. 1993. "The Interpretation of 1 Cor 14:34–35." Pages 219–42 in *Essays on Women in Earliest Christianity.* Edited by Carroll D. Osburn. Joplin: Joplin College Press.

Parker, David C. 1997. *The Living Text of the Gospels.* Cambridge: Cambridge University Press.

Payne, Philip Barton. 1995. "Fuldensis, Sigla for variants in Vaticanus, and 1 Cor. 14.34–5." *NTS* 41:240–62.

———. 1998. "MS. 88 as Evidence for a Text without 1 Cor 14.34–5." *NTS* 44:152–58.

———. 2009. *Man and Woman, One in Christ: An Exegetical and Theological Study of Paul's Letters.* Grand Rapids: Zondervan.

———. 2017. "What about Headship? From Hierarchy to Equality." Pages 141–229 in *Mutual by Design: A Better Model for Christian Marriage.* Edited by Elizabeth Beyer. Minneapolis: CBE International.

Peres, Caio. 2017. "A Deafening Silence: The Transposition of 1 Corinthians 14:34–35 in the Latin Tradition of Ambrosiaster, D, F and G." Unpublished paper, Vrije Universiteit Amsterdam.
Scherbenske, Eric W. 2013. *Canonizing Paul: Ancient Editorial Practice and the Corpus Paulinum*. London: Oxford University Press.
Schmithals, Walter. 1969. *Gnosis in Korint: Eine Untersuchung zu den Korintherbriefen*. Götingen: Vandenhoeck & Ruprecht.
Schüssler Fiorenza, Elisabeth. 1983. *In Memory of Her: A Feminist Theological Reconstruction of Christian Origins*. New York: Crossroad.
Semler, Johannes Salomo. 1776. *Paraphrasis II: Epistolae ad Corinthios; Accessit Latina Vetus Translatio et Lectionum Varietas*. Halle: Hemmer.
Van Lopik, Teunis. 1995. "Once Again: Floating Words, Their Significance for Textual Criticism." *NTS* 41:286–91.
Wasserman, Tommy, and Peter J. Gurry. 2017. *A New Approach to Textual Criticism: An Introduction to the Coherence-Based Genealogical Method*. Atlanta: SBL Press.
Weiss, Johannes. 1910. *Der Erste Korintherbrief*. KEK. Göttingen Vandenhoeck & Ruprecht.
Wendland, Paul. 1968. *Die Briefe an die Korinther*. Göttingen: Vandenhoeck & Ruprecht.
Wire, Antoinette Clark. 1990. *The Corinthian Women Prophets: A Reconstruction through Paul's Rhetoric*. Minneapolis: Fortress.
Wolff, Christian. 1982. *Der Erste Brief des Paulus an die Korinther, Zweiter Teil: Auslegung der Kapitel 8–16*. Berlin: Evangelische Verlagsanstalt.

Reading Paul Obliquely: Reading against the Grain in a Latourian Pluriverse

Cavan Concannon

I read Antoinette Clark Wire's (1990) *The Corinthian Women Prophets* in a seminar on sex and the body in early Christianity when I was an undergraduate, alongside works by Elisabeth Schüssler Fiorenza and Peter Brown. I would like to be able to say that the book immediately changed the way that I read Paul and the Bible more generally; however, the effect was less immediate than I would like to admit. Similar to the biography of some budding New Testament scholars, I was transitioning out of a conservative form of evangelicalism, seeing in traditional forms of historical criticism a way to have my Bible and be liberal, too. And, like some of those male scholars, I thought that believing that women should be ordained in Protestant churches made me feminist enough. Wire's monograph, like the work of Schüssler Fiorenza, called into question the ease with which I accepted both the scientific objectivity of historical criticism and the presumption that the New Testament offered a progressive ethical framework, once it had been properly contextualized by the critical historian. Because of my own gendered blinders, the impact of Wire's work took a while to sink in. But when it did, it had a profound influence on the way I read Paul, and it is truly an honor to be able to offer my own appreciation of Wire and her work in this volume.

Well before my naive undergraduate self came across it, Wire's *Corinthian Women Prophets* drew on and helped to shape feminist biblical studies by reading against the grain of Paul's rhetoric in 1 Corinthians from the position of the women prophets mentioned in 1 Cor 11 and 14. In so doing, Wire offered a nuanced and provocative theological reconstruction of another set of voices in the Corinthian *ekklēsia* beyond Paul's. The juxtaposition of Paul and the women prophets showed that Paul spoke from his own position of interest and was not a neutral arbiter in the debates circulating in Corinth.

In this essay, I imagine how we might expand Wire's reading strategy further by breaking out of the binary structure of reading against Paul. I start with laying out some of the conversations in feminist biblical scholarship that *The Corinthian Women Prophets* engendered or participated in, linking these concerns to similar visions of the politics of assembly in the work of Judith Butler. Next, I discuss how Wire's reading of the women prophets influenced my own work on Paul. Finally, I turn to a potential set of philosophical voices that might broaden out the democratic impulses of Wire's work. Following the work of posthumanist scholars, particularly Bruno Latour's turn to a politics of nonhuman agents, I explore what it might look like to read Paul with Wire toward more radical forms of democratic politics. I conclude with a reading of 1 Cor 6:12–20 that takes into account the agency of nonhuman entities and locates the body as a site where human and nonhuman are entangled together.

The Corinthian Women Prophets and the Politics of Biblical Interpretation

Wire's *Corinthian Women Prophets* helped to shape feminist biblical criticism in many ways, but for my purposes here I put her work in conversation with three lines of argument that work toward the goal of displacing Paul from the center of analysis: the politics of othering, the politics of identification, and authorship in community.[1] While these frames are not taken from Wire's work, I see them as helpful in thinking about how Wire's work challenged entrenched assumptions and ways of reading in Pauline studies. Wire's displacement of Paul gestures toward a conceptualization of politics, ecclesiology, and interpretation that is radically democratic, insofar as it opens up space for hearing other voices at work in the debates of

---

1. On the politics of othering and identification, see Schüssler Fiorenza 1999, 180–88; 2007, 82–89. On authorship in community, see Kittredge 2003. Schüssler Fiorenza adds a third politics to her criticisms of biblical scholarship that I do not discuss directly here: the politics of identity. This refers to the "drive to coherence, unity, and identity [that] is the motivating methodological and ideological force in Pauline studies. It is expressed in the positivistic ethos of 'scientific' exegesis as well as in the essentializing tendencies of Pauline theology" (Schüssler Fiorenza 1999, 182–83).

early Christian collectives.[2] I later suggest that this democratic ethos can be broadened by engagement with posthumanist scholarship.

The Corinthian Women Prophets intervened in the politics of othering that surrounds and infuses Paul's rhetoric by offering an empathetic and positional reading of the women prophets in 1 Cor 11 and 14. Schüssler Fiorenza describes the politics of othering as a hegemonic Western discourse that vilifies and naturalizes difference. Stemming from androcentric Greek debates about who is qualified to participate in the *polis* (hint: propertied, free, male citizens), this discursive strategy stereotypes differences that are then "established as 'relationships of ruling,' in which structures of domination and subordination are mystified as 'naturalized' differences" (Schüssler Fiorenza 1999, 181).[3] Paul's repeated binary constructions (male/female, saved/perishing, wise/foolish) serve to other his opponents, perceived or real, and these binaries, in turn, are deployed by modern scholars when they interpret Paul's letters. In the latter case, the politics of othering encourages biblical scholars to "understand canonical voices as right and true but vilify the submerged alternative arguments as false and heretical" (Schüssler Fiorenza 2007, 84).

The politics of othering means that the Corinthians to whom Paul writes are often stereotyped with negative attributes, such as sexual libertines, ascetics, and factions, or associated with other others, such as gnostics or charismatics.[4] Having been remembered as the heretical other, the Corinthians are marginalized from the theological conversation, able to offer no agency or theological insight that is not already deemed negative or problematic.

---

2. See, e.g., Schüssler Fiorenza 1994; 1999; Castelli 2006; Marchal 2008; Johnson-DeBaufre and Nasrallah 2011.

3. On the androcentrism of the polis, see Saxonhouse 1992.

4. One can take as an example the important study by Walter Schmithals (1971), who argued that the Corinthians were best described as gnostics, part of the great heresiological stream that so exercised early Christian condemnation. This is not to say that Schmithals was himself attempting to smear the Corinthians with a heresiological label. Like those who preceded him in the *Religionsgeshichtliche Schule*, Schmithals was sympathetic to the Corinthians' Gnosticism and thought that Paul himself did not understand it; however, by giving the Corinthians a heresiological label Schmithals gave subsequent scholars ammunition for marginalizing the views of the Corinthians to whom Paul wrote as heretical. See also Castelli 2006, 210; Schüssler Fiorenza 1999, 182.

This concern with how Paul's rhetoric serves to marginalize others and stifle different views is what Wire's book so forcefully resists. As she notes,

> In spite of the great advances in Pauline research in the historical-critical study of 1 Corinthians ... Paul's opponents are still seen as no more than the contrasting background to his own exemplary humility.... Our interpreters remain bound by their heritage in Protestant Orthodoxy to cast these opponents negatively in order to affirm Paul. It is as if every opinion the interpreters hold is Pauline and every opinion of Paul's is their own. (Wire 1990, 10; see also 2000, 127)

We return to Wire's latter point below, but here I note that Wire's resistance to getting caught up in Paul's binary rhetoric gives *The Corinthian Women Prophets* an edge that still cuts through the heart of Pauline studies. By treating Paul's letters as rhetoric, Wire refuses to accept Paul's characterizations as natural or objective descriptions.[5] Further, her empathetic treatment of the women prophets also refuses to follow Paul's lead, taken up by so many Pauline scholars, in demonizing those who clearly articulated an alternative, and occasionally an oppositional, set of positions to those staked out by Paul.

In the quote cited above, Wire questions the ways in which modern scholars often find themselves, consciously or not, aligning themselves with Paul and vice versa. Schüssler Fiorenza (2007, 87) has called this prevalent tendency the politics of identification, in which scholars identify their own interests and concerns with that of Paul and, in turn, "claim Paul's authority for themselves."[6] Without (self-)critical attention to the politics of identification, it is easy for Pauline scholars to use their historical and philological training to authorize themselves as those who can speak for Paul, thus appropriating for themselves the authority that Paul's archive has had in Western theology and history. For many biblical scholars and modern Christian communities, to speak for Paul is simultaneously to speak in the name of God.

Schüssler Fiorenza's challenge to the politics of identification is to push Pauline scholars to recover the voices and visions of those with whom

---

5. See also Castelli 2006, who shows how Paul's rhetoric participates in the ever-shifting relationships of power operative in the Corinthian community.

6. For similar appraisals of Pauline scholarship, see Wire 1990, 10; Stowers 2011, 106–9. Stowers characterizes the dominant strain of Pauline scholarship as "Christian theological modernism."

Paul dialogued, debated, and argued. This is precisely what *The Corinthian Women Prophets* does with such great skill. By treating 1 Corinthians as a form of rhetoric and then reading it for what it can tell us about the complicated rhetorical context to which it was directed, Wire disrupts the ease with which the scholar or the reader can elide their own views with those of Paul. At the same time, by making the goal of interpretation the articulation of alternative views to those expressed by the implied author of the text, Wire displaces Paul's authority as the one who decides on theological or political truth. Resisting Paul's binary rhetoric, Wire lays out an argument for an alternative set of theological commitments to Paul's own that are not then immediately captured in the trap of debates over orthodoxy and heresy.

One potential concern about Wire's empathetic reading of the women prophets is that she merely flips the politics of identification on its head without deconstructing the binary logic that underpins it. Does a reader put down *The Corinthian Women Prophets* thinking that Paul ought now be rendered as the heretic and the women prophets as the new orthodox? Joseph Marchal's work on Philippians underscores the problems with only inverting the politics of identification, particularly since most of those doing the inverting in Pauline studies are, including the present author, academics educated in elite institutions in the West. Marchal (2008, 94) cautions, citing Gayatri Spivak (1993), that we must be careful not to be "the first-world intellectual masquerading as the absent nonrepresenter who lets the oppressed speak for themselves." In other words, we must be careful about how we make the voices haunting the margins of Paul's letters speak. Marchal further cautions that we must also avoid reconstructions that valorize the voices of those other than Paul.[7] Because empires often involve the appropriation of the agency of their subjects in the construction of imperial power relations, one has to imagine those we reconstruct as "both resistant and complicit, both colonized and colonizing" (Marchal 2008, 107–8).[8]

---

7. Speaking of his own reconstructions of Euodia and Syntyche (Phil 4:2–3) within the Philippian community, Marchal (2008, 107) notes, "Recognizing Euodia's and Syntyche's potential position(s) in the intersecting kyriarchal orders of first-century Philippi, though, should not simply lead to an unqualified valorization of them as decolonizing feminist subjects," since women have themselves been a part of colonizing missions in modern empires.

8. For a similar caveat, see Castelli 2006, 209.

While I think that Wire's work is susceptible to such readings, she ultimately evades this potential critique. She does this by the ingenious way in which she chooses whom to reconstruct. Rather than directing her attention to reconstructing the Corinthians in opposition to Paul, as if the Corinthians to whom Paul wrote possessed some essential or cohesive identity, Wire identifies a small subset of Paul's audience: the women who are praying and prophesying in the *ekklēsia*. This group stands in for neither the Corinthians as a whole, nor even all the wo/men among them. The inability for this group to signify an organic whole leaves a remainder that makes it impossible for the politics of identification and othering to function. Clearly Paul, the women prophets, and many others bring their voices to the Corinthian *ekklēsia*. By reading from a particular position within the *ekklēsia*, Wire takes a democratic approach to interpretation. This is not to say that early Christian collectives were democratic, pluralist polities, but that there were always many more voices and perspectives in these gatherings than we can account for, a point to which I return below. The impetus for the modern scholar is to try to expand the possibilities for interpretation rather than attempt to constrain our readings to cohere with Paul's.

A final concern that feminist biblical critics have leveled against scholarly reconstructions in Pauline studies that I find useful in framing Wire's work relates to the question of authorship, or, more specifically, to the ways in which scholars have downplayed or ignored the roles that Paul's audiences played in the construction of Paul's rhetoric and theology. As part of her criticism of the politics of identification, Schüssler Fiorenza (1999, 186) has noted how scholars have largely ignored the independent agency of the communities to whom Paul wrote:

> Insofar as scholars tend to understand Paul as having the authority of the gospel to compel, control, and censure the persons or communities to whom he writes, they tend to read Paul's letters as authoritative rather than as argumentative interventions in the theological discourses of his audience. They thereby fail to understand that "Pauline Christianity" is a misnomer for the early Christian communities to whom Paul writes. These communities existed independently of Paul although we know about them only in and through the letters of Paul.

Though I am wary of positing cohesive and clearly defined communities as the audiences of Paul's letters, Schüssler Fiorenza's point is an important one, in that it reminds us that Paul's audiences had their own perspectives, questions, and beliefs that they brought with them when they heard or read Paul's letters. Equally, Paul's letters themselves are not solely products of Paul's own thought, since they are shaped by Paul's perceptions and knowledge of his audience and by other oral and written sources that he himself did not author.

Wire's work builds from the assumption that Paul's letters must be read in community and not as isolated treatises. On the one hand, Wire's women prophets clearly shape the ways in which Paul's arguments in 1 Corinthians are constructed. Paul takes their practices into account in 1 Cor 11 and 14, and his positions on prayer, head covering, male authority, and wo/men's speech are each worked out as responses to the women prophets, though Wire also suggests ways in which these prophets may have shaped other aspects of Paul's letter.[9] The point is that Paul is not operating outside some form of communal interdependence when writing his letters, and he shapes and is shaped by the rhetorical context in which he finds himself at the time of writing. Paul is thus always already writing in community.

An important example of this line of thought that builds on Wire's work comes from Cynthia Briggs Kittredge (2003), who has questioned the facility with which we can speak of Paul's authorship of his letters. In her work, Kittredge (1998) isolates hymns or theological statements in Paul's letters that were written by others and only quoted or modified by Paul, such as Gal 3:28 or Phil 2:6–11.[10] By isolating these non-Pauline writings, she turns them into resources for the reconstruction of voices in early Christianity other than Paul.

In her reflections on the effects of such textual work, Kittredge (2003, 331) argues that we must shift our way of describing the authorship of Paul's letters:

> It is necessary to use a model for the study of ancient communities that acknowledges the role of the community in the production of creedal and doxological statements and that recognizes the ongoing role of the present community as interpreter of Scripture.… Paul is neither the single author or the central authority in the early Christian movement. Rather,

---

9. See also Castelli 2006 for further exploration of the views of those other than Paul circulating in Corinth.

10. Kittredge is in conversation here with the earlier work of Schüssler Fiorenza (1994, 205–41).

the community experience of the gospel, which for many Christians was unrelated to Paul, is an equally important source for Christian language as well as a resource for theological reflection. This approach recognizes the role of community in producing and employing religious language.

Beyond Paul's own use of preexisting written or oral traditions, Kittredge challenges us to think more critically about the production of Paul's letters in community. When we presume that the communities to which Paul wrote functioned independently from him and that the experience and development of each community was continually worked out on a local level, we can approach the reconstruction of these communities otherwise.[11]

On the Form of the *Ekklēsia*

The Corinthian Women Prophets was a watershed in Pauline studies, even if my undergraduate self could not see it at first glance. By conjuring the voices of wo/men left to the margins of 1 Corinthians, and thus to the margins of modern Pauline studies, Wire opened up space for seeing the Corinthian collective as a diverse combination of theologies, experiences, and practices. As I think about the kinds of community conjured by Wire's work, I imagine those evoked by Butler (1990, 20):

> The insistence in advance on coalitional "unity" as a goal assumes that solidarity, whatever its price, is a prerequisite for political action. But what sort of politics demands that kind of advance purchase on unity? Perhaps a coalition needs to acknowledge its contradictions and take action with those contradictions intact. Perhaps also part of what dialogic understanding entails is the acceptance of divergence, breakage, splinter, and fragmentation as part of the often tortuous process of democratization.

Butler's (2009; 2015) more recent work on precarity, performativity, and assembly builds on this early insight into the possibility of community that forms not just in situations of disagreement, but in breakage, suffering,

---

11. For Kittredge (2003, 326), feminist biblical scholars "operate with a model of theologizing in which communities of worship and praxis are in the process of working out how the gospel will be embodied, rather than a model in which one man's mind must be shown either to be consistent or to have reasonable factors that 'changed' it. This model allows us to imagine conflict between aspects of Paul's vision and elements of other Christian visions."

and in bodies massed in the street. The questions that drive Butler's work circle around questions that also circle around Wire's, though inflected not through the politics of biblical studies but through those of political philosophy: Who has the right to appear? What bodies are given the right to speak? Who is excludable from the social and therefore rendered subject to violence? Can a politics or a movement emerge in fragmentation or around the body or under the threat of precarity? We might rephrase these same questions in Wire's terms: Who has the right to stand in the *ekklēsia*? What bodies are able to speak in the spirit? Who is excludable as a heretic or a sinner or deviant? Can one imagine an *ekklēsia* that could affirm its diversity as the single definition of its community? Wire's work, alongside other feminist biblical scholars, pushes toward a radically democratic rethinking of both the work of the historian of earliest Christianity and the question of how to form and sustain new and more just human socialities.

Women Prophets and Some Corinthians

Wire's pioneering work deeply inspired my own work on Paul's letters to the Corinthians (Concannon 2014). In *"When You Were Gentiles,"* I pay attention to the archaeological remains unearthed through the excavations of Corinth by the American School of Classical Studies in Athens and explore the ways in which they help scholars hear the voices of Corinthians from the first and second centuries. Wire's women prophets helped me to develop an ear for listening for the spectral voices that might be recovered from an inscription, from a broken pottery shard, or from the margins of literary sources written to or about Corinth. I hoped that this attentiveness might bring more Corinthians to the desk of the interpreter to sit alongside Wire's women prophets.

Like Wire, my reconstructions foregrounded the variety of potential readers and readings of the Corinthian correspondence. Where Wire focused on reconstructing a plausible picture of the women prophets of Corinth, I invoked the spectral presence of "some" (*tines*) Corinthians (Concannon 2014, 11–13).[12] *Some* was deliberately chosen to avoid any chance that my reconstructions assumed an essentialized unity for Paul's

---

12. I take the phrase *some Corinthians* from Cameron and Miller (2011), who offered this formulation of reconstructive efforts to highlight the diversity of identities, viewpoints, and boundaries at work in the Corinthian community, noting that any reconstruction can capture only some of the Corinthians to whom Paul wrote.

Corinthian audience. Some Corinthians is a reminder that *the* Corinthians should never be reduced by modern scholars, lest they simply form a binary opposite and foil to Paul. Because my work with the archaeology of Corinth had helped me to see the complex negotiations within the city's landscape around ethnic identity, I focused my reconstructions on how Paul's invocations of ethnic boundaries, both for himself (1 Cor 9) and for his Corinthian audiences (1 Cor 10; 2 Cor 3), might have been heard in Corinth by some in his audiences.[13] Following Wire, I wrote with a commitment to reconstructing a context of plurality and diversity, in which various positions, practices, and identities were up for debate within the Corinthian community and its wider civic context.[14] My hope was that others would continue to follow Wire's lead and conjure more Corinthians who could listen and talk back to Paul.[15]

While my work built on that of Wire and others who focused on the rhetorical context of the Corinthian correspondence, I was particularly interested in reimagining the *reception* of Paul's letters by the Corinthians to whom he wrote. Wire's reconstruction of the women prophets was largely based on a literary reading against the grain of Paul's rhetoric, and focused on how the politics and theology of these women influenced the production of the arguments in 1 Corinthians. Wire's reconstructions also tend to aim at the women prophets as they were at the time of Paul's writing. Her thoughts on their afterlife in Corinth speculate on how Paul's rhetoric would have affected their place in the community were it to be adopted wholesale by the Corinthians. Though my work followed Wire in examining the rhetorical context for the production of 1 and 2 Corinthians, I was also interested not just in the effects of Paul's rhetoric but also in

---

13. While I focused on ethnic boundaries, I think it would be interesting to find ways to bring these issues into conversation with gender constructions in Paul's letters. This is an approach discussed by Schüssler Fiorenza, (2009a), who calls for an intersectional approach that reads race, gender, and status together in the context of ancient and modern kyriarchies.

14. Part of my interest was moving away from readings that focused on trying to read Paul in binary terms to reconstruct Paul's opponents. This is not to say that looking for opponents is itself a flawed endeavor. Such work has been an important part of shaping and refining reading strategies in scholarship on the Corinthian correspondence. See, e.g., Georgi 1986; Sumney 1990.

15. For excellent examples of such conjurings, see Townsley 2017; Hartman 2019; Marchal 2020.

the ways in which we might imagine Corinthians pushing back against or building alternative systems out of Paul's rhetoric, theology, and practice.

Because of this interest in the complicated politics of reception and response, my work looked to how Paul's Corinthian audience was influenced by and participated in larger discourses related to ethnicity and religious practice in Roman Corinth. My approach thus built on Wire's rhetorical analysis by intertwining literary and archeological interpretation as a means of recovering the context in which the Corinthian correspondence was heard and interpreted by an audience living in Corinth. The goal was to reimagine the resources available for Corinthians reading or listening to Paul to think with.[16] The hope was that by paying attention to the complicated and shifting relationships between Paul and the Corinthians and delving deeply into the material and discursive remains from Corinth, we might be able to hear through Paul's letters the spectral presences of the Corinthians who helped to shape the conversations to which these letters were directed and the debates that they sparked.[17] In so doing, I made space for the spectral presences of the Corinthians who heard and interpreted Paul's letters as a means of, in Giorgio Agamben's (2005, 40) phrase, remaining "faithful to that which having perpetually been forgotten, must remain unforgettable."

Networks of Women Prophets

Wire's *Corinthian Women Prophets* was a major force in shaping the currents of feminist biblical scholarship. Feminist scholars such as Wire have pushed Pauline studies to think more critically about the place of Paul in the analysis of his letters, from the ways in which Paul has been treated as an objective observer to the demonization of Paul's opponents and audiences as foils for our own theological interests. In what follows I listen in on a set of conversations that might extend Wire's impact on Pauline studies. Paying particular attention to the work of Latour, I suggest that posthumanist scholarship might offer an interesting site for thinking and

---

16. On the importance of charting what was available for an audience to think with, see Johnson-DeBaufre and Nasrallah 2011.

17. In a similar vein, Mitchell (2005, 323) has suggested that we must also consider the roles that Paul's letters as letters played in the relationship between Paul and the Corinthians: "This means taking very seriously the impact of each missive and its range of perceived meanings on the unfolding relationship between Paul and the Corinthians."

imagining new democratized readings of Pauline texts. I take my first cue from Wire's (1990, 176–80) analysis of Paul's logistical instructions at the end of 1 Cor 16, where she notes that Paul's instructions make it clear that there is more than one network of followers of Jesus connected to Paul's Corinthian audience. As part of thinking about ways to extend Wire's work, I suggest that the often-overused concept of networks, as mediated through the work of Latour, allows for a way of extending the democratic ethos inherent in Wire's historiography.

Network is a word we use quite regularly, almost ubiquitously, in an age in which we are all taught to network with people in our fields and many of us are glued to tablets staring at visualizations of our social networks. Talking in terms of networks can seem banal, but networks are interesting to me precisely because they tend to reflect decentered, rhizomatic lines of connection. Though they are not always so, networks often are comprised of shifting assemblages of nodes and edges, operating at various speeds and intensities, that are constantly in motion. For my purposes here, Latour has theorized the rhizomatic aspects of networks in ways that reflect and extend the diverse and decentered historiographic reconstruction of the early Christian collective in Corinth offered by Wire.

Latour, whose dissertation on Rudolf Bultmann's concept of demythologizing gave way to a long career examining the anthropology of science and modernity, has developed an attentiveness to the radically democratic composition of social and historical assemblages of humans and nonhumans. Latour's (1988, 162–63) philosophical work stems from what was for him the radical realization that the composition of reality could not be reduced and that the immense plurality of being is a moving field of forces that folds and combines together, ever creating new compositions, only to have them decompose in a constant germinal flux.[18] At an ontological level, and in contrast to Plato's conception of reality, Being for Latour is infinite, in the sense that it is characterized by the cacophonous concatenation of an uncountable number of actors, human and nonhuman alike. As a result, Latour (1988, 29) offers the injunction for sociologists and historians: "Replace the singular with the plural everywhere." Latour accounts for order in social and material formations as local and temporary phenomena: "The pluriverse doesn't lack coherent formatting,

---

18. I explore Deleuze's work and its relevance to the study of early Christianity in Concannon 2017.

it just lacks any formatting that is not produced locally and provisionally by the interactions of the multitude itself" (Miller 2013, 16). For Latour, the world is neither a site for difference as a fall from a singular, divinely ordained plan nor a tragic battleground in which varieties of early Christianities battle one another for supremacy; rather, it is a seething flux of creative difference.

Such a framework is interesting to line up alongside Wire and some of the feminist biblical historians discussed above. There was not an early Christianity in which Paul was always already the center and the head, from which divergent groups fell away into heresy and fell apart as a result; rather, there was plurality everywhere, which Wire's reconstructions highlight. Similarly, there was no singular early Christianity, but locally produced and provisional Christianities, made up of the multiple networks that Wire saw in Paul's anxious instructions about competing apostles such as Apollos. We might sum this up with Adam Miller's (2013, 24) summary of Latour's ontology and metaphysics: "Though the One is not, there are unities." In other words, there are no primal early Christian orthodoxies, heresies, or varieties; rather, there are only local, provisional, and postestablished unities.[19] To begin with the presumption of Pauline centrality, to treat him as a fixed and stable source of authority for early Christianity, is to mistake a later theological and political consensus of imperial Christianity for an actual sociological and historical event or object. Ultimately the scholars who make such assumptions about Paul's centrality and authority misread Paul's own place as a node among a shifting series of networks related to the cult of Jesus in the eastern Mediterranean. Both Wire and Latour would see early Christianity as far more diverse and rhizomatic than traditional historiographic models that privilege early Christian unity and Pauline authority. In this they share a vision for community in difference that is similar to that offered by Butler.

Where Latour allows us to extend some of Wire's work into new avenues is in the way in which his own ontological description of reality is rooted in a radical notion of democracy, one that extends beyond humans. Feminist biblical scholars have long sought to bring marginalized voices to the center of their interpretive work, a project that is rooted

---

19. This is perhaps another way of saying that a proper accounting for early Christian difference has to find a way of accounting for both difference and unity (Brakke 2010, 5).

in a fundamentally democratic notion of the Christian *ekklēsia*.[20] The act of bringing the (reconstructed) voices of the women prophets into view reflects a democratic impulse to give every member of a polity the ability to speak and be heard. The centrality of an uncountable multitude of agents involved intimately in every event is central to how Latour understands reality. As such, Latour (1988, 7, 156) pushes scholars to radically democratize our notion of agency: "I start with the assumption that everything is involved in a relation of forces but that I have no idea at all of precisely what a force is.... No, we do not know what forces there are, nor their balance. We do not want to reduce anything to anything else."[21]

Because we do not know what forces or agents are at play or how many there even are, we must "replace the singular with the plural everywhere" (Latour 2004, 29). Latour's injunction makes two interrelated points. First, scholars must avoid the sin of reductionism, of reducing complex phenomena to simplistic or singular causes. By complex phenomena, Latour does not mean just the events that continue to puzzle us, such as the complex negotiations, debates, and political intrigues in the Christian collective in Corinth; rather, Latour would remind us of the radical complexity of even the simplest acts. Second, Latour's (1988, 35) injunction asks that we multiply the agents/actants in any given situation:

> We do not know who are the agents who make up our world. We must begin with this uncertainty if we are to understand how, little by little, the agents defined one another, summoning other agents and attributing to them intentions and strategies.... When we speak of men, societies, culture, and objects, there are everywhere crowds of other agents that act, pursue aims unknown to us, and use us to prosper. We may inspect pure water, milk, hands, curtains, sputum, the air we breathe, and see nothing suspect, but millions of other individuals are moving around that we cannot see.

What is radical about Latour's notion of agency is that it is truly democratic, inclusive of bacteria, hands, water, and air. Latour argues that even nonhuman actants have agency and affect our human socialities in ways that we seldom consider. Latour's (2004) turn toward the agency

---

20. One can see this, for example, in Schüssler Fiorenza (1993; 2009b), where the democratic language of equality is invoked as central to the project of reconceptualizing Christian theology and practice.

21. As Deleuze and Guattari (1987, 9) put it: "All multiplicities are flat."

of nonhuman actants is crucial to thinking through theological, social, and political responses to the catastrophes that face human life on the planet. From massive economic inequality to the eradication of the planet's resources to the warming climate, prevailing forms of politics and organizing have failed to offer an adequate response to these threats to the possibility of life on the planet. Whatever politics emerges to confront or respond to these challenges will have to reckon with the fact that humans can make all manner of political decisions about how their societies will function, but those decisions will mean nothing if the billions of carbon dioxide molecules in the atmosphere are not consulted or if the pH level of the ocean is not taken into account. What we need is a radically democratic form of politics that invites human and nonhuman alike to the table to debate questions of common concern. Wire's work continues to push readers of the New Testament to democratize their reading practices. With Latour, we hear an injunction to go further and reconceptualize our ideas about democracy and agency themselves with an eschatological urgency.

Taking the Women Prophets into the Posthuman

Reading with Latour takes Wire's democratic hermeneutics in the direction of posthumanism, a diverse stream of scholarship that looks to question the underlying premises of Enlightenment humanism and how assumptions about the nature of the human are called into question by our entanglement with other entities and systems. Posthumanist scholarship particularly challenges the unified notion of the human subject, paying attention to the ways in which our selves are entangled rather than autonomous.[22] Much posthumanist work has focused on modern technology and science: genetic modification, artificial intelligence, the virtual landscape of cyberspace (Braidotti 2013; Malabou 2008; Haraway 1997). Some work has focused on interspecies coevolution (Derrida 2008; Deleuze and Guattari 1987; Agamben 2004; Haraway 2016), while others have focused

---

22. "Posthumanism (and transhumanism) denotes the variegated efforts to rethink the human or, at times, to think about transforming the human. It is a misunderstanding of posthumanism to see it as an abandonment of concern for the human; rather, posthumanism considers 'how subjectivity, bodies, agency, and cognition are altered by engagements with' other animals, the 'environment,' and nonorganic matter and technologies" (Buell 2014, 39, citing Weinstone 2004, 4).

on systems analyses that flatten the distinctions between humans and the environment (Delanda 1997; 2006; Crockett 2016). My use of Latour has been connected to the work that I do as a historian who also thinks with archaeological remains and falls within the ambit of posthumanist work that focuses on the agency of objects.[23]

To think about how Latour and other posthumanist scholars might help us shift the way we read Paul's letters in line with the democratizing impulses of Wire's work, I offer a short reading of 1 Cor 6:12–20 alongside the work of Denise Kimber Buell and Dale Martin. Buell (2014) has shown how her work on haunting might be merged in productive ways with aspects of posthumanist thought for use in biblical studies.[24] Buell (32) argues that posthumanist scholarship asks us to pay attention, in ways that we heretofore have not, to how "collective belonging in earliest Christian discourses and rituals was forged through interactions with nonhuman agencies." The texts that we study from antiquity presume that personhood is constructed relationally with human and nonhuman agents and agencies, and to read them without such attention means that we read modern notions of human personhood and subjectivity into these texts (40–41).

Following Buell's lead, I think about how Paul's discussion of the corporate effects of a member of the *ekklēsia* sleeping with a prostitute invokes and ascribes agency to nonhuman entities that have an effect on personhood and the collective.[25] Such a reading takes seriously the need to democratize radically the way we describe agency in the texts we study by adhering to Latour's (2004, 29) injunction to "replace the singular with the plural everywhere." Though not working from within the framework of posthumanism, Martin's work on 1 Corinthians explicitly takes into account the agency of nonhuman entities and their relations with human bodies in ways that complement a posthumanist approach.[26] In my read-

---

23. Beyond Latour, one can see this approach in Bennett 2010; Esposito 2015; Harman 2016.

24. Buell's (2005; 2009) earlier work on hauntology and race and ethnicity have been major influences on my own work.

25. "Paul and his audiences seem to agree that the collision of *pneuma* with *psychē* and *sarx* produces ontological shifts even when they disagree about what these were and their consequences" (Buell 2014, 32).

26. Martin's (1995, 21) approach to reading 1 Corinthians is anchored in his observation that "the ancients by and large view the self as a continuum of substances

ing of 1 Cor 6:12–20, which follows, I follow Martin's (1995, 174–79) path through the complicated relationships that Paul invokes in his argument.[27]

First Corinthians 6:12–20 focuses on the question of what would happen if a member of the *ekklēsia* slept with a prostitute.[28] Paul's polemic in this section relies on assumptions about the ontology and agency of nonhuman entities (the [holy] spirit, Christ, and God) as they affect the individual's body (*sōma*). Paul argues that a member of the *ekklēsia* ought not have sex with a prostitute on the grounds that such an action might affect the complex relationship between the body, (the) spirit, Christ, and God. In other words, Paul's views on sexuality are rooted in how sex alters the relations between certain humans and nonhumans, and not in a logic of individualized sexual morality.

Central to the logic of Paul's argument is the relational constitution of the body (*sōma*), in particular that of the member of the *ekklēsia*. The body was purchased by God in the marketplace as one would purchase an enslaved person (*ēgorasthēte gar timēs*, 6:20) and is therefore not its own owner (*ouk este heautōn*, 6:19).[29] This body that is owned by God, provided it behaves properly, will be raised by God as well (6:14). But the ownership of the individual's body is complicated by God's relationship to the Christ/Lord. As God's agent, the body belongs to the Lord (*kyrios*) and is not for engaging in sexually illicit activities (*porneia*, 6:13).

Paul specifies explicitly how the body belongs to the Lord: each body is a member (*melos*) of Christ (6:15). We learn later in the letter that Paul means this literally: each (baptized) human body is a member of Christ's body (12:12–31). What Paul takes for granted in chapter 6, but spells out in 12:12–13, is that the individual body is grafted into Christ's body by baptism in the spirit (*pneuma*): "For in one spirit we all were baptized into

---

which all, somewhat automatically, interact with and upon one another." This is a perfect illustration of a posthumanist attention to the agency of nonhuman actants.

27. Buell (2017; 2019) has further developed her posthumanist framework in two important articles that push against some aspects of Martin's reading of 1 Corinthians and etiologies of invasion and pollution.

28. It is not clear from the passage whether Paul is addressing a situation where members of the Corinthian *ekklēsia* are actually frequenting prostitutes, a not-uncommon practice in the ancient world, or whether this is a thought experiment (Collins 1999, 240). On ancient prostitution, see McGinn 2004.

29. "*Agorazein* refers not to the sale of a slave to a god by which the slave is actually freed, but to the ordinary sale of a slave by one owner to another owner" (Martin 1990, 63).

one body" (12:13a NRSV). Thus, the relationship between (the body of) Christ and the body of the individual is mediated by the spirit/*pneuma* that joins them together. As Martin (1995, 21) has rightly noted, *pneuma* is not an immaterial entity nor a metaphor for Paul, but refers to a material substance that is immanent in the universe and both in and outside human bodies: "Pneuma is a kind of 'stuff' that is the agent of perception, motion, and life itself; it pervades other forms of stuff and, together with those other forms, constitutes the self." In Paul's argument, the *pneuma* is a substance that is shared between the body of the individual and Christ, connecting Christ's body with that of the individual: "Someone who is joined to the Lord is one *pneuma*" (6:17).[30]

The *pneuma* is not just a connector between bodies but also dwells within them. As Paul notes, a member of the *ekklēsia*, one who has been baptized into the *pneuma*, also has the (holy) *pneuma* within him. This body has been given the *pneuma* by God and is then a temple within which the holy *pneuma* dwells (6:19). The danger, for Paul, of God giving *pneuma* to a human body is that the *pneuma* is now subject to the possibility of pollution by its proximity to the flesh (*sarx*).[31]

The *pneuma* is not the only embodied substance that can connect bodies together. Through an intertextual reading of Gen 2:24, Paul sees sex as the mechanism by which two separate fleshes (*sarkes*) are joined together: "Do you not know that the one who joins with a prostitute is one *sōma*? For, it is said, the two will be one *sarx*" (6:16). Commentators have long argued that *sōma* and *sarx* here are interchangeable, that they refer to the same thing (Collins 1999, 247–48). But recognizing that they are different entities is crucial to understanding how Paul's argument functions. The sexual act links together two separate *sarkes* into one. By virtue of the fact that the *sōma* is the site where *sarx* and *pneuma* intermingle, the joining together of two *sarkes* through *porneia* has a polluting effect when the *pneuma* is also present. And because the *pneuma* is also a substance that is shared by (the body of) Christ, the polluting effect is shared by Christ. This is the logic by which Paul can say, "Do you not know that your *sōmata* are members of Christ? Therefore should I make members of Christ members of a prostitute? Certainly not!" As Martin (1995, 175–76) summarizes the argument, "a Christian's copulation with a prostitute constitutes Christ's

---

30. Unless otherwise indicated, all translations are mine.

31. On pollution and disease etiology in the ancient world, see Martin 1995, 139–62.

copulation with her," which is rooted in that, for Paul, "the individual body has no independent ontological status."

From a posthumanist perspective, what this reading of 1 Cor 6:12–20 shows is precisely that, for Paul, the individual body is not a hermetically sealed and unified self, but is bound up into a series of relationships that involve human and nonhuman entities. The individual body is not a single thing but a constantly shifting site of interaction between a series of substances that link together humans and nonhumans. To follow Wire's impulse further in this direction could involve imagining other constructions of the body by Corinthians, while paying attention to the agency such theoretical bodies might have had for other ancient readers. In reading Paul or other early Christians, we have to democratize our readings and be attentive to the agencies and interactions that our informants consider as actants in their worlds.[32]

Conclusion

Wire's work remains a challenge not just to Pauline or New Testament studies but to ways of thinking about democracy both inside and outside contemporary Christian communities. This work points its readers toward questions about who is included and who is heard, and how we draw our lines around who is inside our polity and who is outside. Such questions remain urgent and must be urgently attended to. Ultimately, such questions can only be answered through alliances and extension, through assembling the kinds of fragmented collectives that Wire, Butler, Latour, Buell, and other posthumanist scholars conjure for their readers. The task for Pauline studies is to continue to imagine how we can radically democratize our readings, conjure the agencies of nonhumans, and imagine new assemblages of people and things. An important recent example of such an approach is Hartman's (2019) rereading of Paul's rhetoric around *porneia* in 1 Cor 5, focusing on how Paul deploys nonhumans (yeast, bread, [paschal] lambs) to animalize those who diverge from Paul's sexual and

---

32. As Buell (2014, 41) notes, taking such an approach allows scholars to account for nonhuman agencies without having to assent to the rhetorical projects within which they are invoked: "Posthumanist writings allow advocates of nonhuman agencies who are not religiously affiliated to engage nonhuman agencies without assenting to the rhetorical terms of the ancient texts and their ethical implications and without assenting to Christian theological frameworks."

communal ethics. Such readings not only help us to move beyond static assumptions of what it means to be human, but also equip us to imagine new forms of sociality between humans and nonhumans as we move ever more rapidly into a period where such imagination will be more and more important for a politics that can address the increasingly dangerous ecological, political, and economic conditions of the Anthropocene.

Works Cited

Agamben, Giorgio. 2004. *The Open: Man and Animal.* Translated by Kevin Attell. CA. Edited by Werner Hamacher. Stanford, CA: Stanford University Press.

———. 2005. *The Time That Remains: A Commentary on the Letter to the Romans.* Translated by Patricia Dailey. Stanford, CA: Stanford University Press.

Bennett, Jane. 2010. *Vibrant Matter: A Political Ecology of Things.* Durham, NC: Duke University Press.

Braidotti, Rosi. 2013. *The Posthuman.* Cambridge: Polity.

Brakke, David. 2010. *The Gnostics: Myth, Ritual, and Diversity in Early Christianity.* Cambridge: Harvard University Press.

Buell, Denise Kimber. 2005. *Why This New Race?: Ethnic Reasoning in Early Christianity.* New York: Columbia University Press.

———. 2009. "God's Own People: Specters of Race, Ethnicity, and Gender in Early Christian Studies." Pages 159–90 in *Prejudice and Christian Beginnings: Investigating Race, Gender, and Ethnicity in Early Christian Studies.* Edited by Laura Nasrallah and Elisabeth Schüssler Fiorenza. Minneapolis: Fortress.

———. 2014. "Hauntology Meets Posthumanism: Some Payoffs for Biblical Studies." Pages 29–56 in *The Bible and Posthumanism.* Edited by Jennifer L. Koosed. SemeiaSt 74. Atlanta: Society of Biblical Literature.

———. 2017. "Embodied Temporalities: Gender, Ethnicity, and Other Transformations." Pages 454–76 in *The Bible and Feminism: Remapping the Field.* Edited by Yvonne Sherwood with the assistance of Anna Fisk. Oxford: Oxford University Press.

———. 2019. "Posthumanism." Pages 197–218 in *The Oxford Handbook of Gender and Sexuality in the New Testament.* Edited by Benjamin Dunning. Oxford: Oxford University Press.

Butler, Judith. 1990. *Gender Trouble: Feminism and the Subversion of Identity.* New York: Routledge.

———. 2009. *Frames of War: When Is Life Grievable?* New York: Verso.

———. 2015. *Notes toward a Performative Theory of Assembly.* MFLBMC. Cambridge: Harvard University Press.

Cameron, Ron, and Merrill P. Miller. 2011. "Redescribing Paul and the Corinthians." Pages 245–57 in *Redescribing Paul and the Corinthians.* Edited by Ron Cameron and Merrill P. Miller. ECL 5. Atlanta: Society of Biblical Literature.

Castelli, Elizabeth A. 2006. "Interpretations of Power in 1 Corinthians." *Semeia* 54:197–222.

Collins, Raymond F. 1999. *First Corinthians.* SP 7. Edited by Daniel J. Harrington. Collegeville, MN: Liturgical Press.

Concannon, Cavan W. 2014. *"When You Were Gentiles": Specters of Ethnicity in Roman Corinth and Paul's Corinthian Correspondence.* Synkrisis. New Haven: Yale University Press.

———. 2017. *Assembling Early Christianity: Trade, Networks, and the Letters of Dionysios of Corinth.* Cambridge: Cambridge University Press.

Crockett, Clayton. 2016. "Earth: What Can a Planet Do?" Pages 21–60 in *An Insurrectionist Manifesto: Four New Gospels for a Radical Politics.* Edited by Ward Blanton, Clayton Crockett, Jeffrey W. Robbins, and Noëlle Vahanian. New York: Columbia University Press.

DeLanda, Manuel. 1997. *A Thousand Years of Nonlinear History.* New York: Zone Books.

———. 2006. *A New Philosophy of Society: Assemblage Theory and Social Complexity.* New York: Continuum.

Deleuze, Gilles, and Felix Guattari. 1987. *A Thousand Plateaus.* Minneapolis: University of Minnesota Press.

Derrida, Jacques. 2008. *The Animal That Therefore I Am.* Translated by David Wills. New York: Fordham University Press.

Esposito, Roberto. 2015. *Persons and Things.* Translated by Zakiya Hanafi. Cambridge: Polity.

Georgi, Dieter. 1986. *The Opponents of Paul in Second Corinthians: A Study of Religious Propaganda in Late Antiquity.* Philadelphia: Fortress.

Haraway, Donna J. 1997. *ModestWitness@Second_Millenium.FemaleMan©_Meets_OncoMouse™: Feminism and Technoscience.* New York: Routledge.

———. 2016. *Staying with the Trouble: Making Kin in the Chthulucene.* Durham, NC: Duke University Press.

Harman, Graham. 2016. *Immaterialism: Objects and Social Theory.* Cambridge: Polity.

Hartman, Midori E. 2019. "A Little Porneia Leavens the Whole: Queer(ing) Limits of Community in 1 Corinthians 5." Pages 143–63 in *Bodies on the Verge: Queering Pauline Epistles*. Edited by Joseph A. Marchal. SemeiaSt 93. Atlanta: SBL Press.

Johnson-DeBaufre, Melanie, and Laura S. Nasrallah. 2011. "Beyond the Heroic Paul: Toward a Feminist and Decolonizing Approach to the Letters of Paul." Pages 161–74 in *The Colonized Apostle: Paul through Postcolonial Eyes*. Edited by Christopher D. Stanley. Minneapolis: Fortress.

Kittredge, Cynthia Briggs. 1998. *Community and Authority: The Rhetoric of Obedience in the Pauline Tradition*. HTS 45. Harrisburg, PA: Trinity Press International.

———. 2003. "Rethinking Authorship in the Letters of Paul: Elisabeth Schüssler Fiorenza's Model of Pauline Theology." Pages 318–33 in *Walk in the Ways of Wisdom: Essays in Honor of Elisabeth Schüssler Fiorenza*. Edited by Shelly Matthews, Cynthia Briggs Kittredge, and Melanie Johnson-Debaufre. Harrisburg, PA: Trinity Press International.

Latour, Bruno. 1988. *The Pasteurization of France*. Cambridge: Harvard University Press.

———. 2004. *Politics of Nature: How to Bring the Sciences into Democracy*. Cambridge: Harvard University Press.

Malabou, Catherine. 2008. *What Should We Do with Our Brain?* PCP. New York: Fordham University Press.

Marchal, Joseph A. 2008. *The Politics of Heaven: Women, Gender, and Empire in the Study of Paul*. PCC. Minneapolis: Fortress.

———. 2020. *Appalling Bodies: Queer Figures before and after Paul's Letters*. Oxford: Oxford University Press.

Martin, Dale B. 1990. *Slavery as Salvation: The Metaphor of Slavery in Pauline Christianity*. New Haven: Yale University Press.

———. 1995. *The Corinthian Body*. New Haven: Yale University Press.

McGinn, Thomas A. J. 2004. *The Economy of Prostitution in the Roman World: A Study of Social History and the Brothel*. Ann Arbor: University of Michigan Press.

Miller, Adam S. 2013. *Speculative Grace: Bruno Latour and Object-Oriented Theology*. PCP. New York: Fordham University Press.

Mitchell, Margaret M. 2005. "Paul's Letters to Corinth: The Interpretive Intertwining of Literary and Historical Reconstruction." Pages 307–38 in *Urban Religion in Roman Corinth: Interdisciplinary Approaches*.

Edited by Daniel N. Schowalter and Steven J. Friesen. HTS 53. Cambridge: Harvard Divinity School Press.
Saxonhouse, Arlene. 1992. *Fear of Diversity: The Birth of Political Science in Ancient Greek Thought*. Chicago: University of Chicago Press.
Schmithals, Walter. 1971. *Gnosticism in Corinth: An Investigation of the Letters to the Corinthians*. Translated by John E. Steeley. Nashville: Abingdon.
Schüssler Fiorenza, Elisabeth. 1993. *Discipleship of Equals: A Critical Feminist Ekklesia-logy of Liberation*. New York: Crossroad.
———. 1994. *In Memory of Her: A Feminist Theological Reconstruction of Christian Origins*. 10th anniversary ed. New York: Crossroad.
———. 1999. *Rhetoric and Ethic: The Politics of Biblical Studies*. Minneapolis: Fortress.
———. 2007. *The Power of the Word: Scripture and the Rhetoric of Empire*. Minneapolis: Fortress.
———. 2009a. "Introduction: Exploring the Intersections of Race, Gender, Status, and Ethnicity in Early Christian Studies." Pages 1–26 in *Prejudice and Christian Beginnings: Investigating Race, Gender, and Ethnicity in Early Christian Studies*. Edited by Laura Nasrallah and Elisabeth Schüssler Fiorenza. Minneapolis: Fortress.
———. 2009b. *Democratizing Biblical Studies: Toward an Emancipatory Educational Space*. Louisville: Westminster John Knox.
Spivak, Gayatri Chakravorty. 1993. "Can the Subaltern Speak?" Pages 66–111 in *Colonial Discourse and Postcolonial Theory*. Edited by Patrick Williams and Laura Chrisman. New York: Harvester Wheatsheaf.
Stowers, Stanley K. 2011. "Kinds of Myth, Meals, and Power: Paul and the Corinthians." Pages 105–50 in *Redescribing Paul and the Corinthians*. Edited by Ron Cameron and Merrill P. Miller. ECL 5. Atlanta: Society of Biblical Literature.
Sumney, Jerry L. 1990. *Identifying Paul's Opponents: The Question of Method in 2 Corinthians*. Sheffield: JSOT.
Townsley, Gillian. 2017. *"The Straight Mind" in Corinth: Queer Readings across 1 Corinthians 11:2–16*. SemeiaSt 88. Atlanta: SBL Press.
Weinstone, Ann. 2004. *Avatar Bodies: A Tantra for Posthumanism*. Minneapolis: University of Minnesota Press.
Wire, Antoinette Clark. 1990. *The Corinthian Women Prophets: A Reconstruction through Paul's Rhetoric*. Minneapolis: Fortress.
———. 2000. "Response: The Politics of the Assembly in Corinth." Pages 124–29 in *Paul and Politics: Ekklesia, Israel, Imperium, Interpretation*;

Essays in Honor of Krister Stendahl. Edited by Richard A. Horsley. Harrisburg, PA: Trinity Press International.

Alternative Futures, Ephemeral Bodies: Untouching the Corinthian Women Prophets

Joseph A. Marchal

What are interpreters after when they turn to the Corinthian women prophets? How do these females function as figures historically or rhetorically in Pauline epistles or interpretations? One can even wonder whether they figure at all, particularly when they are marginalized or obscured in spite of their audacious appearances around twenty centuries ago in Paul's First Letter to the Corinthians, or around thirty years ago in Antoinette Clark Wire's (1990) evocative reconstruction of them through that letter. From another angle, these appearances are all too brief, too slight or subtle to offer much beyond a fleeting glimpse of any of the many people besides Paul in these ancient assembly communities. The archive generated by such glimpses could easily slip through our fingers; yet, as Elisabeth Schüssler Fiorenza (1999, 52) reminds us: "If it is a sign of oppression when a people does not have a written history, then feminists and other subaltern scholars cannot afford to eschew such rhetorical and historical re-constructive work." Despair at the ephemeral nature of these traces, then, could, even *should*, be turned by the political importance of the task for those oppressed and obscured, especially through forms of biblical argumentation. Indeed, here and elsewhere, I share many commitments with Wire, Schüssler Fiorenza (1999, 52), and other feminist interpreters who prioritize "making the subordinated and marginalized 'others' visible again and their repressed arguments and silences 'audible.'" This, in part, accounts for how I and others are persistently drawn, in spite of the obstacles and difficulties, to various figures in these letters—both the passing references and the debased, even stereotyped figures. This pull is related to the countless bodies that have been haunted by the effects of Paul's letters, bodies that many interpreters are still so prone to ignore.[1] One clear exception can be found in Denise Kimber Buell's (2009, 180–81) work around the troubling legacies of ancient Christian materials and those (who claim to be) treating them historically in order to propose origins or ruptures in the creation of our racial, ethnic, and religious categories. This kind of attachment, or what one might call accountability, could, in turn, explain my interest in those targeted or marginalized with and through the letters. To me, these are linked: the ongoing impacts of more recent targeting (in a time that we might initially call "now") require more creative, even urgent responses, responses that involve reflections on those figures evoked in the letters (in a time we might initially call "then").[2]

Such urgency and a corresponding need for creativity do not mean casting aside already argued approaches and results—indeed, I maintain that we need both the approaches and results Wire crafts in her landmark study of the Corinthian women prophets. Rather, by intertwining the bold feminist work of Wire and others, with some more experimental alternatives within queer cultural studies, I signal some of the missed opportunities and striking anticipations in the reception of feminist historical and rhetorical work—a set of alternative futures for the Corinthian women prophets. In this light the work of Ann Cvetkovich and José Esteban Muñoz becomes valuable for the ways they provide and perform examples of alternative archives in the making, drawing on ephemeral materials such as letters. Both sets of approaches, then, recognize the potential significance of slight references, spectral presences, and unsanctified figures.

Careful Confidence around the Corinthians

The approach developed by Wire in pursuit of the Corinthian women prophets should be revisited and, frankly, implemented far more frequently among interpreters of these materials. This would require approaching the letters as neither theology nor history at first, but as rhetoric—as attempts to communicate, argue, and convince an audience. For a rhetorical act to be successful, it must gauge and address an audience successfully. This was

---

1. For some of the first reflections on hauntology and spectrality in relation to the projects of New Testament and early Christian studies, see Buell 2009; 2010; 2014.

2. For the first of several attempts to rethink the relationship between then and now queerly, particularly as a touch across time, see Marchal 2011.

one reason Wire adapted the categories introduced by Lucie Olbrechts-Tyteca and Chaïm Perelman's (1969) new rhetoric to focus on the *function* of a set of arguments, rather than on the act of labeling them with a series of antiquated (and sometimes conflicting) Greco-Roman terms. In keeping with this kind of rhetorical analysis, the interpreter proceeds with the assumption that any rhetor is most concerned with having a particular effect on an audience through the rhetorical act. This has several effects on the interpretive project. First, Paul's letters are not treated as isolated theological treatises but as parts of an exchange between Paul and his audiences. Second, the focus on the operation of these arguments requires recognizing that Paul had hopes for affecting the audience in particular ways; the function of a letter is to persuade or convince, neither of which neatly corresponds to preservation or proselytizing (the work of the historian or theologian). Third, this should, in turn, alter the default (and often unexamined) assumptions of interpreters, particularly those who tend to presume that Paul was *already* authoritative and his arguments always already accepted—then or now. Such an assumption seems to misunderstand how these letters function. As Wire (1990, 10) argues in her introduction: "Because an argument Paul makes cannot be rejected as unconvincing, it also cannot convince. In this way the authority we attribute to Paul prevents him from persuading us." Wire convincingly explains that such an assumption is actually a disservice to Paul and the manifest effort he expended to persuade through these letters (9–11). The assumption of Paul's priori authoritative status ignores what the letters are and what its author appears to have intended to do in and through them. Wire highlights: "The letters do not claim to be authoritative in their own right or this argument would be redundant" (10).

This kind of rhetorical analysis complicates both theological and historical assumptions about the significance of Paul's letters. Once one begins to grapple with their rhetoricity, the letters hardly appear to be straightforward sources for history or theology. These letters are not transparent windows onto historical situations, in either the location of their composition or reception. Rather, Wire's efforts to find out about one group of recipients (the Corinthian women prophets) demonstrates how one must factor in the effects of the persuasive function of the letter, as just one part of a rhetorical exchange, if one wants to postulate historical information about anything or anyone, Paul or other people. Wire (1990, 9) elaborates: "Nothing he [Paul] writes can be considered reliable unless it serves his purpose of persuasion. In other words, everything spoken as description or analysis is first of all an address to the intended readers." One must distinguish between rhetorical and historical situation, because one must work through the rhetoric to get any kind of historical perspective.[3]

Any direct claims or arguments about particular figures in a letter, then, can be helpful, if measured or factored in terms of the letter's argumentative aims. Paul might be basing a claim on a presumed agreement between the audience and himself, yet letters of course reveal other purposes than confirming agreement. Indeed, given the effort and resources needed to compose and send a letter, one should imagine that there were particular concerns that would cause someone such as Paul to send a letter. Once one acknowledges the letters as attempts at persuasion, then, Wire (1990, 9) proposes: "On whatever points Paul's persuasion is insistent and intense, showing he is not merely confirming their agreement but struggling for their assent, one can assume some different and opposite point of view in Corinth from the one Paul is stating." Paul's arguments do not assume agreement or his own unquestionable authority in advance; on the contrary, Wire shows how "Paul expects controversy—provokes it in fact" (11). She suggests that, if one reads the letter's arguments carefully, one can see some audience perspectives in the letter. Through a process compatible with reading against the grain, Wire maintains: "Those in clear disagreement with Paul should be the ones most accessible through his rhetoric" (4).

Grappling with a letter as an act of rhetoric involves a tricky kind of triangulation between the rhetor (Paul), the rhetorical act (the letter), and the audience (recipients such as the prophetic women in Corinth).[4] Indeed, the act is but an *attempt*, an attempt that one must try to measure for its *reliability*; then, to get to other people one must *try to factor* for them, and they can only be accessible if one is *careful*. These are real possibilities, possibilities too frequently ignored or dismissed out of hand (as Matthews's essay in this collection shows); but in taking Wire's approach seriously, one must grapple with how it is simultaneously eye-opening and

---

3. Cynthia Briggs Kittredge (1998, 56, 62–65, 101–10), for instance, stresses that there is a difference between the rhetorical situation inscribed within the letter to the Philippians and the historical situation at Philippi. For the difference between rhetorical and historical situation, see Schüssler Fiorenza 1999, 109, 115–22, 138–42. On rhetorical situation generally, see Bitzer 1968.

4. For previous reflections on this tentative triangulation in rhetorical analysis (and for Philippians specifically), see Marchal 2006, 194–202.

difficult. After all, in the case of 1 Corinthians and the women prophets, a contemporary interpreter has only an artifact of the act (a critical edition of the letter), but seeks information about the rhetor and, especially in my case (following in the footsteps of Wire), the audience. If one is not carefully attentive to the rhetoricity of the act, the rhetor simply remains a saint; if one does not factor for the audience, the women in the assembly community at Corinth can slip through our fingers.

Slight Anxieties

Paul's letters present a set of opportunities, given the way the letters write to a range of audiences, in different places, and mentioning, even addressing specific people in those places.[5] These letters seem like invaluable resources for finding out about more than just the author, who will be canonized and sanctified in succeeding centuries. Nevertheless, there are real challenges in pursuing such people in Paul's letters: the letters are, after all, just presenting one half of a conversation. They maintain one version of Paul's various attempts to persuade. This is particularly troubling when we are looking for and trying to think more about those figures addressed in and by the letters, as we never directly hear their parts of the longer conversation. One would be forgiven if one despaired in one's consideration of these figures once recognizing how each of these references is shaped primarily toward argumentative purposes and, then, encountering just how *slight* these references are and how difficult it might be to factor for those addressed by these passing references within overarching rhetorics.

Of course, in naming this difficulty and the potential anxiety or despair associated with it, I am not proposing a turn away from the sometimes slight, fleeting, or ephemeral. Rather, I maintain that Wire's approach retrains our focus and orientation, and I want to lean even further into it. Indeed, for scholars interested in ancient conceptualizations of gender,

---

5. In this and in many other ways, I am explicitly and implicitly presuming and building on the innovations in feminist biblical scholarship, particularly when feminist interpreters have been interested in historical reconstructions and/or engaged in reading against the grain of these materials. Here, the methodological innovations of Schüssler Fiorenza (1992; 1999; 2001), Wire (1990), and Castelli (1991) come most directly to mind. One could point to a range of other feminist scholars with similar commitments and engaging with these approaches, but for now I simply point to two who have helped me to rethink the uses of these letters: Kittredge 2003; Miller 2015.

sexuality, and embodiment, a lot also rides on how we interpret brief references, such as the inclusion of the *arsenokoitai* and *malakoi* in a longer vice list in 1 Cor 6:9.[6] The former is painfully obscure and hard to determine, while the latter is a more defined pain because we are quite certain of its insulting characterization of femininity as soft and problematic.[7] These pains are hardly slight, particularly for those who are targeted by or with this argument now, *even if* the claim is made in passing: two Greek words, clustered with many others, assembled on the way in an attempt to make some other larger point in the letter. More affirmatively, but still often the product of intensive labors, few feminist interpreters would dismiss out of hand the slight but still precious references to women such as Prisca (1 Cor 16:19; as well as Rom 16:3–5; Acts 18), or the people belonging to Chloe (1 Cor 1:11) in this letter (on the latter, see M. Smith forthcoming). Their places around the edges or margins of these letters need not correspond to their places in the networks of activity within and between these ancient assembly communities, or their places in the stories or arguments we assemble now.

Wire's approach sets the stage for me to emphasize an orientation to the ephemeral—these materials and our approaches to them (likely because humans and other creatures are ephemeral ourselves). Wire reminds us that these letters were not always authoritative, canonized scriptures, but attempts at persuasion, reflections of moments in longer conversations and wider networks. Though they have been raised to the heights of theological authority, each of these letters was once ephemeral ... and to ephemera they might still return.[8] But, for now, what would it mean to linger with the ephemerality of these epistles and the figures deployed and addressed within them? After all, what are we doing but reading other people's mail?! This conception might help us to remember the fleeting nature of these encounters, but it still might imply that this fleeting is still

---

6. On these two terms and the vice lists in 1 Cor 5–6, see Martin 1996; Ivarsson 2007.

7. The two other so-called clobber passages (Gen 19:1–38; Lev 18:22; 20:13) also turn on the meaning of relatively slight terms: *yāda'* (which is quite clear) and *miškəbê 'iššâ* (which is not). For an overview of the former, and the Sodom story in general, see Carden 2004. For the best suggestion for what to do with the manifest difficulties of the latter, see Olyan 1994.

8. Indeed, as Luijendijk (2009) underscores, other early Christian letters were viewed as ephemeral enough to be thrown away. Sometimes we are reconstructing history from garbage.

familiar—we think we know what mailed items are as objects. Even still, approaching the letters again as ephemera helps us to dislodge the letters from their all-too-common and politically, culturally, religiously, and affectively disturbing uses.[9] There is and was nothing necessary about the development in their outsized influence. Here, my political investment, my affective attachment, or just inclination toward the figures targeted and marginalized within these letters can meet with an emphasis on ephemera to help me reconsider, even reconnect, with these figures.

Ephemeral Archives and Affects

Inspired by Wire, then, I treat these letters first as rhetorical and cultural, rather than theological or historical (to start), an effort eased by engagement with queer approaches from outside biblical studies. Cvetkovich and Muñoz focus on ephemeral materials in their bold and improvised experiments with assembling alternative archives in the making.

As Muñoz (1996, 10) stresses, ephemera are "all of those things that remain after a performance, a kind of evidence of what has transpired but certainly not the thing itself … following traces, glimmers, residues, and specks of things." Ephemera involve looking backwards; they point in that direction, even as they persist in the other direction; they are the remainders of a performative act itself—such as, say, an ancient letter. Ephemera, then, require attention to the specific and the particular, rather than the typical or the average. If as Muñoz argues, "Ephemera includes traces of lived experience and performances of lived experience, maintaining experiential politics and urgencies long after these structures of feeling have been lived" (10–11), then ephemera can be the residue, possibly even a repository of materials and sensations, experiences and positions, toward an alternative archive.

Letters, as and alongside ephemera, can be valuable for an alternative archive, nearly absent, often traumatic, but not always finally nor exclusively so. Ephemera are "the stock-in-trade of the gay and lesbian archive," as collections from private donors become public objects *and affects*, "insisting on the value of apparently marginal or ephemeral material" (Cvetkovich 2003, 243–44). The grassroots archives of LGBTIQ people depend on just

---

9. For more traditional approaches to Paul's letters within the conventions of ancient letter writing, see Stowers 1986; Malherbe 1988.

such objects—letters and other occasional documents, alongside other miscellaneous and ephemeral materials (243). As Cvetkovich argues, "In insisting on the value of apparently marginal or ephemeral material, the collectors of gay and lesbian archives propose that affects—associated with nostalgia, personal memory, fantasy, and trauma—make a document significant" (243–44).

Cvetkovich and other cultural critics, then, provide and perform different approaches to ephemera as evidence. Cvetkovich's rich, dynamic, and reflexive work is valuable for many reasons, including its attunement to the ephemeral. She traces the creation of lesbian and queer public cultures, often in relation to an everyday that is shaped by trauma.[10] Indeed, in Cvetkovich's (2003, 12) conceptualization, trauma is the trace of where and how catastrophic histories (large and small) become "embedded within everyday life experiences." Trauma's effects, then, are diffuse and dispersed, requiring different strategies for making archives, attending to marginal, unexpected, and ephemeral materials. This often means grappling with an almost absent archive, a haunting past that is still somehow both hidden and present in cultural texts and surrounding practices (38; drawing on Gordon 1997).

Thus, letters seem to be excellent objects to archive alternatives, even if or perhaps even *because* they were and are ephemeral.[11] Some of Cvetkovich's most fascinating examples, particularly for an interpreter in ambivalent relationship to ancient epistles, come in the form of letters, both within Leslie Feinberg's *Stone Butch Blues* and the Lesbian Herstory Archives. Feinberg's (semi)autobiographical novel is structured as a letter to the protagonist's ex-lover, revealing their painfully buried responses to lesbian and especially butch vulnerability to police harassment, violence, and detention (Cvetkovich 2003, 73–79). Cvetkovich situates this discussion within her extended reflections on butch and femme sexualities in light of trauma and vulnerability (49–82). Since this letter will not be sent to the ex-lover, the novel describes its alternative destination as a public site, not unlike New York's Lesbian Herstory Archives, as a marker of humiliation and helpless-

---

10. For a range of considerations about trauma in relation to the literature now called early Christian, with some reflection on the impact Cvetkovich's practices can make, see Kotrosits 2015.

11. Though it is not my primary (or even secondary or tertiary) interest here, there is the potential for a set of readings of Paul's letters that pursue an ephemeral Paul, or at least ephemeral Paulinisms. See, e.g., Blanton 2014.

ness (78–79), the kind that was left unspoken, unwritten, unsent, unreceived.... The conundrum of the lesbian or the queer archive is that it must somehow reflect and hold these kinds of "traumatic absences" (79). Their affective investment in the objects makes them significant and historical. In the process of "feeling history," then, archives help to constitute a community, even through unexpected objects (Cvetkovich 2012, 124). In such archives, even pulp fiction, with its broad and stereotyped figures, becomes a form of evidence, a slight and seemingly insignificant clue to some, but a clue nonetheless for those who had no other access to the notion of a lesbian public culture (Cvetkovich 2003, 252–53).[12]

Of course, Paul's letters are anything but marginal now, given their religious *and cultural* canonization in the centuries that followed their creation, performance, reception, and circulation. But, as I note above, this was not always the case, nor was it inevitably so. If one wants to unlearn so as to relearn alternative approaches to the past, it is likely a good idea to remember that these objects are letters, not sermons, not doctrines, and certainly not authoritative scriptures in these initial, fleeting settings. If scriptures are orientation devices,[13] we would do well to take a more disorienting approach to these texts that were something else entirely. Indeed, recognizing the oral/aural qualities of the letters' performance and reception, and following Muñoz (1996, 10), one can relearn the ephemerality of epistles as among "those things that remain after a performance." We are already studying ephemera. Multiple acts precede a letter. The significance of a letter does not (exclusively) reside in a (construction of) Paul's intention at composition, nor in the experience of its oral and aural delivery performed in and for the assembly community members at Corinth. Instead, the letters are but remainders, specific traces and reduced residues of a far more extended exchange within a complicated network of people assembling in communities across the northern and eastern Mediterranean.

Ephemeral Options: Untouchable and Uncovered

Wire's approach is important to reconsider, but so are the results of her approach, particularly in the light of these feminist and queer approaches

---

12. Here, Cvetkovich draws on and alludes to previous, and more elaborated work, including her own (for instance, Villarejo 1999; Cvetkovich 2002).
13. See the discussion in Hidalgo 2016; 2018; Wimbush 2012.

to ephemera. In the years since *The Corinthian Women Prophets*, some feminist interpreters of New Testament and early Christian literature have argued that women can only ever function as discursive signs or rhetorical figures in the study of ancient texts.[14] Historically, they can only ever be absent; rhetorically, they remain only vehicles for the message of the text. In a way, then, these kinds of approaches have reduced the female figures to an ephemeral inaccessibility. In contrast, I stand with other feminist biblical interpreters and my queer interlocutors to insist that attention to the inscription of gender (among other factors) in discourse or rhetoric can support historical reconstructive efforts about women and should help us produce alternative archives (see Matthews 2001, 51, 54; Schüssler Fiorenza 1999, 50–52; 2001, 175–86).[15] When even explicitly feminist work on women and gender in relation in 1 Corinthians tends to disavow the possibilities of reconstructing anything about people besides Paul in the Corinthian assembly community (see, e.g., Økland 2004), I believe we have lost something valuable: an alternative past, and a past of some use for our futures, as *an option*. A careful evaluation of these letters' rhetorics can contribute to an alternate archiving—historical reconstructions of *any* of the *many* other people participating in these assembly communities, people whose traces may be ephemeral, but are not entirely absent. Such an approach can contribute in critical and constructive ways to a range of counterkyriarchal projects: attention to the people marginalized in scholarship of the letters and often within the letters themselves provide alternate points of intervention and possibly even identification for those struggling against modes of marginalization and stigmatization now.

In short, the picture Wire constructs of the Corinthian women prophets is an important option. Sadly, otherwise excellent feminist work, reflecting on the dynamics of gender and sexuality on Paul's letters, fails to even consider these prophetic females as compelling historical figures or

---

14. See, e.g., Cooper 1996. For questions about the role of historical reconstructions based on texts that involve female figures, see Matthews 2001. Here Matthews is responding to a set of striking assertions made by Cooper (among others). For a different negotiation of both rhetorical/discursive and historical elements, see Vander Stichele and Penner 2009.

15. My own work's dual interest in the possibilities of textual representation and historical reconstruction marks it as differently influenced by cultural studies and literary theories from some trajectories in biblical studies.

contemporary sociopolitical options.[16] In wider circles scholars' refusal to seriously engage feminist work on this letter often leads to a corresponding inability (or unwillingness) to conceptualize what, how, or why the female Corinthians in this assembly were engaging in specifically embodied practices.[17] Yet, this need not be the case; these interpretive moves are not the only options, as I often find Wire's construction of the Corinthian women prophets both convincing and useful, as a feminist and queer option, even when she is considering seemingly slight references or the kinds of ephemeral traces Cvetkovich and Muñoz summon (for me).

One of the strengths of Wire's treatment of the Corinthian women prophets is an insistence on grappling with the argumentation throughout 1 Corinthians, not only those two texts where women's prayer and prophetic activities come most explicitly into the foreground (11:2–16; 14:26–40). Thus, Wire helps us to archive additional angles on the female figures addressed in this letter. By engaging in such a thorough rhetorical analysis, with the prophetic females always in mind, Wire helps us to piece together how these arguments would sound to them, how the rhetorical efforts could even be responses to these people in the Corinthian assembly community. Suddenly, formulaic notes such as "it is good for a man not to touch a woman" (7:1) ring differently, resounding for longer than a fleeting instant of "on the one hand."[18] A concessive moment before Paul attempts to assert the importance of marriage for some, especially those who lack adequate self-control (7:2–9), thus reflects a principle likely valued among women, given that it restricts male rather than female behavior (Wire 1990, 94). If one combines that formula with others Paul cites, another picture emerges. An assertion of "all things are in my own power" (or, "authorized," or "possible for me," *exestin*, 6:12; cf. 10:23) is a sign of a competing claim to self-authority, one that one can imagine voiced by those who feel the need to assert it in such circumstances. In this light Wire (1990, 94) even suggests that these last two slogans "may have been combined

---

16. For two recent examples, particularly written to be accessible to wider audiences, see Knust 2011, 82–86, 92–94, 159–62; Bird 2015, 107–11.

17. Martin's (1995, especially 229–49) failure to consider Wire's (1990) analysis more carefully (or his absolute lack of curiosity about these women, despite their importance for treating this argument) is symptomatic in this regard. For further reflections on the potential motivations (of both scholars and of prophetic females in Corinth), see Matthews 2015.

18. All translations are mine, unless otherwise indicated.

in a third, 'The woman has authority over her own body' (7:4)."[19] Paul, of course, is trying to limit the application of such slogans in the community, here by quoting the slogan and inserting a *not* into the potentially combined proposition, shaping sexual practice. While he admits that his own unmarried status is good (7:8) and thus preferable (even superior), Paul works to persuade or even prescribe that women should give up this good in their changed lives, whether they were married, widowed, or betrothed.

Nonetheless, this section on sex should not be artificially separated from another section on women. The effort the letter expends on convincing various female figures to return to more conventional sexual roles (7:1–40) indicates that at least some women are withdrawing from sex (with men; Wire 1990, 81–93). This withdrawal is likely an extension or intensification of other positions they held. Wire demonstrates that their experience of prophetic calling is intertwined with their desires to withdraw from sex with males (78–95, especially 93–95). Even Paul notes the association of abstinence with prayer when he concedes their right to occasional sexual refusal, but only to allow for greater attention to prayer (7:5; Wire 1990, 83). This brief effort to place limits on the praying activities of some resonates with the other, more extended passages where Paul specifically attempts to qualify and constrict how and when (and ultimately whether) women should pray and prophesy (11:1–16; 14:26–40). If one set of embodied practice—withdrawal from sex and marriage (with men)—is a reflection or even extension of another set—women's prayer and prophecy—practices that Paul alternatingly practices, approves, and constrains (for others), then it becomes clear that at least some Corinthian females were already drawing different conclusions from Paul about some overlapping practices. There are ephemeral traces of these different conclusions, but they are not yet entirely absent, as some more pessimistic, dubious, or despairing readers might think.

To this end, we can still see how the results of Wire's construction offer alternative negotiations of gender, sexuality, and embodiment, without reducing the terms of the women's transformations to the sexual alone. As such, these first-century female figures look as if they are anticipating feminist and queer options for the twenty-first century. Indeed, these women's withdrawal from sex may prefigure more recent queer critiques

---

19. This third passage uses the same verb of authority or potential as the second slogan discussed above (see Wire 1990, 82).

of reproductive futurity (Edelman 2004; Halberstam 2005), especially if one contextualizes these practices within an ancient assembly shaped by apocalyptic anticipations (see Marchal 2018). To be clear—and queer!—about these almost absent women, I am not imagining them as identical to contemporary queer figures. But their practices fall into the category that social historian Judith Bennett (2000) describes as "lesbian-like." They resisted sex and marriage (with males), they flouted prevailing expectations of sexual propriety, they collaborated with other females, they altered their gendered comportment in their clothing and bodily practices. In an effort to construct an alternative social history, against the sexist and heteronormative tendencies of traditional historiography, Bennett (2000, 15–16) refuses to reduce a category such as lesbian to one sexual dimension, in favor of a more extended, rich, even idiosyncratic set of criteria of "cautious kinship." The term *"lesbian-like"* (with quotation marks intact) simultaneously names what has gone unnamed (lesbian) and destabilizes any certitude about what an identification could connote (-like).[20] *"Lesbian-like"* can be deployed to highlight resemblances and affinities between practices across the centuries. Indeed, closer to the antiquity of these Corinthian females, Bernadette Brooten's (1996, 17–25) landmark study of female homoeroticism stressed that there might be more continuities and fewer turning points in the history of female as opposed to male homoerotic practices. Brooten demonstrated that the term *lesbian* (even without Bennett's qualifying "-like") could index this combination of continuities and discontinuities.

In such light Wire's reading of the Corinthian women prophets begins to resemble Cvetkovich's (2003, 67–71) own reconsideration of other slight references and almost absent archives for butch untouchability. The obstacles for archiving these kinds of butch practices might start with their stigmatization (their departures from prevailing expectations), but they

---

20. "The 'like' in 'lesbian-like' decenters 'lesbian,' introducing into historical research a productive uncertainty born of likeness and resemblance, not identity. It might therefore allow us to expand lesbian history beyond its narrow and quite unworkable focus on women who engaged in certifiable same-sex genital contact (a certification hard to achieve even for many contemporary women), and to incorporate into lesbian history women who, regardless of their sexual pleasures, lived in ways that offer certain affinities with modern lesbians. In so doing, we might incorporate into lesbian history sexual rebels, gender rebels, marriage-resisters, cross-dressers, single-women" (Bennett 2000, 14).

are intensified by their negating definition—or, rather, their positive valuation of not being touched. How does one reach back and find those who think it is good not to be touched? Here, again, I can build on the promise of Wire's constructions of the Corinthian women prophets and the links she traces between multiple passages, the overarching rhetorics of the letter, and the most notoriously difficult passages about women's speech.

Thirty years later, Wire's reading of the rhetorics at work in the most overloaded of these passages—11:2–16—still convinces me in nearly every way. I say "nearly" because, ever the contrarian, I think Wire's breakthrough analysis passed too quickly over one move Paul makes. In particular, when Paul first mentions the Corinthian women doing particular things with their bodies—praying and prophesying uncovered—he claims that such behavior is the same as if the woman's head was shaved (11:5; cf. 11:6).[21] Scholars often trivialize or pass over this particular rhetorical move, characterizing the argument as ridiculous or absurd, as an exaggeration, perhaps even intentionally so on Paul's part. A range of commentaries declares that Paul is being sarcastic in making this equivalence (or in arguing that a woman should cut her hair shortly if she will not cover; Collins 1999, 409; Horsley 1998, 155; Thistelton 2000, 832; Fitzmyer 2008, 414). Wire (1990, 118) combines two common scholarly estimations when she describes Paul's equivalence of prophecy uncovered with head shaving as a "shocking aside." When considered, Paul's argument about shortly cut or shaven hair is seldom deemed relevant for the historical situation in Corinth.[22] It is rarely viewed as central to understanding the historical or rhetorical context of this difficult passage—the reference is slight, but not entirely absent; in other words, it is ephemeral. For Wire (1990, 119), the rhetorical efficacy of Paul offering a "reasonable concession" (head covering during prayer and prophecy) is dependent on shortened head hair being "an unthinkable alternative."

But what if the argument being made here is dependent on being a distinctly recognizable, thus *thinkable* practice and possibility? I suggest that

---

21. Though I focus, here and elsewhere, on what this image of gender variation highlights for the fraught alterities and similarities of such encounters, Buell (2014) considers another exciting if still haunting option given anxious arguments around bodily boundaries, by focusing on human receptivity to spiritual powers and histories of possession and spiritualism.

22. Horsley (1998, 154) insists that this argument is "hypothetical. It does not presume that some women were cutting off their hair."

this particular rhetorical move is more than just an aside, an ephemeral, peripheral, or incidental gesture, completely unmoored from historical dynamics. Lingering over the potential premise "it is shameful (or dishonorable) for a woman (implied: a women's head hair) to be shortly cut or be shaved" (11:6) calls up well-known images of gender variation.[23] Indeed, the capacious, if confused category of ancient androgyny contains at times rather precise ways to think about females with short or shaved head hair, reflecting a range of elite imperial male concerns about women's embodied practices (including both sex and speech). This kind of female is one figure in a range of androgynous figures for Greco-Roman audiences, signs of both female ability and male anxiety, objects of ridicule and occasional, begrudging respect. Such a figuration is not entirely unlike those pulpy stereotypes one also has to trace in order to access an alternative public culture, an almost absent archive for sexual and gender minorities.

In this moment Paul seems to be referencing a known stereotype, or more likely an antitype, a negative form of female gender variation (and one not too distant from more recent characterizations of butch females).[24] Paul deploys this image to elicit a negative reaction from the audience: he aims to get them to link shortened head hair to prayer or prophecy with uncovered head (see also Matthews 2017). Yet, as Wire's work shows, there are perspectives besides Paul's active in these assemblies; we need not agree with Paul's arguments now, particularly because Paul was working so hard then to convince the Corinthians of something they did not already accept: that these embodied practices are outrageous or otherwise problematic. It remains distinctly possible that the prophetic females (and their own followers) did not accept the terms of this potential vilification, just as we now should not accept either these ancient arguments or more recent ones that mock, condemn, or marginalize gender-variant people in the present.

Here, Wire's recognition that Paul's letters function as argument rather than dogma is crucial, since understanding the letters requires keeping open the possibilities for whether (and how) they did or did not convince. Our approach to these epistles and the figures circulating within and with

---

23. Further, as Vander Stichele and Penner (2005, 292) have argued, this claim could even be the "critical lynchpin of Paul's argument in 1 Cor 11."

24. For more on the antitype of the ancient androgyne, and the productivity of juxtaposing ancient and more recent forms of gender variation, see Marchal 2014; and, in longer form, Marchal 2020.

them should not be confined to the perspectives of Paul and the prevailing bodies of interpretation. Thus, again, Wire anticipates or at least resonates with the emphasis on the reception and circulation of objects in the works of Cvetkovich and Muñoz.

Muñoz (2009, 115–30) shows a fleeting, even ephemeral interest in alternative approaches to epistles in his brief reflections on the pre-Stonewall performance art of Ray Johnson and the New York Correspondence School. Muñoz (2009, 119) encounters and then constructs his own ephemeral archive in considering Johnson's mailed collages, information, and ephemera, for which he occasionally asked for responses: "Viewing Johnson's postings, his mail art, was like entering a secret world I had somehow half known. It was edifying. The letter represented a vast system of associations and correspondences that made a world that was not quite here yet nonetheless on the horizon. It was a queer world of potentiality." Muñoz reimagines a secret world of wider networks, of different associations, of unknown potential, a queer life from an earlier era. Further, Johnson's approach to correspondence challenges simplistic views of letters.

> The letter no longer has a "here to there" trajectory. It now takes on a "here to there to there and there too" trajectory, since a piece of mail art will move between a circuit of friends and acquaintances, being altered at every point in the journey. We can call this new temporality one of queer futurity, where the future is a site of infinite and immutable potentiality. (Muñoz 2009, 126–27)

This queer futurity also corresponds in part with how we think Paul's letters could have functioned in antiquity within, between, and among the various assembly communities, with correspondingly open possibilities for how they were (or even still might be) used, particularly by marginalized or obscured figures, now and then.

Circulating an Archive, Instead of Concluding an Essay

I draw on Cvetkovich and Muñoz to help us trace spectral presences through slight references, reminding us of the ephemerality of the exchange within and beyond these epistles, while underscoring that reading for these passing references and debased figures shows how much more can be archived than often assumed within traditional Pauline studies. Wire (1990, 10) has helpfully discussed the problem with presuming biblical and specifically

Pauline authority in advance, since it "excludes the possibility of weighing his arguments in the balance. Because an argument Paul makes cannot be rejected as unconvincing, it also cannot convince. In this way the authority we attribute to Paul prevents him from persuading us." Epistles always signal the possibility to think, feel, organize, and respond otherwise. For instance, if Paul feels the need to deploy a stereotyped figure, at the least he worries that some in these audiences would have identified with features of these figures. Since Paul's view was just one of many in these assemblies, it seems important to pull out the obscured, even pulpy stereotyped figures and place them alongside those figures, like the Corinthian women prophets, who have been more robustly constructed thus far. Cvetkovich reminds us that, in the process of feeling around for history, archiving helps to construct a community, often through ephemeral references and unexpected resonances.

The picture I am developing here might just be such a slight, almost absent archive in the making. The inspiration for this archive draws on more than the feminist and queer approaches of Wire, Cvetkovich, and Muñoz, but the untouched and uncovered subjects occasionally treated as objects in Pauline epistles and interpretations. The exchange between Paul and the Corinthians is stuffed with these alternative futures of the past. I hope it illustrates how these and other alternative futures of the past await, but only if one is willing to (re)consider the methods and results of Wire's landmark project, the rhetorics about and reconstructions of those *Corinthian Women Prophets*.

Works Cited

Bennett, Judith M. 2000. "'Lesbian-Like' and the Social History of Lesbianisms." *JHistSex* 9:1–24.

Bird, Jennifer Grace. 2015. *Permission Granted: Take the Bible into Your Own Hands*. Louisville: Westminster John Knox.

Bitzer, Lloyd F. 1968. "The Rhetorical Situation." *PR* 1:1–14.

Blanton, Ward, 2014. *A Materialism for the Masses: Saint Paul and the Philosophy of Undying Life*. Insurrections. New York: Columbia University Press.

Brooten, Bernadette J. 1996. *Love between Women: Early Christian Responses to Female Homoeroticism*. CSSHS. Chicago: University of Chicago Press.

Buell, Denise Kimber. 2009. "God's Own People: Specters of Race, Ethnicity, and Gender in Early Christian Studies." Pages 159–90 in *Prejudice and Christian Beginnings: Investigating Race, Gender, and Ethnicity in Early Christian Studies*. Edited by Elisabeth Schüssler Fiorenza and Laura Nasrallah. Minneapolis: Fortress.

———. 2010. "Cyborg Memories: An Impure History of Jesus." *BibInt* 18:313–41.

———. 2014. "Hauntology Meets Post-humanism: Some Payoffs for Biblical Studies." Pages 29–56 in *The Bible and Posthumanism*. Edited by Jennifer L. Koosed. SemeiaSt 74. Atlanta: Society of Biblical Literature.

Carden, Michael. 2004. *Sodomy: A History of a Christian Biblical Myth*. BibW. London: Equinox.

Castelli, Elizabeth A. 1991. *Imitating Paul: A Discourse of Power*. LCBI. Louisville: Westminster John Knox.

Collins, Raymond F. 1999. *1 Corinthians*. SP 7. Collegeville, MN: Liturgical Press.

Cooper, Kate. 1996. *The Virgin and the Bride: Idealized Womanhood in Late Antiquity*. Cambridge: Harvard University Press.

Cvetkovich, Ann. 2002. "In the Archives of Lesbian Feelings: Documentary and Public Culture." *CO* 49:107–46.

———. 2003. *An Archive of Feelings: Trauma, Sexuality, and Lesbian Public Cultures*. Series Q. Durham, NC: Duke University Press.

———. 2012. *Depression: A Public Feeling*. Durham, NC: Duke University Press.

Edelman, Lee. 2004. *No Future: Queer Theory and the Death Drive*. Series Q. Durham, NC: Duke University Press.

Fitzmyer, Joseph A. 2008. *First Corinthians: A New Translation with Introduction and Commentary*. AB 32. New Haven: Yale University Press.

Gordon, Avery. 1997. *Ghostly Matters: Haunting and the Sociological Imagination*. Minneapolis: University of Minnesota Press.

Halberstam, Judith. 2005. *In a Queer Time and Place: Transgender Bodies, Subcultural Lives*. SC. New York: New York University Press.

Hidaglo, Jacqueline M. 2016. *Revelation in Aztlán: Scriptures, Utopias, and the Chicano Movement*. BCS. New York: Palgrave Macmillan.

———. 2018. "'Our Book of Revelation … Prescribes Our Fate and Releases Us from It': Scriptural Disorientations in Cherríe Moraga's *The Last Generation*." Pages 113–32 in *Sexual Disorientations: Queer Temporalities, Affects, Theologies*. TTC. Edited by Kent L. Brintnall,

Joseph A. Marchal, and Stephen D. Moore. New York: Fordham University Press.

Horsley, Richard A. 1998. *1 Corinthians*. ANTC. Nashville: Abingdon.

Ivarsson, Fredrik. 2007. "Vice Lists and Deviant Masculinity: The Rhetorical Function of 1 Corinthians 5:10–11 and 6:9–10." Pages 163–84 in *Mapping Gender in Ancient Religious Discourses*. Edited by Todd Penner and Caroline Vander Stichele. BibInt 84. Leiden: Brill.

Kittredge, Cynthia Briggs. 1998. *Community and Authority: The Rhetoric of Obedience in the Pauline Tradition*. HTS 45. Harrisburg, PA: Trinity Press International.

———. 2003. "Rethinking Authorship in the Letters of Paul: Elisabeth Schüssler Fiorenza's Model of Pauline Theology." Pages 318–33 in *Walk in the Ways of Wisdom: Essays in Honor of Elisabeth Schüssler Fiorenza*. Edited by Shelly Matthews, Cynthia Briggs Kittredge, and Melanie Johnson-DeBaufre. Harrisburg, PA: Trinity Press International.

Knust, Jennifer Wright. 2011. *Unprotected Texts: The Bible's Surprising Contradictions about Sex and Desire*. New York: HarperOne.

Kotrosits, Maia. 2015. *Rethinking Early Christian Identity: Affect, Violence, and Belonging*. Minneapolis: Fortress.

Luijendijk, AnneMarie. 2009. *Greetings in the Lord: Early Christians in the Oxyrhynchus Papyri*. HTS 60. Cambridge: Harvard University Press.

Malherbe, Abraham J. 1988. *Ancient Epistolary Theorists*. SBLSBS 19. Atlanta: Scholars Press.

Marchal, Joseph A. 2006. *Hierarchy, Unity, and Imitation: A Feminist Rhetorical Analysis of Power Dynamics in Paul's Letter to the Philippians*. AcBib 24. Atlanta: Society of Biblical Literature.

———. 2011. "'Making History' Queerly: Touches across Time through a Biblical Behind." *BibInt* 19:373–95.

———. 2014. "Female Masculinity in Corinth? Bodily Citations and the Drag of History." *Neot* 48:93–113.

———. 2018. "How Soon Is (This Apocalypse) Now? Queer Velocities after a Corinthian Already and a Pauline Not Yet." Pages 45–67 in *Sexual Disorientations: Queer Temporalities, Affects, Theologies*. TTC. Edited by Kent L. Brintnall, Joseph A. Marchal, and Stephen D. Moore. New York: Fordham University Press.

———. 2020. *Appalling Bodies: Queer Figures before and after Paul's Letters*. New York: Oxford University Press.

Martin, Dale B. 1995. *The Corinthian Body*. New Haven: Yale University Press.

———. 1996. "*Arsenokoitēs* and *Malakos*: Meanings and Consequences." Pages 117–36 in *Biblical Ethics and Homosexuality: Listening to Scriptures*. Edited by Robert L. Brawley. Louisville: Westminster John Knox.

Matthews, Shelly. 2001. "Thinking of Thecla: Issues in Feminist Historiography." *JFSR* 17:2:39–55.

———. 2015. "A Feminist Analysis of the Veiling Passage (1 Corinthians 11:2–16): Who Really Cares That Paul Was Not a Gender Egalitarian after All?" *LD* 2.

———. 2017. "'To Be One and the Same with the Woman Whose Head Is Shaven' (1 Cor 11:5b): Resisting the Violence of 1 Corinthians 11:2–16 from the Bottom of the Kyriarchal Pyramid." Pages 31–51 in *Sexual Violence and Sacred Texts*. Edited by Amy Kalmanofsky. Cambridge: Feminist Studies in Religion Books.

Miller, Anna C. 2015. *Corinthian Democracy: Democratic Discourse in 1 Corinthians*. PTMS 220. Eugene, OR: Pickwick.

Muñoz, José Esteban. 1996. "Ephemera as Evidence: Introductory Notes to Queer Acts." *WP* 16:5–16.

———. 2009. *Cruising Utopia: The Then and There of Queer Futurity*. SC. New York: New York University Press.

Økland, Jorunn. 2004. *Women in Their Place: Paul and the Corinthian Discourse of Gender and Sanctuary Space*. JSNTSup 269. London: T&T Clark.

Olbrechts-Tyteca, Lucie, and Chaïm L. Perelman. 1969. *The New Rhetoric: A Treatise on Argumentation*. Translated by John Wilkinson and Purcell Weaver. Notre Dame: University of Notre Dame Press.

Olyan, Saul M. 1994. "'And with a Male You Shall Not Lie the Lying Down of a Woman': On the Meaning and Significance of Leviticus 18:22 and 20:13." *JHistSex* 5:179–206.

Schüssler Fiorenza, Elisabeth. 1992. *But She Said: Feminist Practices of Biblical Interpretation*. Boston: Beacon.

———. 1999. *Rhetoric and Ethic: The Politics of Biblical Studies*. Minneapolis: Fortress.

———. 2001. *Wisdom Ways: Introducing Feminist Biblical Interpretation*. Maryknoll, NY: Orbis.

Smith, Mitzi J. Forthcoming. *Chloe and Her People: A Womanist Reading of 1 Corinthians*. Eugene, OR: Cascade.

Stowers, Stanley K. 1986. *Letter-Writing in Greco-Roman Antiquity*. LEC 5. Philadelphia: Westminster.

Thiselton, Anthony C. 2000. *The First Epistle to the Corinthians: A Commentary on the Greek Text*. NIGTC. Grand Rapids: Eerdmans.

Vander Stichele, Caroline, and Todd C. Penner. 2005. "Paul and the Rhetoric of Gender." Pages 287–310 in *Her Master's Tools? Feminist and Postcolonial Engagements of Historical-Critical Discourse*. Edited by Caroline Vander Stichele and Todd Penner. GPBS 9. Atlanta: Society of Biblical Literature.

———. 2009. *Contextualizing Gender in Early Christian Discourse: Thinking beyond Thecla*. London: T&T Clark.

Villarejo, Amy. 1999. "Forbidden Love: Pulp as Lesbian History." Pages 316–46 in *Out Takes: Essays on Queer Theory and Film*. Edited by Ellis Hanson. Series Q. Durham, NC: Duke University Press.

Wimbush, Vincent L. 2012. *White Men's Magic: Scripturalization as Slavery*. New York: Oxford University Press.

Wire, Antoinette Clark. 1990. *The Corinthian Women Prophets: A Reconstruction through Paul's Rhetoric*. Minneapolis: Fortress.

The Writing Continues:
The Women Are Still There in 2 Corinthians

Arminta Fox

In her work on the Corinthian correspondence, Antoinette Clark Wire's analysis places a group of Corinthian women prophets, rather than Paul, at the center of interpretation (see further Fox 2020). Wire combines critical theories of rhetoric, social history, and feminism to make an effective social reconstruction of these female prophets. She assumes that Paul, as a good rhetorician, would argue in a way that would measure his audience at every count, using their own language and images to move them in the right direction (Wire 1990, 3). This landmark study has changed the field of biblical studies.

In particular, *The Corinthian Women Prophets* has changed the field of 1 Corinthians scholarship. Wire's work to flesh out a picture of women prophets in Corinth has paved the way for additional feminist, womanist, gender-critical, and queer approaches to 1 Corinthians. In contrast, 2 Corinthians scholarship has been slow to incorporate Wire's work and the presence of women prophets in Corinth. When Wire's work is included in studies of 2 Corinthians, it is primarily in the form of contrasts and negative critiques.[1] This epitomizes what Elisabeth Schüssler Fiorenza

---

1. Witherington (1995, 344 n. 44; Sumney 1990, 85–125), for example, has argued that Wire's analysis is problematic because she does not assume that Paul's assessment of the historical situation is accurate and, instead, sees his assessment as rhetorical. Witherington assumes that there is no reason to doubt Paul's account. When Wire asserts that the Corinthian women prophets stood in opposition to Paul, she is critiqued by Witherington (1995, 344) for mirror-reading, or "assuming that what Paul affirms is the opposite of what his opponents believed," a method that Jerry Sumney (1990, 85–125) denounces in his argument about the use of proper historical-critical methods in 2 Corinthians.

(1999, 180) calls a politics of othering within scholarship. Schüssler Fiorenza terms the multifaceted tendency to either vilify or idealize difference as otherness for the sake of establishing identity as a *discourse of othering*. As scholars identify with Paul, any scholarly identification with others in Corinth seems to represent a threat to Paul's authority and results in the reproduction of defenses of kyriarchy in modern scholarship. *Kyriarchy* is a term coined by Schüssler Fiorenza (2007, 1) to refer to "domination by the emperor, lord, slave-master, father, husband, elite propertied colonizing male." Therefore, it is imperative that feminist analysis be used to interpret 2 Corinthians to resist the politics of othering within scholarship and within the history of the Corinthian early Christ community.

In the next several pages I argue that Wire's analysis of the Corinthian community and the women prophets can be expanded on and applied to 2 Corinthians.[2] Particularly, I analyze 2 Cor 10–13, where Paul writes a passionate defense of his authority within the Corinthian community. Following Wire (1990, 8–9), I assume that this text is dialogic and thus indicates something about those with whom Paul communicates.[3] The places where he argues most creatively and passionately suggest where he anticipates the most resistance to his writing. The images he uses and the assumptions he makes suggest that the audience was familiar with those images. However, some in Corinth undoubtedly thought differently from Paul. His writings, then, are merely indicative of one side of a complex debate. Thus, it is possible and necessary to envision the multiple ways his interlocutors accepted, ignored, or actively resisted his arguments. This type of historical reconstructive work is no less speculative than historical reconstructions put forth by malestream scholars or others who assume

---

2. One of Wire's assumptions is that there were women in Paul's audience. As my title suggests, I also assume that diverse women were there and that they played a role in Paul's rhetoric. Because of studies like Wire's, it is no longer necessary to defend this point. Rather, any studies that assume that women, children, or enslaved people were not present must now defend their assumptions.

3. After stating her assumption that Paul's writing is rhetorical, Wire's (1990, 8) second assumption asserts, "Whatever Paul says about human beings, Corinthians, believers in Christ, women, and prophets is a possible resource for understanding the women prophets in Corinth's church." Wire's third assumption states, "on whatever points Paul's persuasion is insistent and intense, showing he is not merely confirming their agreement but struggling for their assent, one can assume some different and opposite point of view in Corinth from the one Paul is stating" (9). Her fourth assumption is that the women prophets have some role in the rhetorical context (9).

Paul's perspective. Such feminist reconstructive work, too, is based on the work of historians and biblical scholars, and it finds grounding within the literature of the first- and second-century Mediterranean context. While I perform an initial rhetorical analysis of Paul's writing of 2 Cor 10–13, I turn consistently to the question of how the text may have been informed and received by various types of people in Corinth by using a hermeneutics of suspicion and drawing on the work of historians and other biblical scholars. Analyzing the malleability of Paul's own gender performance opens up space to consider the malleability of identity expressions possible in the Corinthian community. An argument for the presence of women in the community starts, in this case, by pinpointing malleable gender expressions in the text. Reading 2 Cor 10–13 with a feminist decentering analysis leads to more historically and ethically plausible interpretations.

Moving Rhetoric and Rhetorical Moves in 2 Cor 10–13

> For, although we walk in flesh, we do not wage war according to the flesh. For the weapons of our war are not fleshly but powered by God for the destruction of strongholds—we are destroying arguments, and are raising up everything that is exalted against the knowledge of God. We are taking prisoner of all thoughts for the obedience of Christ. (2 Cor 10:3–5)[4]

> Who is weak and I am not weak? Who is made to stumble and I am not burning with indignation? (2 Cor 11:29)

In 2 Cor 10–13, the descriptions of the characters move between competing images of power and weakness, strategically sliding along spectrums of identity markers. The weapons of war, the destruction of strongholds, the taking of prisoners, solidarity in weakness and indignation: these and other vivid images invoked in 2 Cor 10–13 assume and depend on a kyriarchal logic. This text consistently relies on the assumptions that gods reign over people, that high-status and wealthy families have strength over lower classes and enslaved people, that men rule over women, that parents rule over children, and that Romans rule over Jews and all other groups. Chapter 10, for example, begins with a God who acts like an emperor at war, sending Paul, like a violent general, to crush the opponents and rescue the

---

4. All biblical translations are my own unless otherwise noted.

obedient Corinthians. But these chapters also assume that identity markers can, at times, be fluid or malleable rather than fixed or static (for more information on malleable identity markers in early Christian texts, see Johnson Hodge 2005; Buell 2005). While someone may appear to have the upper hand in one part of the letter, in another, his or her claims to power are discredited. Paul may begin the section as an imperial general, but he adopts weakness, foolishness, and even slavery before returning to a position of authority by the end of chapter 13. In order for these rhetorical acrobatics to succeed, Paul must also reposition the Corinthians and his opponents. At times, they appear strong or wise; at others, their strength is described as weakness and their wisdom appears foolish.

Indeed, chapters 10–13 feature a rhetorical tour de force. This may be Paul's last known word to convince the Corinthians of the power and wisdom of his voice in a debate about speaking in the community. Such desperate times call for desperate rhetorical strategies, it would seem, as Paul slides from one identity position to another and shifts others around him as well. He openly defends himself on a few counts—speaking ability, ministerial style, position of weakness, and visionary control—even as he also defends against indirect challenges to his masculinity, his strength, and his class status. The kyriarchal logic that underlies Paul's rhetoric ultimately functions to authorize his position of power over others. Paul's final defense relies on a theological program of grace. Paul uses this grace from God in service to his own authority claims over the Corinthians. Grace affects Paul's transformation from weakness to strength, and thus his opponents' shift from strength to weakness. After analyzing Paul's strategic rhetorical shifts in this passage, I envision the lives and afterlives of the text as a communal document.

God the Emperor, the Colonizing Apostle, and the Corinthian Battlefield

Paul presents himself in the image of a strong rhetorician and kyriarchal general in the service of an emperor God in order to claim power in communal debates about authority. As a kyriarchal figure, Paul rhetorically positions himself as powerful in multiple and intersecting ways. One way he claims authority is by appealing to masculinity through highlighting his abilities as speaker or rhetorician and his military strength and violence. Paul presents himself as masculine when he directly addresses the topic of rhetorical abilities as a standard for authority. He claims the right to boast throughout the whole letter (1:12; 3:1; 5:12), but in chapter 10

Paul responds directly to the Corinthian critique recorded in 10:10 that his physical presence is weak and pales in comparison to his strong letters. This critique targets Paul's rhetorical performance and accuses him of being a flatterer, or someone who bows down to others' wishes rather than asserting their own (Larson 2004, 91). Rather than attacking the content of his speech, this common form of critique questions Paul's right to speak by using physiognomics, or the practice of determining one's character, status, or destiny through examination of that individual's body. In examining rhetorical performance, physiognomy would consider vocal tone and clarity, posture, gestures, clothing, and personal appearance (87–90). These critiques of rhetorical performance also functioned as critiques of gender performance (91).[5] Thus, some in Corinth are also attacking Paul's masculinity in 10:10. Gendered bodily performance is at the heart of interactions in this correspondence. In order to defend himself and secure a position of authority in the community, Paul initially presents himself as physically and rhetorically strong.

In response to this Corinthian charge, Paul also defends his masculinity and kyriarchal position when he presents himself as a colonizing male who dominates and effeminizes communities. From the beginning of chapter 10, Paul describes himself as God's imperial warrior who is capable of asserting power over others. Paul commands from afar, arguing that he and his army may live as humans, but they wage war divinely, using divine weapons that conquer and capture thoughts and arguments (2 Cor 10:3–5). This evokes an image of a Roman general who enslaves conquered prisoners of war (Harrill 2006, 53). Warrior Paul demands obedience and punishes disobedience in his God-given mission to build up the Corinthians (2 Cor 10:6–8; on the rhetoric of obedience, see Kittredge 1998). Paul uses vocabulary of measured regions and spheres to present himself as authoritative in Achaia (2 Cor 10:13). As a conquering traveler, Paul declares his hopes to enlarge his territory as the locals submit (10:15). A model general, he describes that he is careful to avoid lands/peoples that are under someone else's authority (10:16). Instead, he keeps to the areas/peoples where he arrived first (10:14). Once he has brought this land and these peoples into obedience, he can make proclamations in farther lands. Paul "will not boast beyond measure," but will follow his orders to stay

---

5. Larson draws from an examination of Seneca and the work of Maud Gleason for this claim. See Seneca, *Contr.* 2, pref. 1; see also Seneca, *Ep.* 114, "On Style as a Mirror of Character."

in his assigned area of duty (10:13–15). By using vocabulary of strength, power, and aggression, Paul is highlighting masculine characteristics. David Clines (2004, 184) argues that Paul presents himself as the "ultimate Can Do male," who looks forward to strength tests with his opponents. In utilizing language of imperial and militaristic action, some in Corinth may have thought of Paul's mission as resembling a Roman conquest of territories and peoples. In the words of Joseph Marchal (2008, 87): "Paul mimes the emperor's authoritative gender while exhorting the community to perform an imitation similar to that demanded of Rome's subjects." By characterizing himself in this way, Paul's goal is to command authority and inspire obedience from the Corinthians.

How would Paul's rhetorical act of identifying himself with a Roman general and God with a Roman emperor have been understood in Corinth? It certainly would not have gone unnoticed by those who heard the letter. Signs and images of Roman colonization surrounded Paul's ancient audience. For example, at the time of Paul's writing to Corinth, 101 of 104 of the inscriptions in Corinth were in Latin, the imperial language, even though the surrounding areas and peoples in Achaia undoubtedly spoke Greek (Murphy-O'Connor 1983, 5; Kent and American School of Classical Studies at Athens 1966, 19). The facts of Roman colonization may have been particularly painful in Corinth as the former center of the Achaian League's rebellion against Rome. In punishment for this rebellion, Corinth was razed by Roman consul Mummius and refounded over one hundred years later, in 44 BCE by Julius Caesar. This split between the Romans and Greeks continued in the later history of Corinth (Murphy-O'Connor 1983, 1). Even cosmological understandings reflected this shift as the gods Poseidon and Helios were replaced with Caesar in the city's founding myth (1). The Greek Achaians may have continued to resent Roman rule and the destruction it wrought. The text of 2 Corinthians is not ignorant of this history. Paul situates Corinth within Achaia at various points throughout the letter (2 Cor 1:1; 9:2; 11:10). Particularly, he states that he wants the boast of his authority to ring out in the regions of Achaia (2 Cor 11:10).

In hearing kyriarchal rhetoric amid the repeated situating of Corinth within Achaia, some in Corinth would have interpreted Paul as taking advantage of this history and the present situation of colonization. Those Corinthians who particularly identified themselves by their Greekness or by their other forms of rebellion against Roman kyriarchy would have heard Paul in this letter as aligning himself with the emperor rather than with the Achaians. Paul's self-constructions and fixed identity claims for his kyriarchal authority are further concretized by his corresponding constructions of the Corinthian Christ community. While Paul constructs himself as an imperial general in chapter 10, he constructs the Corinthians as living territory over which he battles with the superapostles. He repeatedly uses spatial terms referring to measures, spheres, limits, and boundaries. These lands do not talk but passively submit to the uses of others. In describing himself as a bold rhetorician, Paul is dependent on the image of a silently attentive audience. As he makes proclamations throughout the region of his right to boast and to deliver powerful speeches, his loquaciousness is juxtaposed to the constructed silence of the Corinthians. Paul takes advantage of their history of conquest and failed rebellion to construct them as the natural losers and the ones who must accommodate to the new regime and its destruction.

However, from Paul's perspective, God is the emperor, and God lies at the center of the city's founding myth. God, not the Roman emperor, gave Paul his authority through grace. It is God who apportioned this territory, these peoples, to Paul (2 Cor 10:13). Their conquest and their accommodation is divinely sanctioned, says Paul. For the Corinthians, the blending of kyriarchal rhetoric and Paul's message of God's grace would have both reinscribed the power of the Roman empire and drawn awareness to the ways in which God's empire was distinct from the Roman empire. Paul highlights this difference when he specifies that God gave him power for building up rather than tearing down the Corinthians (12:19). Paul also stresses that he does not wish to make them terribly afraid by his letters (10:9). While Paul presents himself as a conquering warrior sent by an emperor, his contrastive arguments serve to distinguish his mission from that of the Roman Empire. He claims power, but he also claims moderation. This moderation also serves his claims to masculinity, as moderation shows that one is the master of the fleshly self and its out-of-control desires. Thus, like his later arguments about weakness, moderation serves to build up Paul's kyriarchal authority claims.

Some individuals in Corinth may have actively resisted Paul's presentation of himself as an imperial warrior or his violent theological vision. Rather than choosing violent or militaristic images of power, there were likely some women in Corinth who saw power embodied in other ways. The life-giving and life-risking power in childbearing, for example, or of bearing divine speech, *logos*, or wisdom may have been images of power from within the *basileia* movement that were more potent for women in Corinth. Using Wire's approach in assuming that the most forceful of

Paul's claims suggests where he felt most threatened suggests that Paul's portrayal of the Corinthians as passive and silent may have been because that is the opposite of how he saw them or how they were. Attempts to portray the Corinthians as a silent battlefield or witnesses to the actions of men point to the activist power of women in the Corinthian *ekklēsia*, particularly around issues of speech, wise argument, and connection to God.

Pater Paul, Jesus the Groom, the Wayward Corinthian Bride, and the Other Men

In the next chapter, Paul also fashions himself as a divinely jealous patriarch who worries about his daughter's virginal status (2 Cor 11:2). By constructing himself as a father to the Corinthians, the kyriarchal relationships between God, Christ, Paul, and the Corinthians are naturalized. Paul describes himself as fatherly in his refusal to accept the Corinthians' offers of material support. Even though he was in great need, he reports that he did not burden anyone in Corinth and instead relied on other communities (11:7-12). Some in Corinth may have interpreted Paul's rejection of Corinthian support in favor of his own independence as a rejection of limits to his masculine autonomy. He appeals to fatherly love and to convention about parents providing for their children to support this refusal (12:14). As a stern father figure, he writes to correct and protect them. By chapter 13, Paul makes it clear that he is coming and will not allow any disobedience. The Corinthians are to listen to him on every point, or else Paul will correct them (13:11).

Where he is described as masculine, powerful, and fatherly, the Corinthians are effeminate, voiceless, passive, and a singular sexually objectified daughter and maiden. Corresponding to Paul's self-construction as father, Paul describes the Corinthian community as his female child whom he has promised in marriage to Christ (Matthews 1995, 212). As Shelly Matthews (1995, 212) argues, this construction serves to denigrate them and place them in a socially inferior and passive role. Paul characterizes the entire Corinthian community as tainted by female sexual promiscuity in that they have not been faithful or chaste. He compares the Corinthians to Eve and the rival apostles to the serpent (2 Cor 11:3). As Matthews argues, this is evidence of his identifying the serpent of Gen 3 with Satan. This comparison also shows that he assumes, along with a popular interpretation at the time, that Eve's actions of eating from the tree were also sexual in nature (Matthews 1995, 212; Dunning 2014). By not listening to Paul, the Corinthians are at risk of being deceived and led astray in thought and body, which would make them unfit for union with Christ, the spouse Father Paul has chosen for them. They are flirting with unfaithfulness and sexual promiscuity in their ready submission to the superapostles' snake-like whisperings in their ears of other Jesuses, other spirits, and other gospels (2 Cor 11:4). By characterizing the Corinthians in the negative image of Eve, Paul effeminizes and sexually objectifies the community. Their obedience is configured as maintaining chastity and sexual purity, for the purpose of pleasing their Lord Christ. Associating the community with sexual transgressions would have been "a direct affront to women who had chosen an ascetic life-style as part of their devotion to God" (Matthews 1995, 212). This association would also have been a denunciation of wo/men who engaged in consensual sexual behavior in their Christ community, or did not shun the family of 1 Cor 5:1, for example. Paul's characterizations may have been an attempt to particularly curb the actions of single or widowed young women active in the Corinthian Christ community. On the other hand, older women in the community may have read these descriptions as attempts to critique their age or vivacity on the basis of gender. Women of any age, no matter how wise, are subject to the control of the patriarch, Paul's rhetoric suggests.

Furthermore, accepting this image of the community as Eve also requires acceptance of the kyriarchal frame that Paul uses in constructing this comparison. Caroline Vander Stichele compares Paul's use of the metaphor of Eve and the sexually seductive serpent to his descriptions of Adam in other letters. Adam exemplifies the universal and old humanity, whereas Christ models a new humanity. In contrast to Adam and Christ, Eve marks the particular, sexual, and physical. Vander Stichele (2012, 751) asserts, "If we look at the way Eve is portrayed in 2 Corinthians, we discover that her sexual identity as a woman stands in the foreground, and moreover, that she is seen to be in a passive role. She herself does not take the initiative; she is simply led astray." In using this image of Eve as a metaphor for the Corinthian community, Paul marks them as passive, sexual, physical, and effeminate. Vander Stichele (2012, 752) points out, "His argument is built on the contrast between the images of two different types of women, the positive image of the virgin (v. 2, *parthenos*), on the one hand, and the negative image of Eve as one at risk of being led astray, on the other." Paul's argument in chapter 11 depends on the notion that women are defined and valued in terms of their sexual purity. Furthermore, it assumes that men and others who may be positioned higher on a kyriarchal pyramid, such as Paul, free male leaders, and God, will judge wo/men according to these standards. Enslaved people and wo/men from low classes had additional challenges in maintaining a virginal status and thus, were more vulnerable to valuing and judgments based on sexual purity. Paul's constructions, in effect, remove these wo/men from the debate about authority, speaking abilities, and wisdom as their sexual and moral purity is in doubt. Similarly, mothers are only valuable in terms of their sexuality and not for their maternal power. Rather than leading or speaking with authority, wo/men, particularly those of low status, are passive, weak, and vulnerable to the whims of others.

Paul not only constructs an image of himself as an imperial general and jealous patriarch, and of the Corinthians as passive territories and sexually compromising wo/men; he also presents the rival apostles as deceptive, false imperial generals and sexually deviant boasters from Satan. This debate about boasting should be seen as a competition of rhetoric and masculinity (2 Cor 10:12, 17; Larson 2004, 91). While Paul "destroys arguments," "enslaves opposing thoughts," and "punishes disobedience," they are responsible for generating these opposing thoughts and arguments (2 Cor 10:4–6). They become a foil for him as he contrasts his own behavior to their extensive bragging and comparisons. Furthermore, in Paul's construction, God supports Paul's boasting, but not the boasting behavior of the other apostles (10:17–18). They merely boast for themselves, says Paul. According to the majority of commentaries, it is the rival Corinthian leaders who critiqued Paul's rhetorical abilities, thus provoking Paul's agitated response (2 Cor 10:10; Bassler 2012; Bultmann 1985; Roetzel 2007; Thrall 1994; Witherington 1995). As I argue above, Paul defends himself and his masculinity by using kyriarchal metaphors and imagery that assert his position above any rival leaders. Paul uses imperial metaphors that claim and map various occupied territories to construct the superapostles as representatives of a false emperor and pseudo-regime as they boast beyond their limits by vying for preaching power over the Corinthians. From Paul's telling, they are clearly in Paul's territory, showing that they do not have the same masculine moderation that he claims for himself (2 Cor 10:15). While Paul boasts in the Lord, they are presented as ministers of Satan in serpent disguise, "false apostles," and "deceitful workers" (11:13–15). While Paul's actions are divinely sanctioned, Paul characterizes the superapostles' actions as foolish (11:19). They attempt to conquer and devour the Corinthians by enslaving them, taking advantage of them, and abusing them (11:20). In identifying them with the serpent, their actions are also sexualized. This enables Paul to construct them as not only opposing him, but also rivaling Christ as suitors for the effeminized Corinthian bride. This characterization of the apostles also participates in the kyriarchal frame that assumes that men have the power to determine how women, and women's bodies, should be treated. As a powerful *paterfamilias* to the Corinthians and warrior for the Lord, Paul claims power over the rival leaders as he portrays them claiming power over the Corinthians.

Strategic Slavery and Forced Foolishness

In stark contrast, Paul also presents himself as weak and slave-like in this passage in order to bolster his arguments for leadership. As he shifts his own self-characterization, he correspondingly shifts his presentation of the community and the superapostles. In descriptions of his bodily weakness, he humbles himself to a slave-like status when he has preached to them for free (2 Cor 11:7). He accepted support from other churches, robbing them, to be a slave for the Corinthians (11:8). Comparing himself to the superapostles, Paul says that he has worked harder and has faced prison and beatings to a greater extent than they have, and that he has even come close to death (11:23). He lists all the various implements that have been used to physically harm him, including lashes, rods, and stones (11:24–25). In many settings he has been in danger at the will of many people and forces. With his own people, Paul has received lashes, which he contrasts to the rival apostles who might gain authority for being a Hebrew, Israelite, and descendant of Abraham. Further evidence of Paul's constructed weakness or enslaved status can be found in the description of his floggings, which would highlight his dishonor by the Roman custom that reserved flogging for noncitizens (Larson 2004, 94). Jennifer Glancy (2004, 99; Barton 1994, 41) argues that wounds on the back and bodily scars from beatings and whippings were distinguished from martial wounds of honor on the front of the body. Indeed, whippable bodies were considered dishonorable, of suspect character, effeminized, and were often enslaved. Paul does not describe his beatings as heroic or manly but rather as weakness (Glancy 2004, 99). Living in subhuman conditions without sleep, food, drink, or clothes, he has had to toil and work (2 Cor 11:26). Not only has he suffered abuses from all people, but even from nature, leaving him often near death, cold, naked, and without food (11:27). He describes himself as the weakest of the weak (11:29). These descriptions contribute to a construction of Paul as sharing the status of the enslaved.

By constructing himself as an enslaved person, Paul strategically negotiates for his authority to speak in the community. J. Albert Harrill (2006) argues that because his opponents use physiognomy to critique his masculinity and power to dominate others, Paul must respond using the same logic. The opponents' charges of Paul's weak bodily presence and contemptible speech in 10:10 portray Paul's rhetorical performance as slave-like, in addition to their related function as attacks on his masculinity, as discussed above. Enslaved people in the Greco-Roman world were likely thought to fall into a category of *unmen* (Moore 2001, 136). In his *Institutes of Oratory*, Roman rhetorician Quintilian remarks that enslaved people generally could not be accomplished orators and warns against adopting a slave-like posture when speaking (1.3.83; 2.11.7; 2.17.6). According to this physiognomic reasoning, observers could identify the enslaved body by poor or submissive posture, hunched shoulders, physical deformity, and small stature and height, which signified weakness, dishonor, and questionable morals (Harrill 2006, 37–38; Bradley 1994, 142–43). Paul responds by his foolish discourse of 2 Cor 11:21–12:10, which resembles rhetorical performances of the enslaved in Greco-Roman comedies. Playing into assumptions of his poor rhetorical performance allows Paul to turn the focus from style to the wisdom of its content (2 Cor 11:6).

For the Corinthians who value wisdom and high rhetoric, Paul's claim that he must speak as a an enslaved person and fool in order to be understood would have acted as a critique of their wisdom. This claim also reinforces kyriarchal associations between the enslaved and foolishness, weakness, and effeminacy. This is in drastic contrast to how some in Corinth may have understood the Christ movement as equalizing. Enslaved people had leadership roles in some Christ communities. What would it be like to be an enslaved person hearing this letter in Corinth? Paul's rhetoric of metaphorical slavery would have highlighted the actual conditions of the enslaved in Corinth. His metaphorical use of a enslaved body would have intensified the uses of and assumptions regarding real enslaved bodies. If some of these these enslaved people were leaders, perhaps due to their wise speech or prophesying, then Paul's rhetoric would have called their leadership into question on the basis of assumptions regarding the control of their bodies.

The Many Faces of Pauline Community Scholars

Scholars who observe the radical differences in Paul's self-fashioning ask whether and to what extent Paul joins in the kyriarchal and oppressive practices of the Greco-Roman world (Stanley 2011). Does he participate willingly, making him a villain to modern liberationist causes, or as a strategic move to reject or critique kyriarchy, which would make him a hero of liberation? On the side of a heroic Paul, Harrill (2006, 54) argues that Paul's construction of himself as slave-like is intended to exaggerate physiognomy to make its use by Paul's opponents seem foolish for its focus on superficial details.[6] Glancy (2004, 134) also sees Paul as powerfully rejecting Greco-Roman norms by identifying with suffering individuals when he boasts of his body as weak and beaten. Similarly, Larson (2004) asserts that Paul rejects Greco-Roman gender physiognomics when he presents himself as weak and effeminate, rather than as strong and masculine. Davina Lopez (2008, 141) makes a similar argument in her work on Galatians: after his call experience, Paul rejects Greco-Roman norms of imperial masculinity by giving up the power to dominate others and identifies instead with the conquered feminized nations living under the power of the empire. Lopez emphasizes Paul's own change in gender status with this rejection: "Paul's masculinity changes from dominant to non-dominant and undergoes further shift toward femininity in Galatians" (141). In other words, Paul's Christlike strength in his weakness allows him to identify with others who are weak or low in status. For Lopez, this signals his countercultural rejection of status systems more broadly.

Others interpret Paul's participation in gender and status discourses as symbolizing his assertions of power and authority over the community. Colleen Conway (2008, 69) argues that Paul draws on a variety of gender discourses and frequently uses athletic and martial imagery to convince the Corinthians that they can achieve masculinity by following Christ. Conway's assertion that Paul claims weakness to achieve power is supported by her observation that strength or power language regularly follows descriptions of Paul's weakness in 2 Cor 10–13. But even this claim for power through gender malleability is also a strategy for survival under empire, Conway (2008; Clines 2004) argues, in which nondominant men and women had to find alternative ways of achieving and displaying gender status. Marchal (2008, 87) views Paul's rhetoric of personal self-lowering and weakness as a performance of identification with suffering that ultimately helps him claim authority in a complex imperial context.

---

6. Harrill uses the works of Betz (1972) and Malherbe (1989) that attempt to locate Paul's writings in the context of competing philosophical and rhetorical schools to support his argument about Paul's response.

Reading 2 Cor 10–13 according to this logic suggests that Paul may pass as effeminate or enslaved, but only in order to affirm his power and status over the community.

Expanding the questions and analysis to include attention to Paul's characterizations of the Corinthians and the other apostles makes possible interpretations in which all parties, not just Paul, are negotiating for authority to speak and for claims to wisdom. Both he and they may have strategically used or rejected the kyriarchal imagery and metaphors available to them when it was advantageous. Rather than classifying Paul (or anyone else) as universally good or universally bad according to modern standards of liberation and justice, it is more ethically responsible and historically accurate to see these interactions and images as particular and local.

When Paul shifts to a self-construction of his weakness, he presents the Corinthians as those whom he loves and serves, even in his weakness (2 Cor 11:7–11; 12:15–19). In Paul's construction, the childlike, passive, feminized, and sexualized Corinthian body is the object over which Paul stages his divinely sanctioned war with the superapostles (10:3–8). The winner takes the prize of full control over the Corinthian body. As the audience, they stay silent, passive, and relatively powerless. While he presents their identity as static, he shifts his own to strategically suit his argument. He presents their role as either accepting or rejecting and makes the case that they should accept him. Paul asserts that they have passively accepted others who have treated them poorly and promises that he will treat them well (11:18–21). Their position remains on the bottom of the status pyramid, as they are described as children, an errant daughter, whose body is under someone else's control. Paul's own identity construction shifts to feature his weakness and service to them. He tells the Corinthians that he will gladly be spent for them (12:15). His every action is in service to them (12:19). Here Paul's self-construction is dependent on his construction of the Corinthians as low in social status. By identifying with Christ in his suffering, Paul's reversal is complete. Paul is both weak/slave-like/effeminate and strong/free/masculine, while the Corinthians are Paul's errant and passive daughter as well as served by Paul in their lowly state. The relational nature of these constructions bolsters Paul's point.

Similarly, when Paul changes his own construction to one of an effeminized, enslaved person, he emphasizes the traits that would seem to give the rival apostles authority in the community: their being Hebrews, Israelites, and of Abraham's seed (2 Cor 11:22). While several commentators argue that these three terms should be taken together to refer to the Jewishness of the rival apostles and to Paul, others have argued that each has distinct connotations that relate different aspects of the Jewishness of these figures (Wan 2000, 138–40). The first term, *hebraioi*, has linguistic connotations, as seen in Acts 6:1, where Hebrew or Aramaic-speaking Jews are contrasted to Greek-speaking Jews. Paul may use this term here in this linguistic sense given the rhetorical context of the passage. If Paul is responding to a critique of his speaking abilities, then it is possible that he is highlighting the speaking abilities of his rivals, in addition to their Jewishness. "Are they Hebrew-speakers? So am I," says Paul. Yet, when Paul speaks as a fool, in the character of an effeminized, enslaved person, these speaking abilities are no longer strengths but weaknesses. Paul highlights the qualities that distinguished his rivals—their lineage, their experience as ministers of Christ, and their linguistic abilities—so that when he inverts the system, these qualities function as evidence of their weakness and inferiority to Paul. Their weakness is further affirmed when Paul claims that his experiences exceed theirs in weakness (2 Cor 11:23). Who is weak if not Paul? The rival apostles are as authoritative neither in their rhetorical performance, nor in their lineage, nor in their commissioning as Paul, but nor are they as weak or as Christlike as Paul.

The constructed silence of the Corinthians continues to ring out in this passage as Paul's own speech and that of masculinized rival apostles becomes the focus. As Corinthian leaders who value rhetoric and wise speech, it would have been frustrating to hear Paul continue to ignore and devalue their speech. Paul's rhetoric in this passage brings the focus to ethnic identity markers. Focusing on the importance of Jewish traits for leaders in the Christ movement both upholds the role of *Ioudaioi* as leaders generally and denigrates the leadership of Greeks, even while also challenging these particular *Ioudaioi* leaders. Greek leaders in the community, who have different lineages or linguistic abilities, are not even worthy of Paul's mention. In particular, Greek leaders who were skilled in rhetoric or divine speech, those invested in the Achaian heritage of speaking out against the Romans, enslaved people, and wo/men would have been insulted by Paul's assumptions regarding leaders in this passage.

By the end of the passage, Paul has regained his power as he discusses his divine authority. Paul now uses language of speaking in Christ in 12:19 and 13:3 alongside the language of speaking as a fool. His foolishness, his comparative weakness gives him comparative authority. While Paul presents himself as speaking from the lowest possible social status, he has raised up the beloved Corinthian community and the so-called superapostles above himself. He does this so that when he redefines the terms of the system—weakness as strength and power, and strength and power as weakness—the rivals and the Corinthians appear exceedingly inferior to him. Paul moves from presenting himself as a divine warrior and *paterfamilias* in chapter 10, to speaking from a position of low status in chapters 11 and 12, to finally returning to the *paterfamilias* of the Corinthian community. His shifts in the presentation of his own malleable identity are dependent on how the community and rival apostles are positioned within his argument, and they shift along with him.

Paul's argument and the constructions that help fortify it are based on the assumption that the kyriarchal system Paul uses will be understood and accepted by those in the Corinthian audience. In vying for power to speak in Corinth, Paul makes use of familiar images and constructions of his day, including those of the empire and of status more broadly. He may be hoping to unite the community in common cause, but he does so at the expense of diversity. According to Vander Stichele (2012, 751), there is no room for particular difference, posed by women and Jews, in Paul's picture of Christianity: "The depiction of unity apparently occurs at the expense of the difference and thus degenerates into uniformity." In other words, it is not just that Paul uses an image of Eve to represent the Corinthians, but that his argument depends on the assumption that women are objects of judgment for how well they fit the two options of Mary's virgin chastity or Eve's scandalous seduction. While it seems that Paul questions standards for authority in terms of rhetorical abilities and displays of wisdom, he also assumes that demonstrable masculinity and imperial shows of force will persuade his audience of his authority. By examining the extent to which he constructs debates about authority using a kyriarchal frame, we see the extent of his metaphors/imagery, suggestive of the gap between the rhetoric and the reality.

Alternative Historical Possibilities

We should not assume that Wire's proposed Corinthian wo/men prophets are no longer participating in negotiations for authority just because Paul, using a kyriarchal frame, presents the Corinthians as passive. Nor should we assume that they were sexually deviant because Paul describes them this way. Indeed, a feminist hermeneutics of suspicion suggests the opposite. Wire's work in 1 Corinthians lays the foundations for envisioning this community and points to some possible avenues for reconstructions in 2 Corinthians. Coupled with identity theories that consider hybridized, multiple, and fluid identities, my work envisions additional historical possibilities. By considering how particular identity markers, such as those of gender, ethnicity, or sociopolitical status, intersect with differences of age, role in the family (child, mother, widow, etc.), and ability, my work opens up additional spaces within Wire's reconstructions.

There are alternative historic possibilities for the wo/men in Corinth and for wo/men in early Christianity. Indeed, as this volume celebrates, Wire has argued that there were Corinthian women prophets who were leaders in the community. The vigor Paul uses in 2 Cor 10–13 to construct the community as a passive, errant, and promiscuous daughter indicates the vibrancy and vitality within the community. The Corinthians may have set a positive example for women and men in other Christ-following communities, especially in regards to gendered practices such as celibacy or marriage. Of the many women leaders mentioned in Rom 16, several are named in ways that could indicate rejection of typical gender or marital roles, such as Phoebe, Mary, Tryphaena and Tryphosa, Priscilla, and Junia. They may be taking their lead from the women prophets and leaders of Corinth.

Rather than assume Paul's perspective on rival leaders in the community, we can consider that they may have seemed threatening to Paul because they were popular or good leaders in the *ekklēsia*. Paul's gendered constructions that describe his rival apostles as male and the Corinthian community as female and passive would have been aggravating to active Corinthian wo/men prophets, who may have been the rival leaders Paul has in mind. By characterizing leaders as aggressive men, the Corinthian women may have taken Paul's constructions as his dismissal of their great efforts within the community, including any offers of support or hospitality they may have extended to him. If some of their work involved a rejection of the veil as a symbol of male authority over women's bodies, or even as a symbol of the pervasiveness of sexual aggression against women, Paul's constructions of them as sexually abusive men would have been infuriating and insulting. Perhaps tension between Paul and the Corinthian community was not due to their seduction or abuse, but rather is Paul's response to their active choice to reject Paul in favor of leaders who are physically present and better suited to lead.

Furthermore, for male and female enslaved and freed people who were participating in a variety of ways with a theology of resurrection,

Paul's assertion that the community was divided along lines of leaders and passive others was dismissive of their contributions. Similarly, if parts of the community came together around egalitarian ethics, or the ethic of Gal 3:28, with a cooperative focus, such as in Acts 2:47–48, then Paul's construction of divisions between leaders and passive others would have been an affront. Rather than judging and selecting leaders as Paul urges, some in Corinth may have doubled their efforts at living with egalitarian resurrection politics. As I argued above, Paul's rhetoric of slavery in 2 Cor 10–13 may suggest that there were enslaved women in Corinth who were leading the community in wise speech, that some of them were of Greek heritage and anti-imperial stance, and that some of them had status in the *ekklēsia* because of how they defied the norms for women and marriage.

Additionally, it is possible to envision that Paul and his Corinthian interlocutors are both participating in *and* resisting imperial norms of masculinity and status. The multiple constructions along malleable lines of gender and status evident in 2 Cor 10–13 suggest that the struggle for how to construct, how to negotiate, and how to interpret is ongoing and evolving. Strategies might contrast or even compete, but this should not mean that one side is good, masculine, or strong while the other is bad, feminine, or weak. Rather, all must negotiate to survive. The power and wisdom of wo/men to envision alternative pasts, presents, and futures continues to flourish, in spite of the obstacles. Wire's continuing legacy within scholarship and the numerous wo/men who have benefited from her ingenuity serve as proof of the ways wo/men are always there, speaking back from the gaps and envisioning new possibilities.

Works Cited

Barton, Carlin. 1994. "Savage Miracles: The Redemption of Lost Honor in Roman Society and the Sacrament of the Gladiator and the Martyr." *Rep* 45:41–71.

Bassler, Jouette. 2012. "2 Corinthians." Pages 566–69 in *Women's Bible Commentary*. Edited by Carol A. Newsom, Sharon H. Ringe, and Jacqueline E. Lapsley. Louisville: Westminster John Knox.

Betz, Hans. 1972. *Der Apostel Paulus und die Sokratische Tradition: Eine Exegetische Untersuchung zu Seiner Apologie 2 Korinther 10–13*. Tübingen: Mohr.

Bradley, Keith. 1994. *Slavery and Society at Rome*. Cambridge: Cambridge University Press.

Buell, Denise Kimber. 2005. *Why This New Race: Ethnic Reasoning in Early Christianity*. New York: Columbia University Press.

Bultmann, Rudolf. 1995. *The Second Letter to the Corinthians*. Edited by Erich Dinkler. Translated by Roy A. Harrisville. Minneapolis: Augsburg.

Clines, David. 2004. "Paul the Invisible Man." Pages 181–92 in *New Testament Masculinities*. Edited by Stephen D. Moore and Janice Capel Anderson. SemeiaSt 45. Atlanta: Society of Biblical Literature.

Conway, Colleen M. 2008. *Behold the Man: Jesus and Greco-Roman Masculinity*. Oxford: Oxford University Press.

Dunning, Benjamin H. 2014. *Christ without Adam: Subjectivity and Sexual Difference in the Philosophers' Paul*. New York: Columbia University Press.

Fox, Arminta. 2020. *Paul Decentered: Reading 2 Corinthians with the Corinthian Women*. Lanham, MD: Lexington/Fortress Academic.

Glancy, Jennifer. 2004. "Boasting of Beatings (2 Corinthians 11:23–25)." *JBL* 123:99–135.

Harrill, James Albert. 2006. *Slaves in the New Testament: Literary, Social, and Moral Dimensions*. Minneapolis: Fortress.

Johnson Hodge, Caroline. 2005. "Apostle to the Gentiles: Constructions of Paul's Identity." *BibInt* 13:3:270–88.

Kent, John Harvey, and American School of Classical Studies at Athens. 1966. *The Inscriptions, 1926–1950*. Princeton: American School of Classical Studies at Athens.

Kittredge, Cynthia Briggs. 1998. *Community and Authority : The Rhetoric of Obedience in the Pauline Tradition*. HTS 45. Harrisburg, PA: Trinity Press International.

———. 2003. "Rethinking Authorship in the Letters of Paul." Pages 318–33 in *Walk in the Ways of Wisdom: Essays in Honor of Elisabeth Schüssler Fiorenza*. Edited by Shelly Matthews, Cynthia Briggs Kittredge, and Melanie Johnson-DeBaufre. Harrisburg, PA: Trinity Press International.

Larson, Jennifer. 2004. "Paul's Masculinity." *JBL* 123:85–97.

Lopez, Davina C. 2008. *Apostle to the Conquered: Reimagining Paul's Mission*. PCC. Minneapolis: Fortress.

Malherbe, Abraham J. 1989. *Paul and the Popular Philosophers*. Minneapolis: Fortress.

Marchal, Joseph A. 2008. *The Politics of Heaven: Women, Gender, and Empire in the Study of Paul*. PCC. Minneapolis: Fortress.

Matthews, Shelly. 1995. "2 Corinthians." Pages 196–217 in *A Feminist Commentary*. Vol. 2 of *Searching the Scriptures*. Edited by Elisabeth Schüssler Fiorenza with the assistance of Ann Brock and Shelly Matthews. London: SCM.

Moore, Stephen D. 2001. *God's Beauty Parlor: And Other Queer Spaces in and around the Bible*. Stanford, CA: Stanford University Press.

Murphy-O'Connor, J. 1983. *St. Paul's Corinth: Texts and Archaeology*. Wilmington, DE: Glazier.

Roetzel, Calvin J. 2007. *2 Corinthians*. Nashville: Abingdon.

Schüssler Fiorenza, Elisabeth. 1999. *Rhetoric and Ethic: The Politics of Biblical Studies*. Minneapolis: Fortress.

———. 2007. *The Power of the Word: Scripture and the Rhetoric of Empire*. Minneapolis: Fortress.

Stanley, Christopher D., ed. 2011. *The Colonized Apostle*. Minneapolis: Fortress.

Sumney, Jerry L. 1990. *Identifying Paul's Opponents: The Question of Method in 2 Corinthians*. Sheffield: JSOT.

Thrall, Margaret E. 1994. *A Critical and Exegetical Commentary on the Second Epistle to the Corinthians*. Edinburgh: T&T Clark.

Vander Stichele, Caroline. 2012. "2 Corinthians: Sacrificing Difference to Unity." Pages 743–54 in *Feminist Biblical Interpretation: A Compendium of Critical Commentary on the Books of the Bible and Related Literature*. Edited by Luise Schottroff. Grand Rapids: Eerdmans.

Wan, Sze-kar. 2000. *Power in Weakness: Conflict and Rhetoric in Paul's Second Letter to the Corinthians*. Harrisburg, PA: Trinity Press International.

Wire, Antoinette Clark. 1990. *The Corinthian Women Prophets: A Reconstruction through Paul's Rhetoric*. Minneapolis: Fortress.

Witherington, Ben, III. 1995. *Conflict and Community in Corinth: A Sociorhetorical Commentary on 1 and 2 Corinthians*. Grand Rapids: Eerdmans.

Out of House and Home: Early Christian Community as Public *Ekklēsia*

Anna Miller

Introduction

In *The Corinthian Women Prophets* Antoinette Clark Wire brilliantly brings the Corinthian women into focus as the target of Paul's rhetorical formulations. Wire's (1990, 182) nuanced analysis reveals Paul's rhetorical differentiation of public from private space, so that he separates "the common life as a public domain from private life." Wire's reconstruction contrasts Paul's portrayal of the Corinthians' common life as a public domain with the Corinthian women's own view of their community as a communal home. Wire parts ways with most scholars in her recognition that the public/private division could be deployed as a rhetorical strategy, an observation that puts into question a natural or accepted division between the public and private in the ancient world. However, Wire's reconstruction of the Corinthian women's *ekklēsia* as a communal home ultimately reinforces scholarship that has commonly identified the earliest Christian communities as private or liminal space. In this model, women's participation and leadership is explicable, in part, by the separation of the Christian *ekklēsia* from a public, political space gendered as male.

In contrast to Wire, my own book *Corinthian Democracy* posits a Corinthian community that understood itself not as a home but as a democratic assembly, an *ekklēsia*, in which Corinthian freeborn women and the enslaved joined freeborn men as equal, speaking participants in the debates and decisions affecting the group (Miller 2015). This vision of early Christians—including early Christian women—as political participants in widespread democratic discourse and practice invites us to question the two-sphere model regularly applied to the ancient world. According to that gendered model, the public realm is male, political space, while women are largely confined to the private sphere of domestic life. Designating the Corinthian community as private space, according to this model, would seem to preclude sustained, authentic political activity, even as identifying the Corinthian community as public space makes it challenging to explain the political engagement of free women or the enslaved. In this essay, I suggest that it is critical that scholars interrogate the two-sphere model that has so dominated our understanding of the ancient world and early Christian groups in classics and New Testament scholarship. We must question it not only because its scholarly origins owe so much to modern, exclusionary political theory with roots in the Enlightenment, but also because it has effectively masked the robust political participation of marginalized groups within the ancient world. I argue that, whereas modern political theory bears some responsibility for acceptance of this gendered, two-sphere model as fixed in the ancient world, other iterations of political theory can also expand our vision of political participation. First Corinthians is not the only early Christian text that yields new insights about Christian practice and community in light of such a revised consideration of the two-sphere model. In the second part of the essay, I apply these insights to 1 Timothy, a text that itself brings forward and intensifies ideas present in 1 Corinthians. Even as 1 Timothy seeks to forward Paul's distinction of public space from private to the detriment of women's voice and authority, this text also evidences contest and struggle that substantiate women's participation in a communal, public sphere.

The *Ekklēsia* Closed to the Public

In *The Corinthian Women Prophets* Wire (1990, 17) hypothesizes that when Paul rhetorically disassociates public from private spheres in 1 Corinthians, "he may be trying to send back home a Pandora's box of women's spiritual and physical energy that has given the church the richness and disruptiveness of a home." Wire's detailed rhetorical analysis illuminates Paul's use of the public/private dichotomy to limit women's participation in the *ekklēsia* (17, 157). However, her reconstruction of the Corinthian *ekklēsia* as a communal home also contributes to a body of scholarship that envisions the gatherings of the earliest Christians as differentiated in critical ways from public, political space in the ancient world. Many ascribing to this model, like Wire herself, suggest women's inclusion and agency in the Christian *ekklēsia* is made possible by its separation from public space.

Wire's definition of the Corinthian community as a communal home is only one example of the creative and varied ways in which scholars have distinguished between the Christian *ekklēsia* and ancient, public, political space over the last decades. For instance, Ross Kraemer (1992, 141–42) proposes that the early Christian use of familial language helped to make the public realm an "extension of the domestic." Carolyn Osiek and Margaret MacDonald (2006, 4) likewise envision the Christian community meeting in houses as a liminal location, describing it as a "crossroads between public and private." By contrast, Jorunn Økland (2004, 67–71) posits that Paul's utterances on women in 1 Cor 11–14 seek to identify the Corinthian gathering as sanctuary space that, as neither fully public nor private, allowed for the presence and participation of women—even if such space was itself structured by a gendered hierarchy. Karen Torjesen (1993, 127) more definitively locates the early Christian *ekklēsia* in private space, suggesting that in common with ancient voluntary associations she labels as private, Christian communities were distinguished by their "nonpublic, nonpolitical character."

Despite their contrasting perspectives on the nature of the early Christian *ekklēsia*, these scholars all reinforce the essential difference between the space and identity of the Christian community and public, political space in the ancient world. Likewise, these scholars also hypothesize that the practices that stem from this distinction enabled women's participation and/or leadership, whether by allowing Christian women to engage practices in community they habitually performed in domestic space or by rendering the Christian *ekklēsia* a private or liminal location where women were released from strictures adhering to the public, political realm.

The claim that the *ekklēsia*'s distinction from public space made possible women's freedom, participation, or leadership leaves largely uncontested a construction of public space in the ancient world as male political space. In turn, acceptance of this construction tends to mask or mark as exceptional examples of ancient women's political participation. This implicit acceptance of a gendered public/private division in the ancient world can also obscure struggles around gender and political participation, including ways in which the public/private dichotomy was mobilized to foreclose women's political agency. An understanding of the origins of the two-sphere model as it has been applied to the ancient world illuminates the limitations of this model for envisioning the full extent of ancient women's political participation. An expanded vision of ancient political participation can allow for more sophisticated comprehension and analysis of democratic participation of freeborn men, women, and the enslaved in early Christian communities such as the ones represented in 1 Corinthians and in 1 Timothy.

Antiquity and Modernity according to the Two-Sphere Model

The depiction of ancient women that has flourished in both classics and New Testament studies owes much to the two-sphere model originating with the Enlightenment (Katz 2004, 296). From the Enlightenment forward, political thinkers have described the public sphere as the realm of political action, of justice and freedom. By contrast, private space has been linked with "particularity, interest, and partiality" (Landes 1998b, 143). Certainly, theorists have drawn the private sphere so as to include intimate domestic space. However, the private realm has also been identified as the space of moral and religious conscience and economic freedom.

From its Enlightenment origins, this modern explanation of the public/private dichotomy has also been deeply gendered. The drawing of the boundary between the two spheres assigned women to private domestic space. Meanwhile, this model suggested men moved freely between the public realm, in which they engaged developing rights of justice, freedom, and equality, and the domestic sphere, where the adult man's patriarchal authority held sway. Herbert Marcuse explains, "Running parallel to the liberation of man as a 'citizen' whose whole existence and energies are devoted to 'society' and its daily economic, political, and social struggles is the commitment of the woman and her whole being to her house and family and the utilization of the family as a 'refuge' from daily struggles" (cited in Möhrmann 1984, 108). Scholarship on the development of the bourgeois family recognizes ongoing tensions between the model of equality and justice that came to define the political realm in modern democracies and the "non-consensual, non-egalitarian assumptions" that cohered with the private sphere (Stone 1979). Indeed, the private, domestic space was largely exempted from questions of justice that drove political debates in the public sphere.

Essentializing constructions of gender have been critical to maintaining the private/public boundary in political theory. As Iris Marion Young (1998, 432–33) explains, the exclusion of women from the public, political sphere[1]—and thus from the equality and freedom associated with democratic citizenship—relied on a conception of woman as irrational, wild, and representative of bodily appetites. Such a construction rendered women unsuited for public, political affairs and made woman a foil for the male citizen painted as the ideal and universal human being. Young and others point out that women were not alone in this construction of their essential inability to exercise the strength, reason, and stability necessary for citizenship. Similar inability was ascribed to racialized others, likewise described as unsuited to the responsibilities and rights of citizens (Young 1998, 432–33).

Marilyn Katz observes that from the eighteenth century forward, scholarship on the ancient world served this conception of the modern two-sphere model, asserting a limitation of ancient women from the public sphere that helped justify their political exclusion in modern democracies. During the Enlightenment, intellectuals no longer saw the ancient Greeks and Romans as simply two among many other exotic cultures to be investigated with a developing science of anthropology. Instead, the Greek and Roman political systems figured as possible models for "new and invigorated forms of antimonarchical political organization" (Katz 2004, 296). Ancient Greek women were of particular interest to these Enlightenment thinkers, since "the status and social role of women in ancient Greece were, likewise, invoked as reference-points for the development of an ideology of women's place in the new social orders of the eighteenth and nineteenth centuries" (296). Katz notes that the parameters and topics that defined investigations of women's status in antiquity were formulated in conversation with the public/private ideology. Scholars investigated the status of ancient women according to their domesticity, education, arranged marriages, and social life—topics closely linked with "the principal issues around which the ideology of separate spheres was originally formulated" (297).

Many classics scholars working in the shadow of this legacy continue to present as unproblematic, or in need of analysis, the depiction of the exclusion of ancient women from civic political life (Ober 1989, 5; Finley 1985, 51). This contrasts with more rigorous evaluation of the political status of others excluded from citizenship. For instance, much scholar-

---

1. I understand *public* and *political* to be coordinate adjectives both describing the noun *sphere*.

ship has chronicled the impact of the enslaved and resident foreigners on ancient Athenian democracy (Bakewell 2013; Ismard 2017). Accepting that two spheres shaped ancient society and that women were firmly located in the private sphere, scholars have failed to investigate women's status as "properly understood—that is, about their legal, social, and political rights and disabilities" (Katz 2004, 297). Such an omission is striking in part because ancient authors such as Aristotle, Plato, and Aristophanes did not regard women's exclusion as political subjects unworthy of debate or argument.[2]

Like our classics counterparts, scholars of early Christianity have not intensively interrogated the two-sphere model when it comes to the male gendering of ancient public, political space. Scholars in our field continue to represent this ancient, public political sphere as closed to women in any meaningful way. Korinna Zamfir (2014, 527) gives a concise recent example when she argues that 1 Timothy sees the church as public space, and thus women are excluded from leadership since "just as in contemporary society, the [Pastoral Epistles] assign men to the public, women to the private sphere." As I discuss in this essay, the effort to account for women's active involvement and critical leadership roles in early Christian communities has led to a range of creative explanations for ways in which the Christian *ekklēsia* stands distinct from fully public space. As in classics, scholars of early Christianity have not, by and large, genuinely addressed the question of women's public, political status in the ancient world, and the implications of that status for the earliest Christian communities.

When it comes to reevaluating the public/private dichotomy as applied to the ancient world and, more specifically to ancient women, I agree with Katz that scholars have been constrained by narrow definitions of ancient political participation. In particular, Katz questions the adequacy of Aristotle's most limited definition of political participation as citizens engaging judicial functions and the civic offices that include *ekklēsia* attendance (*Pol.* 1275a20–26). Not only does this definition fail to encompass the fullest expression of political participation by male citizens, but it also limits our understanding of the complex interaction between civic political insti-

---

2. Plato's *Republic* certainly offers an example of this debate over women's role in the polis. Aristotle's *Politics* (1252a1–1260a15) also devotes considerable space to the question of women's fitness to exercise citizenship in the polis. By contrast, Aristophanes's *Ekklēsiazousae* and *Lysistrata* use comedy to imaginatively engage the potential of women's active political participation within the democratic polis.

tutions such as the *ekklēsia* and other "domains of communal life" in which free women, the enslaved, and foreigners participated (Katz 2004, 306).

Expanding the Public: Habermas and Feminist Theory

Modern political theory may have limited scholarly vision of ancient women's political participation, but its recent iterations also offer strong tools to conceptualize broader and more inclusive political participation in antiquity. Some of these tools may be found in the ongoing debates about the nature of public space. Liberal political theory postulates a restricted vision of the public that finds common ground with Aristotle's focus on civic institutions in describing citizenship. This theory not only suggests a strong division between public and private but also envisions public space primarily as the arena of official politics. Benjamin Barber (1988, 18) and others have critiqued liberal political theory for its "preference for 'thin' rather than strong versions of political life where citizens are spectators and clients while politicians are professionals who do the actual governing."

The political theory of Jürgen Habermas has served as a foil for the limited vision of public space in liberal political theory and thus for many has been a starting point for a "non-state dominated sphere of public life" (Landes 1998a, 5). Habermas puts forth a model of public, political space that is procedural, defined by participation through speech and debate. For Habermas, the public comes into existence when and where those affected by social norms and political action gather to debate those norms and actions. The normative constraints governing this practical debate in Habermas's (1984) model are universal moral respect and egalitarian reciprocity.

Cultural theorists Seyla Benhabib (1992, 103) and Nancy Fraser (1990, 57) suggest that Habermas's discursive model makes a better fit for "the realities of highly differentiated and pluralistic modern societies" than the state-centered model of liberalism. In particular, Habermas's theory better accounts for the disagreements and debates within democratic practice, a contrast to liberalism's artificial conversational restraint of neutrality (Benhabib 1992, 96). However, Benhabib and Fraser also argue that we must engage Habermas's democratic theory with an awareness of the significant critiques that feminists level regarding the division between public and private in political theory—including those relating to Habermas's theory.

Feminist scholarship on the two-sphere model in political theory and practice offers critical insights. This scholarship illuminates issues of power regarding who has been able to set the boundary between public and private and how that boundary has been drawn.³ As Benhabib (1992, 110) notes, "Traditional modes of drawing this distinction have been part of a discourse of domination which legitimizes women's oppression and exploitation in the private realm." Feminist theorists and historians have done much to question the public/private boundary as set and natural, not least by interrogating its reliance on essentialist claims of the two-sex model (Schüssler Fiorenza 2000, 10). These scholars have demonstrated the changing and gendered contents of the public/private divide and the way that, historically, this divide has been a matter of constant negotiation (Landes 1998a, 2).

Habermas's theory has also received significant feminist critique. Like liberal political thinkers, Habermas is "gender blind" when he ignores the issue of difference in the "experience of male versus female subjects in all domains of life" (Benhabib 1992, 109). Indeed, his theory has also contributed to the view that justice only concerns the public realm, thus leaving power relations in the intimate realm unexamined. Meanwhile, his idealization of bourgeois public space for its accessibility masks the way in which this space was constituted over time through exclusions based on gender, race, and class (Fraser 1990, 59).

If Habermas's theory occasions valid critique, this theory also provides the basis for comprehending a broader and more wide-ranging political engagement. Habermas's procedural model allows for the negotiation of boundaries between public and private. Such negotiation enables matters traditionally consigned to the private sphere to become part of a public debate that includes all those affected by these matters. Benhabib (1992, 105) argues that Habermas's theory opens the possibility for not just one universal public, but multiple locations and configurations in which the public appears—so that "there may be as many publics as there are controversial general debates about the validity of norms."⁴ Indeed, Fraser (1990,

---

3. In an article that examines the public/private dichotomy with regard to Anita Hill's testimony in the confirmation hearings for Supreme Court Justice Clarence Thomas regarding sexual harassment, Fraser (1998, 331) argues that "the feminist project aims in part to overcome the gender hierarchy that gives men more power than women to draw the line between public and private." At the same time, Fraser also insists that the public/private divide must be analyzed in terms of a racial-ethnic dimension which means that historically, this divide has been drawn in different ways for White and Black women.

4. Fraser offers another feminist argument for multiple publics. For her part, Fraser (1990, 68–69) contends that in both stratified and egalitarian societies par-

61) contends that along with the appearance of a male bourgeois public in the eighteenth century, there arose a multiplicity of competing publics that "contested exclusionary norms, elaborated alternative styles of political behavior and alternative norms of public speech." In these terms, any portrayal of women's absolute exclusion from the public in recent centuries must ignore their participation in publics beyond the male bourgeois public space. In turn, such a portrayal of exclusion can only be seen as ideological, resting "on a class and gender biased notion of publicity" (Fraser 1990, 68–69). Fraser and Benhabib suggest that multiple publics are not detrimental to democracy but essential, as they provide arenas in which subordinated groups participate in formulating counterdiscourses and identities that are directed toward, and in conversation with, what one may call the "wider public."[5] In this way, multiple publics help to question and expand the boundaries of citizenship and its attendant rights, even as they help to expand the list of issues and concerns that are part of public debate (Fraser 1990, 67–72; Benhabib 1992, 112–13).

When read in critical dialogue, Habermas's discursive theory and feminist analysis of public and private spheres open new vistas for the way to understand political engagement in antiquity—including the political engagement of the early Christian *ekklēsia*. Habermas encourages us to look for public, political engagement based in democratic debate and discernment. For Habermas, the restraints of such debate are found in an egalitarian reciprocity that enables those affected by norms to debate and decide those same norms. Benhabib and Fraser's analysis of Habermas suggests scholars may use his theory to envision not just one state-centered space of public engagement, but multiple publics that appear when and where such egalitarian debate and decision takes place. At the same time, feminist exploration of the public/private boundary encourages us to recognize the way that this boundary has been and still is constantly renegoti-

---

ticipatory parity is more closely approximated by "contestation among a plurality of competing publics than by a single, comprehensive sphere."

5. Schüssler Fiorenza provides an example of the value of multiple publics in her description of the *ekklēsia gynaikon* or women-church, the "movement of self-identified women and women-identified men in biblical religion." She envisions this community as seeking to realize the radical, democratic potential of the ancient civic *ekklēsia* and argues that the women-church is "the dialogical community of equals in which critical judgment takes place and public freedom becomes tangible" (Schüssler Fiorenza 1984, xiv–xv). Elsewhere, she speaks of this *ekklēsia* as a "counter-public-sphere from which a feminist biblical rhetoric can speak" (1992, 7).

ated (Davidoff 1998). During the first centuries of the Roman Empire, I suggest that ongoing democratic practice and discourse helped to create such multiple publics—including the public space of the Christian *ekklēsia*.

Creating the Public:
Democratic Discourse and Practice in the Early Roman Empire

In New Testament studies, a view of ancient democracy as effectively confined to the classical past has had a direct impact on debates over the wider political context for early Christian communities and Christian use of the title *ekklēsia* (Miller 2015, 69–72). The vast majority of studies on politics during the first centuries CE have investigated imperial power dynamics, implicitly or explicitly asserting empire as the political model conditioning expectations for group organization and leadership in the Greek East. Meanwhile, the civic, democratic associations for *ekklēsia* as civic assembly are commonly recognized, only to be dismissed as inoperative in the early empire.[6] A few scholars of early Christianity have acknowledged *ekklēsia* as a term significant for its civic, political associations into the first centuries CE. However, these scholars have tended to give only a generic political meaning to the *ekklēsia*, failing to fully realize the *ekklēsia*'s continuing place in civic politics and its connection with a robust discourse of democracy (Zamfir 2014; Peterson 2010, 9–83; Berger 2006, 173–206).

With a small group of scholars in classics and New Testament studies, my own work has seriously questioned both the irrelevance of the civic *ekklēsia* and also the disappearance of democratic discourse and practice in the early empire. Textual and inscriptional evidence demonstrates the ongoing legislative authority of civic *ekklēsiai* in the Greek East (Salmeri 2000; Ma 2000a; 2000b; Rogers 1991; Zuiderhoek 2008; Rhodes and Lewis 1997; Korner 2017; Payne 2019). This continued meeting and decision-making of civic *ekklēsiai* corresponds to the pervasiveness of thought and practice associated with democracy in early imperial sources. The early empire was permeated by what I have described as *ekklēsia* discourse. *Ekklēsia* discourse coheres with the logic and topoi that marked constructions of democracy in the early empire as authors and public speakers continued to engage the reality and the ideal of an empowered citizen body,

---

6. Horsley (2000, 79) gives one example in his contention that "under imperial Roman rule, then, the last vestiges of democracy were undermined as the oligarchies gained control of or simply abolished the city assemblies."

its collective power of decision, and individual citizen equality realized in free speech and decision within the *ekklēsia*. The civic assembly represents only one institution that sustained and replicated this *ekklēsia* discourse. This democratic discourse expanded into other fields of the Greco-Roman world to constitute a prevalent kind of social knowledge and cultural logics, defining debates over power and authority in a variety of contexts. Michel Foucault (1972, 45) recognizes that discourse is sustained through but not limited to particular institutions. A range of institutions such as education maintained *ekklēsia* discourse as a vital part of the Greek cultural context in the first century (Miller 2015, 14–39). These institutions and their practices helped to form the democratic citizen as a speaking and discerning subject in the first centuries of the empire.

This construction of citizenship had its roots in democratic, classical Athens, where the exercise of speech in the context of the *ekklēsia* was not only the mark of full citizenship but also a realization of the freedom and equality associated with that citizenship (Hansen 1999, 85; Ober 1989; Saxonhouse 2006). Euripides gives voice to this principle in his play *Suppliant Women*, when he defines freedom by quoting the formula used to open the assembly: "This is freedom: 'Who is willing, having good counsel, to bring it before the city?'" (Euripides, *Suppl.* 435, my translation). As *ekklēsia* speech defined free and equal citizenship, discernment of this speech rendered each member of the assembly an active participant in the process of democracy, their judgment circumscribing the exercise of political authority (Ober 1989, 79). With democratic assembly leadership and participation based in freedom of speech and debate, ancient authors repeatedly invoked the necessary partnership of wisdom and speech on the part of assembly speakers and audience.[7]

In the first two centuries of the common era, authors such as Plutarch, Dio of Prusa,[8] and Josephus all witness the continuing association of the

---

7. Demosthenes tells his audience in the *ekklēsia*, "You the many are not expected to speak as well as the orators, but you, especially the older ones of you, are expected to have intelligence equal or better than that of the speakers" (*Exord.* 45.2 [trans. Ober 2000, 164]. Dio and Plutarch continue this close connection of wisdom with *ekklēsia* speech and discernment (e.g., Plutarch, *Praec. ger. rei publ.* 801e–802f; Dio Chrysostom, *Or.* 42.1; 47.1).

8. Giovanni Salmeri (2000, 71–72) states, "It is above all the writings of Plutarch and Dio that show the *ekklēsia* as a far from negligible element in the political life of the *polis* during the imperial age."

ekklēsia with debate and negotiation between citizen speakers and audiences (Miller 2015, 40-89). These authors vividly depict the creation of public space through speech, debate and discernment. Likewise, such authors register their own participation in *ekklēsia* discourse through a construction of leadership and citizenship based on the exercise of persuasive speech before a discerning audience. This pervasive democratic discourse in the Greek East offered a model of political practice that, like Habermas's vision of democratic participation, was deeply procedural, realized in egalitarian speech and discernment. The appearance of such democratic discourse and practice in a range of institutions, such as education or voluntary associations, speaks to the creation of public spaces, of multiple publics, beyond the arena of official politics located in any individual civic *ekklēsia*.

Tensions and struggles around women's public speech had their own place in early imperial democratic discourse. Ancient authors commonly gendered speech and wisdom as male so as to assert women's inability to exercise full citizenship that was itself based in speech and discernment (Miller 2015, 117-30). This construction of women as unsuited to full citizenship relied on an assertion that public, political space was male and that women's natural location was in domestic space. Certainly one must be cautious in suggesting that the construction of the public and private divide was necessarily the same in antiquity as in the modern period.[9] Nevertheless, early imperial sources richly attest that ancient writers, like their modern counterparts, deployed a gendered public/private dichotomy to limit political participation—especially that of free women and the enslaved. Feminist theorists encourage us to recognize not only the utility of this dichotomy toward political exclusions but also the way that free women and the enslaved in antiquity constantly threatened to exceed— and indeed *did* exceed—the limitations set on their political participation (Landes 1998a, 9). If scholars apply Benhabib and Fraser's vision of multiple publics to antiquity, we may be able to better recognize and chart this boundary-crossing political participation.

---

9. I agree with Katz (2004, 299) and others that major differences may be identified between ancient and modern conceptions of public and private. Notably, I believe scholars must question anachronistic reconstructions that exclude both religion and economics from the ancient, public sphere. A contention that economics and religion can be excluded only artificially from public life of antiquity finds common ground with theorists who argue such a separation is artificial even for the modern period (Benhabib 1992, 100).

To demonstrate the inadequacy of the two-sphere model for illuminating ancient women's political participation, we must consider women's roles in creating public space in a range of ancient civic, religious, and political institutions, including those that are often seen as distinct from official civic institutions. For instance, John Kloppenborg (2017) has recently shown that voluntary associations in Greek democratic cities engaged the vocabulary and practice of civic politics, while their membership included free women, the enslaved, and foreigners alongside male citizens. Early Christian texts such as 1 Corinthians and 1 Timothy reveal other ancient public spaces created, in part, by the deliberating voices of both women and men. Such texts have an advantage over inscriptional evidence such as that connected to voluntary associations in that these texts reveal not just women's participation but the nature of the ongoing contest and struggle around that participation. Even as these texts show an author such as 1 Timothy deploying a public/private distinction in order to silence women's voices, they also suggest that not only democratic discourse but also Christian theology could empower those same voices.

The Public *Ekklēsia* in 1 Timothy

First Timothy, like 1 Corinthians, is distinguished within the Christian canon by the focus on women's speech paired with an effort to locate women within domestic space, an effort that articulates public from private space. First Timothy intensifies the restrictions Paul seeks to impose on women's speech in 1 Corinthians, marshaling additional theological and social arguments in order to block women's vocal participation in the *ekklēsia*.[10] Scholars have regularly explained 1 Timothy's restrictions on women's participation as an attempt to bring the Christian community in line with traditional or conventional cultural mores of the Greco-Roman world (Verner 1983, 135; Towner 2006, 193–200; Johnson 2001, 204;

---

10. I understand 1 Timothy as pseudonymous and part of the larger corpus of the Pastoral Epistles together with 2 Timothy and Titus. Likewise, I read the recipient *Timothy* as part of the pseudonymity of this author's construction. In this way, the Pastoral Epistles are examples of what some scholars have labeled double pseudonymous writings (Bassler 1996, 32–34). For extended arguments regarding the Pastoral Epistles as pseudonymous see Oberlinner 1994, xxxiii–xxxix, xlii–xlvi; Donelson 1986; Marshall 2006.

Osiek and MacDonald 2006, 233–34; Horrell 2008, 124).[11] The two-sphere model is readily visible in these arguments that 1 Timothy seeks to mold the community to accepted conventions reserving public, political speech for men, while relegating women's speech—and their person—to private space. Johnson (2001, 234) provides a particularly strong illustration of this reasoning when he speaks of "a cultural context in which men are the public speakers in any assembly (*ekklēsia*) … and a tradition in which women's roles were defined in terms of the domestic sphere rather than the public forum." These scholars intimate that the Christian *ekklēsia*, as it becomes an authentically public space in line with the wider society, has little place for women's voices. Some argue this as an evolutionary path away from "the fairly open possibilities for women's leadership in Paul's day toward increasing restriction within the household" (Osiek and MacDonald 2006, 234). By contrast, I argue that 1 Corinthians and 1 Timothy *both* offer evidence that freeborn men, women, and the enslaved in the communities they address have together created a public, democratic space in the gathered *ekklēsia*. The author of 1 Timothy, like Paul, contests women's participation in helping to constitute this public space, even as this author contests Paul's own legacy in fostering women's public participation.

First Timothy's discussions over women's speech and participation are part of a larger, pervasive focus on speech throughout the text. First Timothy makes speech a central theme as this author seeks to limit the speech of some while authorizing that of others. At the same time, this author also works to delegitimize certain types of speech. As in 1 Corinthians, 1 Timothy's engagement with democratic, *ekklēsia* discourse registers not just in the title *ekklēsia*, but more significantly with the rhetorical effort to shape and to constrain the exercise of communal speech. With Wire and Elisabeth Schüssler Fiorenza, I understand that an author's rhetoric is directed toward particular audiences with the intent to persuade. An analysis of the rhetorical situation in a text such as 1 Timothy can help us to better understand the complex relationship between author and audience, in which

---

11. Osiek, MacDonald, and Horrell are among those who see this as part of the apologetic mission of this author to make the Christian *ekklēsia* less open to criticism from the wider society. My work here and elsewhere suggests women's public participation was not an anomaly in the ancient world, thus questioning whether the apologetic thesis can adequately account for the restrictions that 1 Timothy seeks to impose on women in this community.

certain constraints govern "the argumentative possibilities of the speaker as well as the possible expectations of her audience" (Schüssler Fiorenza 1999, 108). In what follows, I argue that democratic discourse figures in the constraints on both speaker and audience in 1 Timothy, and is thus critical for determining the rhetorical situation—and working toward historical reconstruction of the community which this author seeks to persuade. First Timothy itself opens with the author privileging one model of communal speech and interaction over another. Analyzing this opening rhetoric on speech in 1 Tim 1:3–7 and its implications for democratic discourse sets the stage for considering 1 Tim 2:8–15 and the gendering of speech practice that takes place in that passage.

After identifying Paul as the letter writer and Timothy—his child—as recipient, the author turns in 1 Tim 1:3 to a commission for the purported Timothy. This commission includes significant critique of speech practices taking place in the community. The author urges Timothy to remain in Ephesus to protect the teaching that Paul has passed down, so that certain people do not teach differently. First Timothy further describes both right teaching and its contrast in what follows. Timothy's guidance of the community is connected to divine stewardship (*oikonomian theou*) in faith (1 Tim 1:4). The goal of this guidance is love, which itself springs from "a pure heart, good conscience, and sincere faith" (1:5).[12] Thus, in 1 Tim 1:3–6, the author holds up correct teaching defined by apostolic legitimacy and its association with faith and love.

The author insists that this legitimate divine speech be used to combat diversions into "myths and endless genealogies that promote speculation" (1 Tim 1:4). Indeed, 1 Tim 1:6 describes people in the community turning from legitimate teaching to engage in "meaningless talk" (*mataiologion*).[13] These talkers want to be teachers of the law, but the author insists that they do not even understand their own speech (1:7). As 1 Timothy has immediately linked the letter's preferred speech with the divine, with faith and love, this author critiques others' speech as marked by speculation, empty expression, and ignorance. The contrast that the author creates in these early verses suggests that even as Paul and Timothy's teaching may

---

12. All biblical quotations in this chapter follow the NRSV.

13. *Mataiologia* is a biblical *hapax legomenon*, but *mataiologoi* does appear in Titus 1:10. Johnson (2001, 166) describes this accusation of opponents' speech as foolish as a common topos in philosophical discourse, citing Lucian, *Jupp. trag.* 27; Epictetus, *Diatr.* 2.1.31, among others.

be understood as divinely perfect, the speech the letter condemns can only be human in its misunderstanding and fallibility.

Scholars have difficulty identifying with any confidence the content of the teaching 1 Timothy opposes. When it comes to the "myths and endless genealogies" of 1 Tim 1:4, hypotheses range from 1 Timothy's opponents as gnostics or protognostics theorizing the pleroma to Judaizers focused on genealogies from Jewish literature—or even a hybrid heresy Dibelius describes as "Judaizing Gnosticism" (Johnson 2001, 163; Towner 2006, 110; Dibelius and Conzelmann 1989, 65). If scholars have been split over the nature of the teaching 1 Timothy confronts, they have shown greater agreement that these verses betray 1 Timothy's preoccupation with speech itself and the way he shapes his rhetoric toward identifying certain speakers as worthy and some as lacking legitimacy. In his analysis, Luke Timothy Johnson (2001, 163) suggests the possibility that the author's language of "myths and endless genealogies" can be located in conventional rhetoric regularly deployed by ancient authors to label the talk of others as "foolish chatter." For his part, Philip Towner (2006, 111) claims that regardless of the exact nature of myths or genealogies to which the author refers, the adjective *endless* (*aperantois*) applied to genealogies in this case must be "polemical, meant to discredit protracted arguments that go nowhere." With Deborah Krause (2004, 37, 124), I submit that such debate, rather than any particular theological teaching, is the author's real target. More specifically, I understand that the author's preoccupation in this and other passages of 1 Timothy is to uphold one dynamic of communal speech against another he seeks to discredit as false, lacking in wisdom, and dangerously argumentative.

In these initial verses, the author of 1 Timothy portrays an ideal in which communication moves in one direction from Paul and Timothy to the communities they lead. First Timothy here asserts a kyriarchal model of authority and community interaction that calls to mind the ancient, elite household. With his own words guaranteed by his father, Paul, Timothy's teaching is associated with stewardship, *oikonomia*, even as he is urged to curb different teaching by others.[14] Certainly the language of *oikonomia* anticipates the author's claim in 1 Tim 3:15 that the *ekklēsia* is

---

14. The verb *heterodidaskaleō*, "to teach differently," which appears here and in 1 Tim 6:3, is a New Testament *hapax legomenon* used only in this book but present elsewhere in Ignatius, *Pol.* 3.1.

the household of God[15] and his insistence that the bishop's ability to lead this *ekklēsia* corresponds to his ability to manage his own house (1 Tim 3:4–5). Throughout, the rhetoric of 1 Timothy works to impose the kyriarchy of the elite ancient household arranged according to the age, gender, and enslaved/free status of its members. In this opening to the letter, the author sets the stage for later arguments by suggesting that this vision of *ekklēsia* has a foundation in divine will and Paul's own hopes for the Christian community.

If 1 Timothy uses these early verses to ground his vision of an *ekklēsia* with the power relations, the kyriarchy, of a household, these same verses reveal interaction within the community that recalls not the elite household but the democratic *ekklēsia* itself. These verses suggest a group choosing discussion and deliberation. Instead of a singular authority instructing the community, multiple figures within the group aspire to a speaking, teaching role. The author's preference for monovocal, authoritative instruction contrasts with a group engaging multiple viewpoints and multiple authority figures. The discussion and speculation mentioned in these verses conjure up an open exchange of ideas. Such an exchange is substantiated by 1 Tim 6:4–5, another passage that shows just how concerned this author is by the community's preference for "controversy and for disputes about words" (*zētēseis kai logomachias*). Such evidence for a community embracing egalitarian debate and discernment evokes the participation model of the civic *ekklēsia*. Likewise, the rhetoric of ignorance and disorder that the author of 1 Timothy uses against those community members participating in discussion and debate in 1 Tim 1:3–7 has its own place in democratic discourse. The author's tight correlation between proper speech and wisdom in a discussion of *ekklēsia* speech—and the corresponding correlation of inadequate speech with ignorance—is an important marker of democratic discourse in the ancient world (Miller 2015, 95–99). As ancient authors regularly defended democracy and its practice by claiming wisdom on the part of *ekklēsia* speakers and audiences, critiques of democracy depended on assertions of deficient wisdom in citizen speakers and decision makers.[16] Like other ancient authors enabled and constrained by democratic

---

15. This part of 1 Tim 3:15 reads, "if I am delayed, you may know how one ought to behave in the household of God, which is the *ekklēsia* of the living God."

16. For Thucydides's explanation of the necessity of wisdom on the behalf of speakers and decision-makers within ancient democracy, see *Hist.* 6.39.1–2; likewise, Plutarch, *Dem.* 1.1; 8.71. In the early empire, see: Plutarch, *Praec. ger. rei publ.* 802f;

discourse and practice, the author of 1 Timothy questions the wisdom of his audience in order to end debate in the *ekklēsia* in favor of harmonious agreement with his own position.

The dynamics of open discussion and debate in a community identifying as an *ekklēsia* certainly recalls the space and practice of the civic assembly of the Greek polis. The community of 1 Timothy not only shares a title with the civic assembly; this group's debate also creates a public space according to the theory of Fraser and Benhabib. In the case of 1 Timothy, the extent of the author's arguments regarding speech, and specifically women's speech (1 Tim 2:8–15; 5:3–16), indicates that women and men in this community were together, in Habermas's terms, performing speech that made this communal space a public *ekklēsia* with its own ties to the wider ancient public. A consideration of 1 Tim 2:8–15 reveals additional implications for women's speech in this public *ekklēsia*.

First Timothy further defines and genders speech for this group in 1 Tim 2:8–15. While the passage as a whole centers on women's speech, this passage begins with the author's ideal for male speakers. These men should speak in prayer, with lifted hands, and most critically without "anger or argument" (*chōris orgēs kai dialogismou*).[17] First Timothy's attempt to impose male *ekklēsia* speech without passion may be located in ancient constructions of masculinity, which held up "control, including self-control, as the key masculine trait" (Glancy 2003, 240). The call for such self-control on the part of male speakers provides a strong contrast for the author's subsequent portrayal of women and their speech as dangerously lacking in such control. However, this verse serves to shape not only *who* can speak in the *ekklēsia*, but *how ekklēsia* speech should be performed. This author's ideal of *ekklēsia* speech omits the key component of democratic participation: debate. Indeed, this author connects lack of self-control with such debate, suggesting the only *ekklēsia* speech he authorizes, (free) men's speech, cannot be controlled if exercised in debate.

The lion's share of this passage concerns women's speech, an observation that has led scholars to conclude that women within this group

---

Dio Chrysostom, *Or.* 43.3. For a critique of the democratic assembly's wisdom, see Dio Chrysostom, *Or.* 32.26–27.

17. Krause (2004, 58) offers the intriguing hypothesis that 1 Timothy attempts to end men's *ekklēsia* argument because some men were arguing on behalf of women's authoritative speech.

were indeed speaking and teaching within the *ekklēsia* (Verner 1983, 171; Krause 2004, 57; Tamez 2007, 39). First Timothy's requirements for women that start in verse 9 and extend to verse 15 pose a stark contrast to the author's characterization of ideal men's speech. For one, the author's arguments about women's speech begin with the order that women should dress with modesty (*meta aidous kai sōphrosynēs*) and avoid the extravagance of pearls, gold, and braided hair. As Rebecca Solevåg (2013, 115–18) observes, a topos developed during the early empire that connects women's adornment with immorality, even as the plain look denotes women's proper morality and control. Plutarch gives an especially apt example of this topos in his *Advice to Bride and Groom*, where he insists that a woman's lack of ornament not only will ensure her virtue but also will keep her within the house. In particular, Plutarch emphasizes that the virtuous, unadorned woman keeps her speech within the house since "her speech ought to be not for the public."[18] Like Plutarch, the author of 1 Timothy begins with a call for women's lack of adornment that links to a gendered public/private dichotomy in which women's virtue coheres with their constraint within the private sphere and, critically, the exclusion of their speech from public space.

First Timothy follows directions for women's clothing, hair, and jewelry with a direct command that women learn silently with full submission (*en pasē hypotagē*). Women's role as perpetually silent learners is underlined by 1 Timothy's next declaration that "I permit no woman to teach or to have authority over a man; she is to keep silent" (1 Tim 2:12). First Timothy here shares key vocabulary with the requirement for women's *ekklēsia* silence in 1 Cor 14:33–36, notably in the call for women's silence as well as their submission.[19] However, 1 Timothy also intensifies the limitations of 1 Cor 14:33–36 by specifying that a woman may never hold any authority over a man.

---

18. Plutarch, *Conj. praec.* 142c–d (Fowler). Plutarch here tells the story of Theano, Pythagoras's wife, who when her arm was exposed said it was not for the public. Plutarch adds, "Not only the arm of the virtuous woman, but her speech as well, ought to be not for the public."

19. Johnson (2001, 200) notes that 1 Tim 2:9–15 shares with 1 Cor 14:33–36 not only the order that women should be silent (*en ēsuchia*) and in submission (*en pasē hypotagē*), but that they should do so in order to learn (*manathanetō*). I have engaged the scholarship on 1 Cor 14:33–36 and made my own argument for that passage as genuine Pauline material (Miller 2015, 176–84).

Like Paul in 1 Cor 11:2–16, 1 Timothy appeals to the second story of creation in Genesis to justify gender difference and hierarchy within the *ekklēsia*, in this case to argue for women's silence. First Timothy follows Paul in citing Gen 2:7 as part of that justification, specifically that the male Adam is created before the female Eve. Moreover, he extends his interpretation to claim not just woman's secondary place in the order of creation but also their lack of judgment displayed in the presumed act of disobedience in the garden: "And Adam was not deceived, but the woman was deceived and became a transgressor" (1 Tim 2:14). First Timothy, like his near-contemporary Philo of Alexandria, uses Genesis's second creation story to posit woman's lack of reason and justify her necessary subordination to men (Philo, *Opif.* 167). Philo's reading of Genesis genders mind and judgment as male, even as his interpretation also genders the senses and susceptibility to pleasure as female (D'Angelo 2007, 82–83). Solevåg (2013, 124–25) argues that 1 Timothy too has in mind Eve's sexual susceptibility and lack of self-control, which is a common element in Hellenistic and early empire interpretations of Genesis. When it comes to the close association in democratic discourse between wisdom and correct *ekklēsia* speech, ancient authors from Aristotle on similarly correlate women's lack of intellect and self-control with a call for women's public silence and, thus, the exclusion of their voices from the civic assembly.[20]

First Timothy ends this pericope with the claim that women's salvation comes through childbearing.[21] Like Paul in 1 Cor 11:12, 1 Timothy makes a fundamental connection between women's identity and the childbearing role. However, 1 Timothy strengthens the role of childbearing in

---

20. Aristotle claims that the essential difference between freeborn men on one side and freeborn women and slaves on the other lies with their souls. Aristotle (*Pol.* 1260a12–15) writes, "And all possess the various parts of the soul, but possess them in different ways; for the slave has not got the deliberative part at all, and the female has it, but without full authority, while the child has it, but in an undeveloped form." Arius Didymus gives a notable example of the continuing place of this reasoning in the early empire when he repeats Aristotle's formulation concerning the differing souls of men, women, and slaves (see Stobaeus, *Ecl.* 149.7). For another argument gendering the intellect in order to enforce women's silence in the public sphere, see Plutarch, *Conj. Praec.* 139a–145d.

21. While I recognize the complexity of the arguments regarding the meaning of being saved in this passage, I am persuaded by the careful work of Porter 1993; Tamez 2007, 43–47; Solevåg 2013, 129–35; and others that in this case the author uses this terminology in a soteriological sense.

defining the worth of women. The traditional role of mother becomes the key to explaining not only the relationship of women to men in this world but also women's hope for "eschatological or salvific reward" (Porter 1993, 101). Again, in common with 1 Corinthians 11:2-16, 1 Timothy works to define woman (*gynē*) as "wife" by emphasizing kyriarchal hierarchy and the critical childbearing role (Tamez 2007, 46). Such a definition not only conceals the situation of those enslaved women in the *ekklēsia* who could not marry (Glancy 1998; Shaner 2017, 172)—or those widows who chose not to (re)marry—but also locates women's purpose and worth entirely in the domestic realm. Just as Wire demonstrated that Paul's rhetorical efforts to silence and refute in 1 Corinthians reveal voices and arguments that contrast with Paul's own position, 1 Timothy's intense argumentation here intimates a positive valuation others in the community are placing on asceticism and/or women's public participation.

Solevåg has argued convincingly that 1 Timothy uses this passage to create an ontological difference between men and women that necessitates a special salvation for women based on the difference—and for women the particular transgression—established in Gen 3. Solevåg (2013, 133) contends that 1 Timothy's equivalence of house and "God's *ekklēsia*" in this text blurs the boundaries between the community and the individual household so that he can argue women's salvation depends on living "according to *oikos* ideology and submitting to marriage and potential child-bearing." Envisioning 1 Timothy as enabled and constrained by democratic discourse, I would reframe Solevåg's contention. In the company of other ancient authors, 1 Timothy seeks to impose the household model onto the public, democratic *ekklēsia* in order to foster kyriarchal structures of power (see: Philo, *Ios.* 36-38, 63-73, 148; Aelius Aristides, *Or.* 24.22-42). Such an identification between the hierarchical, harmonious household and the polis could be used to limit, shape, and mask the debate and equality in free speech that was the foundation of democratic practice and discourse. However, even as this author imposes the household model onto the *ekklēsia*, his arguments gendering speech and *ekklēsia* participation also depend on an assertion of a public/private dichotomy. In 1 Tim 2:8-15, he deploys this dichotomy to insist that women's person and speech should be contained largely within the house. In turn, the intensity of this author's effort to gender public and private spaces reveals struggles around who will be able to act—and perhaps most critically, who will be able to speak—in the public space of a democratic *ekklēsia*.

In 1 Tim 2:8–15, this author initiates a process of gendering speech and space that is intensified later in this text and in the other Pastoral Epistles. First Timothy not only establishes hierarchy between men and women in this passage but also genders both speech and wisdom according to logic commonly used to exclude women's speech in the public realm. Likewise, the last verse in this pericope locates women's essential worth and thus their place in domestic space. First Timothy's rhetoric in this passage thus establishes a public space characterized by men's serene, passionless speech and women's silence, even as women's purpose and worth coheres with roles occurring in private. This pattern is strongly reinforced elsewhere in this text. In 1 Tim 5:11–14, this author warns about the dangers of young widows freely moving between houses, speaking to other women in their travels. He draws on the ancient gossip discourse to present their speech as foolish and even dangerous, a form of secret or private communication that contrasts to public, male speech.[22] The author uses this suspect speech, combined with the women's lack of control over sensual desires, to call for these women's containment in domestic space where they should "marry, bear children, and manage their households" (1 Tim 5:14). In this way, women and their speech are relegated to domestic, private space differentiated from the public space that surrounds it. Indeed, in the only passage in the Pastorals that specifically sanctions women's speech to others in the community, older women are prompted to teach the younger how to love husband and children, manage their household, and be "submissive to their husbands" (Titus 3:4–5).[23] Thus, the only speech the author upholds for women is communication about domestic matters between women who are devoted to the kyriarchally structured household and its concerns.

First Timothy's efforts to define debate, speech, and wisdom in an *ekklēsia* context attest to the engagement of this author and his audience with ancient democratic discourse. Passages such as 1 Tim 1:3–9; 2:8–15;

---

22. Marianne Kartzow identifies these characterizations of speech as key indicators of the gossip discourse in antiquity. Kartzow (2009, 41–66, 209) argues that the author of the Pastoral Epistles mobilizes this discourse and thus evokes these characterizations of gossip in order to turn the young widows toward a domestic ideal that requires them to "give up any alternative discourse."

23. Solevåg points out that the author uses the word *kalodidaskalous*, "teachers of good," in Titus 2:3 to denote women as teachers. This is a *hapax legomenon* that Solevåg (2013, 103) suggests this author uses in order to avoid "highly charged verbs and nouns connected with male teaching."

and 6:3–5 reveal a struggle over both who will speak and the type of speech that will be practiced in this *ekklēsia*. The author of 1 Timothy champions men's *ekklēsia* speech lacking animated debate. The attempt to impose the kyriarchy of the ancient, elite household onto the *ekklēsia* claims authority for "fathers" such as Paul, Timothy, and the bishop that renders debate as dissention and disorder endangering the right teaching of these leaders. Meanwhile, the author seeks to silence women with familiar arguments utilized by other ancient authors to construct women as unsuited to public speech and thus unsuited for full democratic citizenship.

At the same time, with Wire, scholars may recognize that close rhetorical analysis can recover other voices and perspectives that allow a fuller understanding of early Christian groups. In this case, 1 Timothy's rhetoric reveals voices in the community choosing vigorous *ekklēsia* debate with multiple teachers. The specificity of this author's restrictions regarding women's speech and his efforts to confine women to private, domestic space suggest that women in this community, married and unmarried— and likely enslaved and free—are participating in this debate and thus helping to manifest this communal space as public. Such an *ekklēsia* space hosting lively and egalitarian debate connects with the ideals and practice of civic democracy and its principal institution, the citizen assembly. However, vocal, political participation of both men *and* women in an *ekklēsia* setting also works to expand the boundaries of citizenship and its rights as traditionally defined in political institutions of the Greek polis. Likewise, such participation strains the two-sphere model, showing the radical potential of democratic discourse and Christian theology to empower by challenging such citizenship boundaries.

If the community of 1 Timothy, like that of 1 Corinthians, participated in democratic discourse centered on *ekklēsia* discernment and debate, one may understand speech functioning as a marker of equality and citizenship. The claims of democratic discourse to provide universal equality and freedom for citizens imposed a burden of explanation for those who would exclude certain groups from that circle (Wolin 1996, 80). Early Christian authors such as Paul or 1 Timothy who engaged democratic discourse and wished to champion hierarchy and the exclusions of certain groups from full participation had to struggle with not only the egalitarian claims of democratic discourse but the egalitarian claims of Christian theology as well. Like Paul, 1 Timothy asserts women's essential difference from men, locating this difference in the order of creation. However, 1 Timothy also uses the second Genesis creation story to assert women's lack of judgment.

Like other ancient authors, 1 Timothy suggests that women's flawed reason precludes them from public, political speech even as he locates their virtue in decency, modesty, and silence. However, 1 Timothy parts ways with other ancient authors, and in particular with other Christian authors, with his claims that women's salvation only comes through childbearing.

First Timothy's insistence that women's inherent social and theological worth lies with bearing children contradicts liberating elements of Paul's uncontested letters, including the radical promise of the baptismal formula in Gal 3:28 that "patriarchal marriage—and sexual relationships between male and female—is no longer constitutive of the new community in Christ" (Schüssler Fiorenza 1994, 211).[24] Likewise, 1 Tim 2:15 directly opposes Paul's preference for celibacy for both men and women in 1 Cor 7. By locating women's essential worth in domestic roles, 1 Timothy not only departs from such liberating elements of Paul's letters but also intensifies the gendered public and private dichotomy that Paul sought to create in 1 Corinthians.

In the case of 1 Timothy, the author's arguments for silencing women in the public sphere, and his insistence on their procreation, must be balanced with signs in the letter that women's voices were part of the public *ekklēsia*. In passages such as 1 Tim 4:3 and 5:3–16, this author also intimates that some of these women were choosing the celibacy Paul earlier offered as an ideal. Readers must consider whether women in this community found empowerment in egalitarian elements of Christian theology—including elements from Paul's letters—even as the author of 1 Timothy sought to intensify gender difference and hierarchy also present in Paul's letters. If there is a change between Paul and 1 Timothy regarding women's agency and participation in the Christian *ekklēsia*, I argue that it is not in accelerating acceptance of the wider society's traditional gender roles. First Timothy shares with 1 Corinthians, and indeed with evidence from the wider Greco-Roman world, signs of ongoing debates and struggles around the place of women in public spaces. However, 1 Timothy, when read in conversation with other early Christian texts such as the Acts of Thecla,

---

24. Consideration of the political implications of Gal 3:27–28 within early Christian communities distinguishes Schüssler Fiorenza and Wire from other scholars who have held up an eschatological meaning of the formula. Wire (1990, 126) observes that the place of "male and female" alongside "neither slave nor free" and "neither Jew nor Greek" suggests "overcoming in Christ a division cutting across the whole of society, which privileged one group at the expense of another."

suggests an evolution in which Pauline texts themselves become part of the arsenal used by both sides in a struggle over women's full participation in the public space of the *ekklēsia* (Krause 2004, 59; MacDonald 1983).

Conclusion

Wire's sophisticated investigation of Paul's rhetoric in 1 Corinthians reveals the logic and intent of that rhetoric in relationship to an audience led in part by influential, spiritually powerful women. By situating Paul's rhetoric in relationship to this audience and by recognizing that Paul's engagement of the Corinthian women signals their authority in the community, Wire opened up significant new avenues of investigation in a range of Christian texts. My own work on democratic discourse in early Christian texts owes a great debt to Wire's insightful rhetorical analysis of Paul's negotiation with his audience. Wire's vision of Paul's rhetoric as shaped and constrained by an audience with voices, commitments, and beliefs sometimes significantly differing from Paul's own helped me to further explore Paul's relationship with the Corinthian community. In *Corinthian Democracy* I recognized Paul as not just any speaker but a speaker within a democratic *ekklēsia* context defined, in part, by debate, the power of a discerning audience, and free speech open to all members of the assembly.

In these terms, even as I am indebted to Wire's rhetorical analysis, I depart from her reconstruction of the Corinthians' self-identity as a communal home that serves to separate the Christian community and the Corinthian women's participation from public, political space in the ancient world. This reconstruction contributes to a gendered two-sphere model that locates ancient women's agency and participation in private space, while accepting that political participation primarily occurs in public space gendered as male.

I suggest the need to seriously question the two-sphere model, which continues to limit our understanding of early Christianity and of women in the ancient world by obscuring women's robust political status and participation and fostering an artificial separation of the Christian *ekklēsia* from the public, political realm. Together, feminist theory and the work of Jürgen Habermas offer new possibilities for imagining multiple publics in the ancient world, and thus expanded possibilities for discerning women's political involvement.

The multiple ancient publics created through participation in the democratic discourse and practice that continued to infuse the early empire deserve more scholarly attention. Habermas's theory together with the concept of multiple publics allows scholars to better comprehend "highly differentiated and pluralistic modern societies" (Benhabib 1992, 103), even as this theory allows scholars of antiquity to better recognize public, political participation in the Roman Empire—itself composed of highly differentiated and pluralistic societies.

I bring these observations to 1 Timothy, a text that shares with 1 Corinthians evidence of engagement in democratic discourse together with women's vocal *ekklēsia* participation. First Timothy's efforts to address and contain debate and decision in a space named as *ekklēsia* alert the reader to the presence of democratic discourse and practice in this community. First Timothy's work to eliminate women's *ekklēsia* speech witnesses that women's voices have already helped to create public space within this community. I argue that 1 Timothy's deployment of a gendered public/private dichotomy that places women's agency and value entirely in the private realm is part of an ongoing and widespread struggle around women's public participation. First Timothy draws on common ancient arguments gendering both public speech and wisdom itself as male, even as it intensifies theological arguments for largely limiting women to the private sphere. As Wire herself has demonstrated, such an author's rhetorical efforts must be read with an awareness of the audience the author seeks to persuade. In 1 Timothy, as in the case of 1 Corinthians, this audience includes women who have found a path to public speech in democratic discourse and egalitarian elements of Christian theology.

Works Cited

Bakewell, Geoffrey. 2013. *Aeschylus's Suppliant Women: The Tragedy of Immigration*. Madison: University of Wisconsin Press.
Barber, Benjamin. 1988. *The Conquest of Politics: Liberal Philosophy in Democratic Times*. Princeton: Princeton University Press.
Bassler, Jouette. 1996. *1 Timothy, 2 Timothy, Titus*. Nashville: Abingdon.
Benhabib, Seyla. 1992. *Situating the Self: Gender, Community and Postmodernism in Contemporary Ethics*. New York: Routledge.
Berger, Klaus. 2006. "Volksversammlung und Gemeinde Gottes: Zu den Anfängen der christlichen Verwendung von '*ekklesia*.'" Pages 173–206 in *Tradition und Offenbarung: Studien zum frühen Christentum*. Edited by Matthias Klinghardt and Günter. Röhser. Tübingen: Francke.

D'Angelo, Mary Rose. 2007. "Gender and Geopolitics in the Work of Philo of Alexandria: Jewish Piety and Imperial Family Values." Pages 63–88 in *Mapping Gender in Ancient Religious Discourses*. Edited by Todd Penner and Caroline Vander Stichele. Boston: Brill.

Davidoff, Leonore. 1998. "Regarding Some 'Old Husbands' Tales': Public and Private in Feminist History." Pages 164–94 in *Feminism: The Public and Private*. Edited by Joan B. Landes. ORF. Oxford: Oxford University Press.

Dibelius, Martin, and Hans Conzelmann. 1989. *The Pastoral Epistles*. Translated by Philip Buttolph and Adela Yarbro. Hermeneia. Philadelphia: Fortress.

Donelson, Lewis. 1986. *Pseudepigraphy and Ethical Argument in the Pastoral Epistles*. HUT 22. Tübingen: Mohr Siebeck.

Finley, Moses I. 1985. *Democracy Ancient and Modern*. London: Hogarth.

Foucault, Michel. 1972. *The Archaeology of Knowledge and the Discourse on Language*. Translated by Alan M. Sheridan Smith. New York: Pantheon.

Fraser, Nancy. 1990. "Rethinking the Public Sphere: A Contribution to the Critique of Actually Existing Democracy." *SocText* 25–26:56–80.

———. 1998. "Sex, Lies, and the Public Sphere: Reflections of the Confirmation of Clarence Thomas." Pages 314–37 in *Feminism: The Public and Private*. Edited by Joan B. Landes. ORF. Oxford: Oxford University Press.

Glancy, Jennifer. 1998. "Obstacles to Slaves' Participation in the Corinthian Church." *JBL* 117:481–501.

———. 2003. "Protocols of Masculinity in the Pastoral Epistles." Pages 235–64 in *New Testament Masculinities*. Edited by Stephen D. Moore and Janice Capel Anderson. SemeiaSt 45. Atlanta: Society of Biblical Literature.

Habermas, Jürgen. 1984. *The Theory of Communicative Action*. 2 vols. Translated by Thomas McCarthy. Boston: Beacon.

Hansen, Mogens Herman. 1999. *The Athenian Democracy in the Age of Demosthenes: Structure, Principles, and Ideology*. Translated by John A. Crook. Norman: Oklahoma University Press.

Horrell, David. 2008. "Disciplining Performance and 'Placing' the Church: Widows, Elders and Slaves in the Household of God (1 Tim 5,1–6,2)." Pages 109–34 in *1 Timothy Reconsidered*. Edited by Karl Paul Donfried. Leuven: Peeters.

Horsley, Richard. 2000. "Rhetoric and Empire—and 1 Corinthians." Pages 72–102 in *Paul and Politics: Ekklēsia, Israel, Imperium, Interpretation; Essays in Honor of Krister Stendahl*. Edited by Richard Horsley. Harrisburg, PA: Trinity Press International.

Ismard, Paulin. 2017. *Democracy's Slaves: A Political History of Ancient Greece*. Translated by Jane Marie Todd. Cambridge: Harvard University Press.

Johnson, Luke Timothy. 2001. *The First and Second Letters to Timothy: A New Translation and Commentary*. AB 35A. New York: Doubleday.

Kartzow, Marianne Bjelland. 2009. *Gossip and Gender: Othering of Speech in the Pastoral Epistles*. New York: de Gruyter.

Katz, Marilyn. 2004. "Women and Democracy in Ancient Greece." Pages 292–312 in *Ancient Greek Democracy: Readings and Sources*. Edited by Eric W. Robinson. Malden, MA: Blackwell.

Kloppenborg, John S. 2017. "Associations, Christ Groups, and Their Place in the *Polis*." ZNW 108:1–56.

Korner, Ralph J. 2017. *The Origin and Meaning of* Ekklēsia *in the Early Jesus Movement*. Ancient Judaism and Early Christianity 98. Boston: Brill.

Kraemer, Ross Shepard. 1992. *Her Share of the Blessings: Women's Religions Among Pagans, Jews, and Christians in the Greco-Roman World*. New York: Oxford University Press.

Krause, Deborah. 2004. *1 Timothy*. Readings: A New Biblical Commentary. New York: T&T Clark.

Landes, Joan B. 1998a. "Introduction." Pages 1–17 in *Feminism: The Public and Private*. Edited by Joan B. Landes. ORF. Oxford: Oxford University Press.

———. 1998b. "The Public and the Private Sphere: A Feminist Reconstruction." Pages 135–63 in *Feminism: The Public and Private*. Edited by Joan B. Landes. ORF. Oxford: Oxford University Press.

Ma, John. 2000a. "The Epigraphy of Hellenistic Asia Minor: A Survey of Recent Research (1992–1999)." *AJA* 104:95–121.

———. 2000b. "Public Speech and Community in the Euboicus." Pages 108–24 in *Dio Chrysostom: Politics, Letters, and Philosophy*. Edited by Simon Swain. New York: Oxford University Press.

MacDonald, Dennis R. 1983. *The Legend and the Apostle: The Battle for Paul in Story and Canon*. Philadelphia: Westminster.

Marshall, I. Howard. 2006. *A Critical and Exegetical Commentary on the Pastoral Epistles*. New York: T&T Clark.

Marshall, John W. 2008. "'I Left You in Crete': Narrative Deception and Social Hierarchy in the Letter to Titus." *JBL* 127:781–803.
Miller, Anna C. 2015. *Corinthian Democracy: Democratic Discourse in 1 Corinthians*. PTMS 220. Eugene, OR: Pickwick.
Möhrmann, Renate. 1984. "The Reading Habits of Women in Vormärz." Pages 104–17 in *German Women in the Nineteenth Century: A Social History*. New York: Holmes & Meier.
Ober, Josiah. 1989. *Mass and Elite in Democratic Athens: Rhetoric, Ideology, and the Power of the People*. Princeton: Princeton University Press.
———. 2000. "Political Conflicts, Political Debates, and Political Thought." Pages 111–38 in *Classical Greece: 500–323 BC*. Edited by R. Osborne. Oxford: Oxford University Press.
Oberlinner, Lorenz. 1994. *Die Pastoralbriefe: Kommentar zum ersten Timotheusbrief*. HThKNT. Freiburg: Herder.
Økland, Jorunn. 2004. *Women in Their Place: Paul and the Corinthian Discourse of Gender and Sanctuary Space*. London: T&T Clark.
Osiek, Carolyn, and Margaret Y. MacDonald. 2006. *A Woman's Place: House Churches in Earliest Christianity*. Minneapolis: Fortress.
Payne, Steven. 2019. "Pneumatic Bodies and the Afterlives of Ancient Democracy in Early Paulinism." PhD diss., Fordham University.
Peterson, Erik. 2010. "Ekklesia: Studien zum altkirchlichen Kirchenbegriff." Pages 9–83 in *Ausgewählte Schriften: Sonderband*. Edited by Barbara Nichtwiss and Hans-Ulrich Weidemann. Würzburg: Echter.
Plutarch. *Moralia, Volume X*. Translated by Harold North Fowler. LCL. Cambridge: Harvard University Press, 1936.
Porter, Stanley E. 1993. "What Does It Mean to be 'Saved by Childbirth' (1 Tim 2:15)." *JSNT* 49:87–102.
Rhodes, Peter J., and David M. Lewis. 1997. *Decrees of the Greek States*. New York: Oxford University Press.
Rogers, Guy M. 1991. *The Sacred Identity of Ephesos: Foundation Myths of a Roman City*. New York: Routledge.
Salmeri, Giovanni. 2000. "Dio, Rome, and the Civic Life of Asia Minor." Pages 53–92 in *Dio Chrysostom: Politics, Letters, and Philosophy*. Edited by Simon Swain. New York: Oxford University Press.
Saxonhouse, Arlene. 2006. *Free Speech and Democracy in Ancient Athens*. Cambridge: Cambridge University Press.
Schüssler Fiorenza, Elisabeth. 1984. *Bread Not Stone: The Challenge of Feminist Biblical Interpretation*. Boston: Beacon.

———. 1992. *But She Said: Feminist Practices of Biblical Interpretation*. Boston: Beacon.

———. 1994. *In Memory of Her: A Feminist Theological Reconstruction of Christian Origins*. Tenth anniversary edition. New York: Crossroad.

———. 1999. *Rhetoric and Ethic: The Politics of Biblical Studies*. Minneapolis: Fortress.

———. 2000. *Jesus and the Politics of Interpretation*. New York: Continuum.

Shaner, Katherine. 2017. *Enslaved Leadership in Early Christianity*. New York: Oxford University Press.

Solevåg, Anna Rebecca. 2013. *Birthing Salvation: Gender and Class in Early Christian Childbearing Discourse*. Boston: Brill.

Stone, Lawrence. 1979. *The Family, Sex and Marriage in England*. New York: Harper & Row.

Tamez, Elsa. 2007. *Struggles for Power in Early Christianity: A Study of the First Letter to Timothy*. Translated by Gloria Kinsler. Maryknoll, NY: Orbis.

Torjesen, Karen. 1993. *When Women Were Priests: Women's Leadership in the Early Church and the Scandal of Their Subordination in the Rise of Christianity*. San Francisco: HarperSanFrancisco.

Towner, Philip H. 2006. *The Letters to Timothy and Titus*. NICOT. Grand Rapids: Eerdmans.

Verner, David C. 1983. *The Household of God: The Social World of the Pastoral Epistles*. SBLDS 71. Chico, CA: Scholars Press.

Wire, Antoinette Clark. 1990. *The Corinthian Women Prophets: A Reconstruction through Paul's Rhetoric*. Minneapolis: Fortress.

Wolin, Sheldon. 1996. "Transgression, Equality and Voice." Pages 63–90 in *Demokratia: A Conversation on Democracies, Ancient and Modern*. Edited by Josiah Ober and Charles Hedrick. Princeton: Princeton University Press.

Young, Iris Marion. 1998. "Impartiality and the Civic Public: Some Implications of Feminist Critiques of Moral and Political Theory." Pages 421–47 in *Feminism: The Public and the Private*. Edited by Joan B. Landes. ORF. Oxford: Oxford University Press.

Zamfir, Korinna. 2014. "Is the *Ekklēsia* a Household (of God)? Reassessing the Notion of οἶκος Θεοῦ in 1 Tim 3.15." *NTS* 60:511–28.

Zuiderhoek, Arjan. 2008. "On the Political Sociology of the Imperial Greek City." *GRBS* 48:417–45.

A Posthumanist Lens on Paul and Corinthian Agency

Antoinette Clark Wire

Inspiration from These Essays

All the above essays chart new directions these scholars have taken since my efforts to reconstruct the Corinthian women prophets from Paul's rhetoric in 1 Corinthians. Shelly Matthews gives her attention to the shorn woman Paul derides in 11:6. She points us beyond the traditional mourner, exposed adulteress, or enslaved woman who is shorn to a possible chosen gender performance like that of Thecla, who takes on the robe of an itinerant preacher. Gender, Matthews shows, cannot be charted as a binary but stretches across a wide spectrum. Anna Miller asks what kind of speech characterized the Corinthian assembly and finds in contemporary usage of Josephus and Plutarch that *ekklēsia* points not to home-based meals and devotions, but to civic deliberations and common actions. I hear this telling us to expect that women's prophecy in Corinth was often political, social, and economic. Joseph Marchal's essay is another challenge to extend our archive of specific groups in Paul's audience in Corinth. He asks about men and women whom Paul classifies only as wrongdoers, among them Sodomites and prostitutes (6:9–11). He wants to know how these people are living when, as Paul says, they are "justified in the name of the Lord."

This kind of work keeps moving us toward a more accurate and fruitful reading of 1 Corinthians. Yet I take my start in this response from certain points made in the three other essays. Arminta Fox (2019) carries us into 2 Corinthians in her new *Paul Decentered: Reading 2 Corinthians with the Corinthian Women*, and in her essay here on Paul's contentious rebuttal to the Corinthians being persuaded by rival apostles (2 Cor 10–13). I agree that 1 Corinthians can no longer be read in isolation from the letter that followed, and both need to be taken into account, not only in the ways they reinforce each other, to which Fox contributes here, but also in the ways they contest each other.

Jorunn Økland has taken up the challenging task of defending the integrity of 1 Cor 14:34–35, on which *The Corinthian Women Prophets* depends, both in her critique of the history of interpretation and in a careful analysis of the manuscripts. Such work is crucial because American interpreters continue to skip the passage or a larger unit as an interpolation from the margin, a quotation that Paul refutes, or a command restricted to a specific group of women. She and some others in European scholarship see these explanations as recent efforts to keep Paul pristine from the gender bias of the church since his time. Økland also reminds us that scholars today are becoming less ready to attribute difficulties they have in interpreting a text to faulty transmission or later editing, recognizing that the writer's rhetoric, perhaps especially where it is rough, may be our best clue to the process of writing. Concerning 2 Corinthians, this means that there is new energy for hearing how this letter reads as a whole and how it follows 1 Corinthians.

Finally, it is Cavan Concannon's piece in this collection that has provoked my thinking, his warning that binary othering naturalizes domination, also when an interpreter identifies with or against an author to authorize himself or herself. In fact, he argues, a letter is shaped by the traditions it reflects and the audiences it anticipates as much as by the composer, and beyond that by all the audiences it actually gets, who shape the traditions of its hearing down to ourselves. If this is not enough to complicate our reading, Concannon insists with Bruno Latour's posthumanism that attention be given to the nonhuman agencies that Paul speaks of, from the common clay pot that holds a treasure to the *pneuma* or spirit animating both the bodies of believers and Christ's body. The interest of these posthumanist thinkers is not at all to dismiss the role of humans on the earth but to challenge the human assumption that nonhumans exist to serve our interests. Because all things that exist have agency in their own ways and on their own schedules, human exploitation of other animals, plants, and minerals threatens the common ecosystem and shifts us into a posthuman era, whether to our enlightenment or our eclipse.

Posthumanism

Latour applies the term *actant* to these nonhuman actors, not only to the living animals, plants, and bacteria, but equally to the so-called inert things such as mountains, metals, and motes. Here Jane Bennett's (2010, 3) small book, *Vibrant Matter: A Political Ecology of Things*, presents most clearly "the not-quite-human capaciousness of things," a vitality intrinsic to materiality in all things and in ourselves, who are each a shifting network or assemblage of diverse and interacting parts. She helps us recognize that we are not humans in a passive or simply hostile environment but we are one aspect of vital materiality, "nested microbiomes" that share with others the problems and possibilities we face (20–38, 112–14). Humans and nonhumans already share political responsibility for this process. Latour ends his *We Have Never Been Modern* with a call to convene the Parliament of Things, and recently in *Facing Gaia* describes his own experiment at realizing a posthumanist world by convening a simulation called "Making It Work." At this parliament not only people groups but also the ocean, atmosphere, and land are vocally represented in the hall, in addition to endangered species, nongovernmental organizations, and cities (Latour 1993, 142–45; 2017, 255–70). A scientist was present in each delegation as a nonvoting consultant. The results were lively and contentious, if not conclusive.

Integral to the posthumanist conviction that all things have agency and make their distinctive claims is the corollary that the many precede the one. The validity of any claim to exist does not depend on an external source or system to which something owes its allegiance, but is integral to the thing that persists in being itself. So subordination is not built in, and all the shifting networks by which life functions reflect alliances among things, both organic and inorganic, that seek to persist, rather than reflecting set affiliations. When in *Facing Gaia* Latour (2017, 135) insists that the parts are necessarily superior to the whole, he explains: "Superior does not mean more encompassing. It means more connected." Therefore, he says, an Anthropocene grasp of our situation is not obtained by ramping up the scale toward global thoughts but by attending to local loops in the networks of things, by making "numerous relationships, and especially reciprocal ones" (136). Here Gaia is the name proposed for all the unpredictable consequences of each agent pursuing its own interest by engaging its environment (142). Conflicts abound, but those who are sensitive are able to deal with them by better networking with others, organic and inorganic.

This posthumanist priority of multiple actants over any single species or principle has also been articulated in terms of the rhizome rather than the rooted plant (Deleuze and Guattari 1987, 3–25). Most trees and plants and many animals grow from seed in a generational cycle, drawing sustenance through roots and leaves or by ingesting plants and animals until they reach their lifespan and die; but some are rhizomes. Like the tuber, the potato, and most wild grasses, they grow by extending themselves, always producing one more piece that is neither the seed nor the fruit but the middle again. Deleuze and Guattari's volume *A Thousand Plateaus*—itself a rhizome at near that many pages—sees those plants and animals that propagate by seed favoring a kind of affiliation of dominant and dependent parts, whereas rhizomes form networks that do not distinguish beginning and end, center and periphery. The tree as a self-standing structure is commonly taken as a model for living things, but there is also the rhizome. It provides no generic model but can only be mapped, and that provisionally, since as a network it is always incomplete and open to modification (Deleuze and Guattari 1987, 12-13). Among animals the rhizome appears not in the lone wolf but in the shifting wolf pack that sustains itself over wolf generations, likewise not in the human self but in human society (26-38). All these networked things and a myriad more meet up with one another, struggle or negotiate with one another, and shape wider networks as they seek the resources they live on. Need this mean perpetual war? Posthumanists do speak of Gaia (from *gē*, "earth, ground, dirt") not at all as a fertility goddess, but as a perpetual threat of the worst (Loveloch 2000, 3; Latour 2017, 130-42, 281-92).[1] The scramble for life ends life for many individuals and species. But Gaia means correspondingly a perpetual hope for life. Hope remains possible because the networks are not determined and closed but incomplete and open.

Posthumanism and Paul

Using posthumanist thinking to understand the letters of Paul may not seem promising. In the first place, Paul has little curiosity about or knowledge of the natural world, being an urban man promoting a social movement in scattered cities of the Roman East. Just compare his metaphors to Jesus's parables—a Roman triumph to a harvest payday. More importantly, he does not hold to the posthumanist first principle that the many precede the one, that each actant persists from itself by shifting interactions with others, rather than from any necessity imposed on it from its origin or end.

---

1. As one of the oldest Greek gods, Gaia is linked to earthquakes, storms, and other acts of retribution. For ancient sources on Gaia see Burkert 1985, 418.

For Paul "there is one God, the Father, from whom are all things and for [or toward] whom we live" (1 Cor 8:6 NRSV). Finally, Paul presents himself as God's messenger to the nations carrying news of a recently executed man named Jesus the Christ whom God raised from the dead, offering life to whomever will trust God's life-making power. Paul is obsessed with spreading news of this transformation of all things that he sees happening through God's Spirit active in the assemblies of these people.

Though easy communication between Paul and the posthumanists seems fraught, there are people today who live in a posthumanist world and ask whether it is possible to draw Paul toward posthumanist perceptions and draw these insights toward Paul. Is it possible to be a Christian posthumanist in a way consonant both with Paul's discoveries and the insights of this thinking? Similar questions may also be asked by Jews and Muslims, as well as by nonaffiliated people who want to integrate a posthumanist cosmology with their spiritual life and ethical commitments. This exploration can only be suggestive because posthumanism and Paul's thought are far more complex than first appear and are formulated in many different ways—witness the range of interpreters of posthumanism and the range of theologies in Paul's different letters. Taking only one slice of the evidence on each side, I restrict myself to Latour and his circle as described above to represent posthumanism and to the Corinthian correspondence to represent Paul.

I should say before turning to Paul that posthumanists make no a priori exclusion of spirit or even God from agency, having affirmed the agency of all things, each in its own way. They make no decision in advance that all reality is material in the same sense. What is rejected is any concept of the divine or any originary principle that programs other things and therefore denies them the agency that is their life. Already in *We Have Never Been Modern*, Latour (1993, 77) asks, "How can we shift from immanent/transcendent Society towards collectives of humans and nonhumans? How can we go from the transcendent/immanent crossed-out God of origins to the God who should perhaps be called the God below?" Twenty-five years later in *Facing Gaia*, Latour (2017, 69) begins by asserting that all modes of agency function in interacting networks of events in what he calls a metamorphic zone. Animism of all kinds is present, he claims, in that all things are actants with impact. Yet this is not at all a consequence of one creative impulse. Each agency modifies itself to survive, countered or assisted by others "within a distributed intentionality of all agents" (101). The result is waves of action that respect neither borders nor any fixed scale.

In an effort to overcome the gulf between what are often seen as extremes, belief in one God and belief in one nature, Latour (2017, 181, 195-99) sketches a provisional chart that links the authority of the laws of nature and the authority of an ordering God. In place of each he proposes the authority of the multiverse and the authority of the "God of ends/ends of God." While the former concepts of nature and God take themselves to be universal and undisputable, the latter are the chosen province of scientists and of religious groups respectively. The former nature and God are conceived to be off the ground and otherworldly, the latter networked and earthbound; the former claiming a radical break with the past, the latter temporal and unstable; the former either deanimated (nature) or overanimated (religion), the latter simply animated in both its scientific and religious modes.[2]

Most interestingly, Latour does not reject out of hand the apocalyptic expectations of religious movements in their early stages. In a lecture titled "The End of Time or Not" he calls for living in the end times within time, taking up the "reprise of tension" reflected in Pope Francis's *Laudato Si* by avoiding any degeneration of apocalyptic into a past event that assures salvation for the few (Latour 2017, 193-206). Latour argues that we have colonized matter, ignored its agency, and shaped from it a materialism to serve our own ends. He concludes that we now face the material Gaia, who announces, "Let matter go." This puts us as material beings not before or after the apocalypse but during it. Latour (206-19) nonetheless says that Gaia as apocalypse is not yet the end but the face that can possibly prevent the end by making it visible, shocking us finally to our feet to rematerialize our belonging to the world.

Turning to Paul no longer seems like such an impossible stretch. But he must be read out of his own world and in light of the threats he faced as he wrote the letters to Corinth. These threats were not planetary but social, yet what he faced bears comparison to the crisis faced in the posthumanist situation. To read Paul, I must take up his understanding of God, the point where he anchors his thought, although it is often ignored in our focus on the diverse voices in his letters. When we leave the task of figuring out the theological conflict in Corinth to the historians of dogma, they hold the heavy weapons in the battle for the text's meaning and keep us on the

---

2. Compare here the work of Denise Kimber Buell (2009; 2014) on hauntology, the study of specters of the past, spirits that haunt and inspire communities that have suffered violence on the way to claiming their agency.

margins. Yet I want to keep this theology decentered as I observe the multiple agencies that shape the text. My question is how other-than-human powers affect the active agency of the marginal humans with whom we have chosen to ally ourselves—the women and enslaved people and foreigners and prostitutes and "men who sleep with men" who appear here. I argue that these people are the representatives in Paul's Corinthian correspondence of the posthumanists' "vibrant matter," agents that have not been allowed agency. They have been used as instruments of other people in the textual and reading world who are serving their own power. Only when we take all the agencies in the text and its interpretation as integral to its comprehensive network of life and no longer assume privileged human and superhuman realities do we enter the theological debate in Corinth and broaden the scope of the text to incorporate ourselves and the people there with whom we ally ourselves.

Posthumanism challenges us to take seriously agencies that are not human down to the peat that produces methane when the permafrost melts. So it follows that we cannot understand Paul's letters and their significance for reconstructing marginal voices when we dismiss the agency of God that Paul says has made a new creation in them through the death and resurrection of Jesus Christ. But how can we identify that agency in a way that does not take our attention off the agency of the enslaved foreign woman? I suggest that we take soundings in Paul's theology at a few points where Paul appeals to the agency of God either to restrict or to stimulate the agency of the Corinthians. This may allow us to distinguish between his theological moves that are destructive and those that may be constructive for the people who are considered nothings (1 Cor 1:28). For a time we can park our prejudices pro and con concerning the dogmas that Paul's theology has since generated and consider what impacts he sees God's agency having on the agency of various people in this community.

Paul in 1 Corinthians

I begin with the verb *hypotassein* ("to subordinate"), which appears in three contexts in 1 Corinthians, and its cognate noun *hypotagē* ("subjection"), appearing once in 2 Corinthians. I start with a text where the subordination term itself is not used, but a metaphor or pun about heads serves the same purpose. In Paul's first response to Corinthian worship practices, he requires that women cover their heads when praying and prophesying on the grounds that "the head of every man is Christ, the head of a woman is the man, and the head of Christ is God" (1 Cor 11:3).[3] The subordination of woman to man, pinched between the subordination of man to Christ and Christ to God, not only restricts woman's agency but orders the man's relation to Christ and Christ's to God in terms of subordination. Women's subordination then appears explicitly when Paul excludes all women's speech from the assembly at the final climax of his guidelines for worship:[4] "Let the women be silent in the assembly since it is not proper for them to speak, but let them be subordinate as the law also says" (1 Cor 14:34; see Jorunn Økland's essay in this volume defending the integrity of this passage within Paul's letter).[5]

In a further 1 Corinthians context Paul speaks of subordination to describe the final victory when all will be subordinated to God. Quoting Pss 110:1 and 8:7 (NRSV 8:6), Paul projects a sequence in which Christ will overcome "every ruler and every authority and power," then will overcome death itself, and finally will subordinate himself to God "so that God may be all in all" (1 Cor 15:24–28 NRSV). This suggests a cosmic dualism in which Christ wins out on behalf of God in a zero sum game against "the rulers of this age" or "the god of this world" (1 Cor 2:8; 2 Cor 4:4 NRSV). His victory will give life to people through their incorporation into him, the resurrected human being, who will finally subordinate himself to God.

The language of subordination appears once more when Paul closes 1 Corinthians by instructing his hearers to be subordinate to the household of Stephanas and to those who work with him (1 Cor 16:15–18). On opening the letter, Paul mentioned this household among the few early believers whom he had baptized (1 Cor 1:16–17), but now they have apparently lost favor among other Corinthians because Paul speaks on their behalf. This shows that Paul expected subordination also among people in the community, specifically subordination to those allied with him. Modern embarrassment with this is evident in the NRSV's softening "subordinate yourselves" into "put yourself at the service of such people" (16:16).

Compare all these 1 Corinthians references to subordination with the single reference in 2 Corinthians that does not call for subjection to other

---

3. Unless otherwise indicated, biblical translations are mine.

4. On the significance of Paul's beginning and ending his worship instructions by restricting women's speech see Wire 1990, 152–56; 1994, 155–56, 176, 188; Marshall 2017.

5. See also Wire 1990, 149–52, 229–32; 284–86; Niccum 1997.

people or to God. Here Paul uses the term only when he tells them to be subject to "your confession of the good news of Christ" by giving liberally to the poor in Jerusalem (2 Cor 9:13). This suggests a change in Paul's approach to the Corinthians between the two letters.

Even the subordination Paul advocates in 1 Corinthians is not narrated as a myth of divine cosmic conflict such as we find in Rev 12–20. Paul's argument against eating sacrificed meat points in another direction. He realizes that the Corinthians in Christ already know that no idol exists and that sacrificed meat is harmless since there is "one God from whom are all things and toward whom we live, and one Lord Jesus Christ through whom are all things and through whom we live" (1 Cor 8:4–6). Yet he tells them not to eat what is sacrificed with anyone who might consider it holy, not so much because this could mislead the other person than for their own sakes, warning them with Deut 32:17: "What they devote to demons is not devoted to God" (1 Cor 10:20). If the Corinthians sacrifice at every god's table, they ignore their own human limitations and therefore slight God. This human overconfidence, not any cosmic divine power, is suggested to be the actual threat to God's all-sufficiency.

The threat that appears in Paul's Letter to the Romans as the power of sin rising up in people to defy God's righteousness appears here as the Corinthians' boasting in their own wisdom in competition with God's distinctive wisdom (1 Cor 1:18–25). Though Paul is not writing to the elite of Corinth, but to a group "not many wise by human standards, not many powerful, not many of note" (1:26), he says, and I translate literally, "The world's foolish things are what God chose in order to shame the wise; the world's weak things are what God chose in order to shame the strong; the world's common and despised things are what God chose—things that are nothing, in order to shame things that are something—so that that all flesh could not boast before God" (1 Cor 1:27–28). Yet when Paul interprets God's purpose this way to be the humbling of the powerful in a cosmic conflict between God's power and human power, this seems to leave only secondary place for the positive transformation of the foolish, weak, and despised. Paul does go on to affirm, "It is God's doing that you yourselves are in Christ Jesus who became for us wisdom from God—and justice and holiness and freedom—so that as it is written, 'Let the one who boasts boast in the Lord'" (1 Cor 1:30–31; Jer 9:22). Yet it seems to be the wisdom of Christ humbling the proud that they are to boast on God's behalf rather than a new agency in their own lives.

Corinthian Agency in 2 Corinthians

So in 1 Corinthians it is not clear that God provides an opening for the human agency of those who are foolish, weak, or despised, or God does this only by choosing them to shame the wise and shift the balance of power from powerful humans to God. Second Corinthians is another story. Any reader can see that Paul is less secure in this letter about his authority in Corinth. No longer is he giving advice by affirming the Corinthians' claims in order to contain or restrict their conduct (compare to 1 Cor 6:12–13; 7:1–2; 8:1–9; 10:23; 11:2–3; 14:31–32; 39–40). Now he is defending himself and seeking their affirmation of him (2 Cor 1:10; 3:1–3; 4:1–2; 5:11–12; 6:11–13; 7:2–4; 13:3–5). He persists in denying himself the rights he has in the gospel (see 1 Cor 9) and takes on every trial and abuse in order to get out the news of Christ (2 Cor 4:8–10; 6:4–10; 11:23–29), but he no longer asks them to pattern their lives after his example, as he often did in the earlier letter (1 Cor 4:10–16; 9:22–24; 10:31–11:1). Instead, he takes the life in them to be the result and proof of his effective work: "You yourselves are our letter, written in our hearts, known and read by all people" (2 Cor 3:2); "So death is active in us, but life in you" (4:12); "We rejoice when it is we who are weak, but you who are strong" (13:9). Note that it is not Jesus's death that Paul finds in them, but Jesus's resurrected life. Paul claims that he embodies Christ's death as agent of the news he carries, and this in turn enables them to embody Jesus's life, which finally makes him confident that God will one day also raise him with them (1:14; 4:13–14; 11:2).

Paul makes the same point about how Jesus's death generates life in them with several other metaphors in 2 Corinthians: "On your account Jesus Christ became poor so that you in his poverty might become rich" (2 Cor 8:9). "The one who did not know sin was made sin on our account, so that we might become the righteousness of God in him" (5:21). "For it is the God who said, 'From darkness let light shine!' who has shown in our hearts to make the knowledge of God's glory shine in the face of Jesus Christ" (4:6). The point in each case is that a great loss or lack in one has led to a gain in the others, in fact, a total reversal. Yet it takes them both to reflect Christ's dying and rising, Paul in his own limited and harsh work, and they in their consequent faith and expressive life. The agency is attributed to God, or to Christ, who became poor, and the benefits fall to the Corinthians, who become rich, righteous, and shining, in spite of, or better through, Paul's many deficiencies. This is his defense.

But does Paul recognize the agency of the Corinthians here, or is he claiming all credit for God and for himself as God's instrument? Second Corinthians when read as a whole makes clear that he is totally dependent on them to respond favorably to his pleas for their reconciliation with God and with himself before he can ask them to share in the collection for Jerusalem (2 Cor 5:18–7:15, especially 6:11–12; 7:2–4). Even his closing third-person attacks on rivals who compete with his interpretation of Christ are carefully distinguished from his simultaneous second-person challenges to the Corinthians not to tolerate their abuses (2 Cor 10–12). Finally, after general warnings against contention and immorality (12:19–21; cf. Gal 5:19–21), he returns the ball to their court, leaving it up to the Corinthians to examine themselves whether they are "in Christ" (2 Cor 13:5–10).

The clearest evidence that Paul recognizes their agency in 2 Corinthians is that he has stopped giving advice and correcting their deficiencies, and now confirms their positive experience of Christ, defending himself as God's instrument in their transformation. I propose in my recent 2 Corinthians commentary that Paul's unrelenting self-defense in this letter makes most sense if they had ignored his initial instructions in 1 Corinthians (Wire 2019). The Corinthians have apparently continued to exhibit their newfound wisdom and demonstrate publicly their freedom to eat sacrificed food, the women to lead in prayer and prophesy uncovered, spouses to continue to set aside marriages, the sexually distinctive to live their lives.[6] Only one person was disciplined and has repented (2 Cor 2:5–11; 7:5–13). Instead of Paul changing their ways according to his instructions, they have changed his way and challenged him to prove that Christ is speaking in him (2 Cor 13:3). Paul is the one who has had to reconfigure. Although the zero-sum contest between God and the boasts of the powerful still hovers in the background of Paul's theology, threatening to reduce the role of the once foolish and weak Corinthians to shaming the wise and powerful, the foreground is now a celebration of the Corinthians' life that comes out of Paul's death. This life is also affirmed as riches out of poverty, light out of darkness, treasure in clay, all this in the lives of people "not many wise, not many powerful" who did not accept a marginal role in someone else's drama. I call that their agency. When people defect until Paul must defend himself and recognize that in Christ they have been given God's

---

6. See also the recent work on the responses and actions of the Corinthian women in Fox 2019.

life and light and power and wisdom, God's agency is working not simply against the proud to assure divine sovereignty, but for—or rather in—the once weak and dismissed to establish their power and life.

God's Agency in the Corinthian Letters

This sign of the Corinthians' agency provokes another question. Is God's life-giving power, which Paul celebrates in 2 Corinthians, so overwhelming that the one swallows up the many, absorbing the Corinthians into God's glory and making even a cosmic dualism seem like a relief? This might be the case if the divine agency aimed to reproduce itself endlessly and determine all things from one will. But does God have such a program in Paul's letters to Corinth? The term Paul uses most consistently for God's impact is *charis*, often translated "grace." God's grace is what Paul says keeps him going in spite of his hardships (1 Cor 3:10; 15:10; 2 Cor 12:9), empowering him to say what he knows directly and openly, if not fluently or with visible wisdom (2 Cor 1:12; 4:1–2; 10:10; 11:6). But God's grace is also understood to be given "to you [Corinthians] in Christ" and is evident in their speech, knowledge and spiritual gifts, their sufficient support and their good works (1 Cor 1:4–7; 2 Cor 8:1, 9; 9:8, 14).

Yet, does *charis* then become the single divine will that monopolizes all agency? *Charis* seems rather to be given away in performative speech. Whenever Paul's letters are read in Corinth, the hearers receive *charis*, at the opening, "Grace to you and peace," and again at the closing, "the grace of the Lord Jesus Christ … be with you" (1 Cor 1:3; 16:23; 2 Cor 1:2; 13:13). Moreover, the word *charis* is also used for benefits or privileges that one human provides another human (2 Cor 1:15; 8:4), so that it becomes a name repeatedly used for the collection that Paul challenges the Corinthians to take up for the poor in Jerusalem, making them the givers of grace (1 Cor 16:3; 2 Cor 8:6, 7, 19). To complete the process, *charis* is also the word normally translated "thanks" in each of Paul's many exclamations of thanksgiving to God: literally, "Grace be to God for his inexpressible gift!" (1 Cor 10:30; 15:57; 2 Cor 2:14; 8:16; 9:15). So God receives as well as gives grace, and, one could say, the circle is complete with no privilege gained, no obligation incurred.

The meaning of *charis* in Paul's thought has been richly interpreted in several studies, with particularly fresh insight by Magdalene Frettlöh (2001) and Marlene Crüsemann (2014).[7] One Latourian theorist has even

---

7. See also the discussion in Barclay 2015, 562–74; Wire 2019, 178–82, 255–57.

articulated Latour's thought as a reformulation of grace for our time (Miller 2013). Yet, I still wonder when Paul recounts Christ's words to him, "My grace is enough for you since power is realized in weakness" (2 Cor 12:9), is human weakness made the condition for God's grace? And has the debt common in gift exchange become a stranglehold if the ability to give is itself a gift passed back in thanks for having been received? Can the creature ever be more than an instrument of the creator? Or is it the case that life can actually generate life, that what is given from a boundless source, an artesian spring, if you will, requires no responding gift and therefore generates a boundless response? Paul does seem to see the vicious cycle of "give to take" broken through in a gracious cycle by God's grace in Christ (*charis apo theou*, 1 Cor 1:3; 2 Cor 1:2) that gives rise to the Corinthians' grace for the Jerusalem poor (*eis hymas kai tēn charin tautēn*, 2 Cor 8:6; cf. 8:7, 19), which in turn overflows in grace/thanks to God (*charis tō theō*, 1 Cor 15:57; 2 Cor 2:14; 8:16; 9:15). Parallel to other scholars' interest in the *pneuma*/spirit that is both a human and nonhuman agency in Paul's letters,[8] *charis*/grace is another image for the broader-than-human palette in 2 Corinthians.

So we see, in Paul's use of both *charis*/grace and *pneuma*/spirit, that these powers with a nonhuman origin are found in humans (1 Cor 3:1–4, 16; 13:11–12; 15:45–59; 2 Cor 4:16; 13:9). They become spiritual people (*pneumatikoi*) who can decide whether to give *charis* to the poor in Jerusalem and whether to return *charis* to the source from which it came. Rather than becoming competitors with the nonhuman origin of their gifts, Paul concedes that he and they are full participants in the creativity they receive (2 Cor 9:11–15).

My language here of *human* and *nonhuman* for people and God proves itself inadequate for Paul, since we would have to include the entire animal, plant, and mineral world in the human category to reflect Paul. He sees these also originating in God's creation, fallen into decay, and "joined in groaning and wailing in labor pains until now" as each one struggles for its fulfillment, what Paul calls "the glorious freedom of God's own progeny" (Rom 8:19–23). Are we then thrown back into traditional theological language that speaks of Paul's letters in terms of a superhuman creator of everything else? Or is it closer to Paul to change the metaphor from a super-

---

8. See Concannon's essay in this collection, as well as Buell 2014; 2017; Hartman 2019. Kraftchick (2015) deals more with the interface of humans and technology.

human God above to a grounding God below, the power of a multifarious rhizomatic network that keeps generating its independent and interacting progeny? Then we would see the human being within the fluid animal, plant, and mineral whole, and leave behind the gap we were taught between the human and these others as a vestige of our humanist era. Or perhaps we would retain the distinction as an act of modesty to identify our analysis as a human project among other projects to claim agency rising from animal, plant, and mineral beings. Yet because each thing, each bit of vibrant matter, struggles to sustain, express, and develop itself, and this always occurs in networks of relations to other beings, Paul's affirming such a whole is not an antipode to the agency of the many but an enabling context of each life, not as program but as a fresh becoming of creative life.

Agency in Christ

We circle around Paul's theology but do not touch bottom until we ask how it is shaped by his experience of Jesus Christ. Jesus is not a metaphor for Paul but a man in his own time who was crucified by "the rulers of this age" (1 Cor 2:8), stimulating a messianic movement that Paul himself had suppressed until God "revealed his son in me" (Gal 1:16). Paul is reticent about this experience (in contrast to his biographer in Acts) and speaks only of having "seen the Lord" (1 Cor 9:1; 15:8). But on this basis Paul proclaims Jesus Christ risen from the dead and giving life to all who trust in him. Paul never mentions in any letter the Jesus of Galilee who ate with tax collectors and prostitutes, healed the sick and taught disciples, nor does he tell stories about Jesus's birth, baptism, or transfiguration, or what provoked his execution. We supply all this when he says "Jesus," but it is not there.

What he seems to claim from having "seen the Lord" is the vindication of a crucified man in a world where the word *crucified* meant the state-imposed violent death of a defenseless person, usually a slave, deviant, or criminal. Though Paul occasionally uses traditions of a sacrifice to interpret Jesus's death—"Christ our pascal lamb has been sacrificed" (1 Cor 5:7); "This cup is the new covenant in my blood" (1 Cor 11:25)—the point is not any agency of God in Jesus's death. He is crucified by "the rulers of this age," and God's agency appears in raising Jesus from the dead (1 Cor 2:8; 6:14; 15:15; 2 Cor 4:14).[9] Here again Paul does not tell accounts of the risen Jesus speaking or

---

9. The same distribution of agency—the ruler kills and God gives life—appears in early Jewish martyrdom texts (2 Macc 7:36; 4 Macc 7:18–19; 16:24–25; 17:5–6;

eating, but tells Jesus's effect on the agency of others: "He died for all so that the living might no longer live for themselves but for him who died and was raised for them.... If anyone is in Christ—a new creation! What's old is gone—look, what's new has come! All this is from God" (2 Cor 5:15, 17-18). Jesus's resurrection is also claimed to be the firstfruit or foretaste of the resurrection of the dead, not only those who identify with him but in some comprehensive way of all the dead: "As in Adam all die, just so in Christ all will be made alive" (1 Cor 5:20-22; 2 Cor 4:14; Rom 5:18). In 2 Corinthians Paul affirms in particular Jesus's resurrection in the living: "We, the living, are always being given up to death on Jesus' account so that Jesus' life might become visible in our mortal flesh. So death is working in us, but life in you" (2 Cor 4:11-12); "And all of us, seeing with uncovered faces the Lord's glory as refracted in a mirror, are being transformed into the same image from glory to glory, this from the Lord, the Spirit" (2 Cor 3:18; on glory, see Wire 2001).

Can posthumanism allow us to hear what Paul is affirming in a contemporary light? Paul goes beyond saying that the world he knows has been affected by something not strictly human. He says that the impact has been one of grace (*charis*), of spirit (*pneuma*), and, perhaps most precisely due to his experience of Christ, of life (*zōē*). This not only dissolves the elevation of one class of humans over another and of human agency over other animal, plant, and mineral agencies, but it claims what cannot be proven by human testing, that the rhizomatic network of emergent agency is at bottom giving and life, rather than taking and death. This echoes Martin Luther King's words, "The arc of the universe bends toward justice." Paul struggles to believe this against all evidence to the contrary, insisting over and over until we doubt his words, "We have this confidence"; "We do not lose heart" (2 Cor 3:4; 5:6; 4:1, 16). Yet in the span of his letters that survive, he does not give up, and he challenges others to have this faith. He attributes his confidence to "the mercy of God" (2 Cor 4:1; 1 Cor 7:25), a mercy that makes all that receive it—people and things—free agents of this spirit/grace/life.

Marginal Corinthians and Posthumanism

This open agency takes us back to the questions that others have tackled in the essays in this volume. How did people other than Paul, the marginal

---

18:20-23). These martyrs' deaths are also taken to be able to save others (4 Macc 6:28-29; 17:20-22; 18:4-5).

majority, practice this agency in the Corinthian assembly? What impact did they have on Paul, on each other, and on other people and things in Corinth? As one contribution to answering these questions, I argue here that the people Paul was restraining in 1 Corinthians have made him concede in 2 Corinthians that their new life is not a shameful violation of good order but is the best evidence he has that his work in Corinth was effective. This has shifted his theological emphasis away from God's overpowering human boasts by a sequence of not-always-voluntary subordinations until all are reduced to the one. To defend himself, he has begun to depict God empowering created beings that are, each in their own distinctive way, creative agents of giving and receiving within an emergent and multiplex bundle of life. Those who were once without wisdom and power and who now have new wisdom and power have ignored his restrictions and taught him this.

By way of summary, I point to some resonances shared by Paul's gospel here and the message of the posthumanist proponents. First, they both announce that all beings that have long been used as instruments for the fulfillment of others are entitled to realize their own agency. This came to Latour in what others have called his "Damascus Road experience." In 1972 after years of philosophical effort when he was walking on the road from Dijon to Gray, he stopped and said, "Nothing can be reduced to anything else" (Latour 1988, 162–63). I suggest Paul discovers this more than once and specifically in his struggle with the Corinthians. He finds that his own experience of life can only be defended by conceding their experience of life, and this through negotiating with each other. The multitude will articulate itself.

Second, no one is alone, but all things function in networks that are continually being contested and negotiated. Here we have on the posthumanist side the rhizome of life that cannot be a model to imitate but can be mapped provisionally as it emerges, adapts, and discards. Paul's God, who is rejected and chooses the ignorant to shame the wise, could well fit here (1 Cor 1:21–31), a God who tries one thing and then another, reaching out for some kind of reconciliation that Paul begins to imagine because he himself cannot do without it in Corinth (2 Cor 5:17–31; 7:2–3). This rhizomatic network may be the source and end of being, but only in an emergent and reactive way that remains in process among the many as each one seeks to sustain its life.

Third, this system is highly vulnerable. Other systems built on a model of given authority and involuntary subjection have dominated the earth for millennia. Now they threaten to destroy it through depletion of limited resources, technologies of violence, and fear of loss. Latour warns that we are facing Gaia at our peril. Paul warns that all will get the consequences for what they have done (2 Cor 5:10; 11:10; Rom 14:12). Yet neither has slackened in his effort to make the apocalypse visible. Both are evangelists of the possibility within impossibility, Latour proclaiming Gaia as a hope to "rematerialize our belonging to the world," Paul proclaiming Christ embodied in a death for all and in a life for all, one that Paul has to concede is visible in the nothings of Corinth. Both Latour and Paul learn to look for what happens in specific, local places where life is a struggle. There they find that out of darkness light shines and new conduct is being tested.

Works Cited

Barclay, John M. G. 2015. *Paul and the Gift*. Grand Rapids: Eerdmans.

Bennett, Jane. 2010. *Vibrant Matter: A Political Ecology of Things*. Durham, NC: Duke University Press.

Buell, Denise Kimber. 2009. "God's Own People: Specters of Race, Ethnicity, and Gender in Early Christian Studies." Pages 159–90 in *Prejudice and Christian Beginnings: Investigating Race, Gender, and Ethnicity in Early Christian Studies*. Edited by Elisabeth Schüssler Fiorenza and Laura Nasrallah. Minneapolis: Fortress.

———. 2014. "Hauntology Meets Post-humanism: Some Payoffs for Biblical Studies." Pages 29–56 in *The Bible and Posthumanism*. Edited by Jennifer L. Koosed. SemeiaSt 74. Atlanta: Society of Biblical Literature.

———. 2017. "Embodied Temporalities: Gender, Ethnicity, and Other Transformations." Pages 454–76 in *The Bible and Feminism: Remapping the Field*. Edited by Yvonne Sherwood with the assistance of Anna Fisk. Oxford: Oxford University Press.

Burkert, Walter. 1985. *Greek Religion*. Translated by John Raffan. Cambridge: Harvard University Press.

Crüsemann, Marlene. 2014. "Christologie der Beziehung: Trost, *charis*, und Kraft der Schwachen nach dem 2. Brief an die Gemeinde in Korinth." Pages 191–97 in *Gott ist Beziehung: Beiträge zur biblischen Rede von Gott*. Edited by Claudia Janssen and Luise Schottroff. Gütersloh: Gütersloher Verlagshaus.

Deleuze, Gilles, and Félix Guattari 1987. *A Thousand Plateaus: Capitalism and Schizophrenia*. Minneapolis: University of Minnesota Press.

Fox, Arminta M. 2019. *Paul Decentered: Reading 2 Corinthians with the Corinthian Women*. PCC. Minneapolis: Lexington/Fortress Academic.

Frettlöh, Magdalene. 2001. "Der Charme der gerechten Gabe." Pages 123–36 in *"Leget Anmut in der Geben": Zum Verhältnis von Ökonomie und Theologie*. Edited by Jürgen Ebach, Hans-Martin Gutmann, Magdalene Frettlöh, and Michael Weinrich. Gütersloh: Gütersloher Verlagshaus.

Hartman, Midori E. 2019. "A Little Porneia Leavens the Whole: Queer(ing) Limits of Community in 1 Corinthians 5." Pages 143–63 in *Bodies on the Verge: Queering Pauline Epistles*. Edited by Joseph A. Marchal. SemeiaSt 93. Atlanta: SBL Press.

Kraftchick, Steven John. 2015. "Bodies, Selves, and Human Identity: A Conversation between Transhumanism and the Apostle Paul." *ThTo* 72:47–69.

Latour, Bruno. 1988. *The Pasteurization of France*. Translated by Alan Sheridan and John Law. Cambridge: Harvard University Press.

———. 1993. *We Have Never Been Modern*. Translated by Catherine Porter. Cambridge: Harvard University Press.

———. 2017. *Facing Gaia: Eight Lectures on the New Climate Regime*. Translated by Catherine Porter. Cambridge: Polity.

Loveloch, James. 2000. *Homage to Gaia: The Life of an Independent Scientist*. London: Oxford University Press.

Marshall, Jill E. 2017. *Women Praying and Prophesying in Corinth: Gender and Inspired Speech in First Corinthians*. WUNT 2/448. Tübingen: Mohr Siebeck.

Miller, Adam S. 2013. *Speculative Grace: Bruno Latour and Object-Oriented Theology*. New York: Fordham University Press.

Niccum, Curt. 1997. "The Voice of the Manuscripts on the Silence of Women: The External Evidence for 1 Cor 14.34–5." *NTS* 43:242–55.

Wire, Antoinette Clark. 1990. *The Corinthian Women Prophets: A Reconstruction through Paul's Rhetoric*. Minneapolis: Fortress.

———. 1994. "1 Corinthians." Pages 153–95 in *A Feminist Commentary*. Vol. 2 of *Searching the Scriptures*. Edited by Elisabeth Schüssler Fiorenza with the assistance of Ann Brock and Shelly Matthews. New York: Crossroad.

———. 2001. "Reconciled to Glory in Corinth? 2 Cor 2:14–7:4." Pages 263–75 in *Antiquity and Humanity: Essays on Ancient Religion and Philosophy; Presented to Hans Dieter Betz on His Seventieth Birthday*.

Edited by Adela Yarbro Collins and Margaret M. Mitchell. Tübingen: Mohr Siebeck.
———. 2019. *2 Corinthians*. WisC 48. Collegeville, MN: Liturgical Press.

Contributors

Cavan Concannon is Associate Professor of Religion at the University of Southern California. He is the author of *Profaning Paul* (University of Chicago, 2021), *Assembling Early Christianity: Trade, Networks, and the Letters of Dionysios of Corinth* (Cambridge University Press, 2017), and *"When You Were Gentiles": Specters of Ethnicity in Roman Corinth and Paul's Corinthian Correspondence* (Yale University Press, 2014).

Arminta Fox is Associate Professor of Religion and Director of the Varenhorst Center at Bethany College in Lindsborg, Kansas. She also founded and codirects the Women's and Gender Studies Program. Fox earned her PhD in New Testament from Drew Theological School. She is the author of *Paul Decentered: Reading 2 Corinthians with the Corinthian Women* in the Paul and Critical Contexts Series (Lexington/Fortress Academic, 2020). In addition, she is grateful to have received generous grant funding from NetVUE and IFYC to develop initiatives to engender social responsibility and combat systemic injustice in the local and academic communities.

Joseph A. Marchal (any pronouns used with respect are welcome) is Professor of Religious Studies and affiliate faculty in Women's and Gender Studies at Ball State University. He is the author of four books—most recently *Appalling Bodies: Queer Figures before and after Paul's Letters* (Oxford University Press, 2020)—and editor (or coeditor) of six collections, three with SBL Press, including *Bodies on the Verge: Queering Pauline Epistles* (2019) and *The People beside Paul: The Philippian Assembly and History from Below* (2015), with more in preparation. They are currently serving as chair of the Society of Biblical Literature's first-ever LGBTQ+ Task Force and a founding coeditor of *QTR: A Journal of Queer and Transgender Studies in Religion*.

Shelly Matthews is Professor of New Testament at the Brite Divinity School. She is the coauthor, with Barbara Reid, OP, of the two-volume feminist commentary *Luke* for the Wisdom Commentary Series (Liturgical Press, 2021). She is the general editor for the SBL Press Early Christianity and Its Literature series and the cofounder and inaugural cochair with Tat-Siong Benny Liew of the Society of Biblical Literature Racism, Pedagogy, and Biblical Studies program unit.

Anna Miller is Associate Professor of New Testament and Early Christianity at Xavier University in Cincinnati, Ohio. Her research interests center on politics and gender in the earliest Christian communities. These interests are represented in her book *Corinthian Democracy: Democratic Discourse in 1 Corinthians* (Pickwick, 2015). Miller has also written on disability and scripture, collaborating with Arthur Dewey on a lengthy article on Pauline literature for the volume *Disability and the Bible: A Commentary*. Most recently, Miller has been researching and writing a book on 1 Timothy, gender, and the public.

Jorunn Økland is Director of the Norwegian Institute at Athens and Professor of Gender Studies in the Humanities at University of Oslo, Norway. Her latest volume is *From Akershus to Acropolis: Norwegian Travelers to Greece* (2019); her edited volumes in biblical gender studies include two journal special issues on masculinities and biblical studies (2015) and *Marxist Feminist Biblical Criticism* (Sheffield Phoenix, 2008). She is the author of *Women in Their Place: Paul and the Corinthian Discourse of Gender and Sanctuary Space* (T&T Clark, 2004). With SBL Press, she was responsible for setting up the English version of the encyclopedia on The Bible and Women and was English coeditor of the first volume, *Torah* (2010); she is currently serving as a member on Society of Biblical Literature Council. She is founding coeditor of the *Journal of the Bible and Its Reception* (*JBR*), on the Translation and Redaction Committees of Norwegian Bible Society, and a member of the Norwegian Academy of Science and Letters.

Antoinette Clark Wire is Professor of New Testament Studies Emerita at San Francisco Theological Seminary and the Graduate Theological Union. Her research ranges from the theology of Paul and his interlocutors to women in early Christianity and the gospel as oral story. She spent nearly ten years each on five main projects: a dissertation on Paul's implicit theology (1974), *The Corinthian Women Prophets: A Reconstruction through Paul's Rhetoric* (Fortress, 1990), *Holy Lives, Holy Deaths: A Close Hearing of Early Jewish Storytellers* (Society of Biblical Literature, 2002), *The Case for Mark Composed in Performance* (Wipf & Stock, 2011), and Wisdom Commentary's *2 Corinthians* (Liturgical Press, 2019). High points have been teaching small classes, learning about China's church and its oral songs, and growing vegetables.

Ancient Sources Index

Hebrew Bible

Genesis
1	54, 184
1:27	54–57
2	55
2:7	54, 56, 184, 187–88
2:24	184
3	116
19:1–38	152, 185
	128

Leviticus
18:22	128
20:13	128

Numbers
5:18	61
30	29

Deuteronomy
32:17	203

Psalms
8:7	202
110:1	202

Jeremiah
9:22	203

Deuterocanonical Books

2 Maccabees
7:36	208–9

4 Maccabees
6:28–29	209
7:18–19	208–9
16:24–25	208–9
17:5–6	208–9
17:20–22	209
18:4–5	209
18:20–23	208–9

Ancient Jewish Writers

Philo, *De Iosepho*
36–38	185
63–73	185
148	185

Philo, *De opificio mundi*
134	54
167	184

Philo, *Legum allegoriae*
1.31–32	54

New Testament

Acts
	29, 93, 208
2:47–48	162
6:1	159
12	29
18	128

Romans
	15–16, 203
1:12	16
1:18–32	16
1:18–2:11	16

Romans (cont.)

5:18	209
8:19–23	207
14–15	16
14:12	211
16	161
16:3–5	29, 128
16:7	29

1 Corinthians	5–6, 8, 9, 14, 18–19, 22, 25, 28, 30, 33, 64, 69–70, 72, 77–78, 85, 89–90, 93, 99, 102, 105, 123, 127, 132, 145, 160–61, 166, 168, 177–78, 185, 187–90, 195–96, 205, 210
1	64
1–4	62
1:3	206–7
1:4–7	206
1:11	128
1:16–17	202
1:18–25	203
1:18–31	62
1:21–31	210
1:25–30	64
1:26	203
1:27–28	203
1:28	201
1:30–31	203
2:8	202, 208
3	9–10
3:1–4	207
3:10	206
3:16	207
4	16
4:1–2	206
4:6–21	28
4:8	49
4:10–16	204
4:13	62
4:20–21	16
5	50, 115, 117–18
5–6	16, 62, 128
5–7	10, 60
5:1	49, 153
5:7	208
5:20–22	209
6	6, 28, 50, 55
6:9	128
6:9–11	195
6:12	133
6:12–13	204
6:12–20	34, 100, 114–17
6:13	115
6:14	115, 208
6:15	49, 115
6:15–18	60
6:16	62, 64, 116
6:17	116
6:19	115–16
6:20	115
7	188
7:1	133
7:1–2	204
7:1–16	55
7:1–40	34, 134
7:2–9	133
7:4	133–34
7:5	134
7:8	134
7:12–16	12, 22
7:18–24	55
7:25	209
7:25–40	55
8:1–9	204
8:4–6	203
8:6	199
9	108, 204
9:1	208
9:22–24	204
10	108
10:10	206
10:20	203
10:23	49, 133, 204
10:30	206
10:31–11:1	204
11	6, 13, 16, 25–26, 28, 53, 85, 99, 101, 105, 137
11–14	70, 167
11:1–16	27, 134
11:2–3	204

11:2–16	17, 30, 34, 56, 60, 85, 133, 136, 184–85	16:23	206
11:3	49, 201–2	2 Corinthians	9–11, 30, 34, 35, 78, 108, 145–62, 195–96, 201–11
11:5	34, 60–64, 136		
11:6	62, 136–37, 195, 206	1:1	150
11:7–10	56	1:2	206–7
11:12	56, 184	1:10	204
11:16	85	1:12	148, 206
11:25	208	1:14	204
12:12–13	115	1:15	206
12:12–31	115	2:5–11	205
12:13	55, 115–16	2:14	206–7
13	28	3	108
13:11–12	207	3:1	148
14	6, 16, 28, 53, 69, 73, 91, 93, 99, 101, 105	3:1–3	204
		3:2	204
14:6–14	31	3:4	209
14:11	31	3:13–16	26
14:26–40	133–34	3:18	209
14:31–32	204	4:1	209
14:33	75, 80, 85	4:1–2	204, 206
14:33–35	73, 85	4:4	202
14:33–36	12, 17, 52, 73–74, 79–80, 85–87, 92, 183	4:6	204
		4:8–10	204
14:33–38	73	4:11–12	209
14:33–40	81	4:12	204
14:34	80, 202	4:13–14	204
14:34–35	17, 34, 72–85, 90–93, 196	4:14	208–9
14:34–40	74–75, 92	4:16	207, 209
14:36	75	5:6	209
14:36–39	76, 79	5:10	211
14:36–40	80–81, 83	5:11–12	204
14:39–40	204	5:12	148
14:40	74, 76, 80	5:15	209
15:8	208	5:17–18	209
15:15	208	5:17–31	210
15:24–28	202	5:18–7:15	205
15:45–49	207	5:21	204
15:49	54	6:4–10	204
15:57	206–7	6:11–12	205
16	110	6:11–13	204
16:3	206	7:2–3	210
16:15–18	202	7:2–4	204–5
16:16	202	7:5–13	205
16:19	29, 128	8	78

2 Corinthians (cont.)

Reference	Page
8:1	206
8:4	206
8:6	206–7
8:7	206–7
8:9	204, 206
8:16	206–7
8:19	206–7
9	78
9:2	150
9:8	206
9:11–15	207
9:13	203
9:14	206
9:15	206–7
10	147–49, 151, 160
10–12	205
10–13	34, 146–62, 195–96
10:3–5	147, 149
10:3–8	158
10:4–6	154
10:6–8	149
10:9	151
10:10	149, 154, 206
10:12	154
10:13	149, 151
10:13–15	149–50
10:14	149
10:15	149, 154
10:16	149
10:17	154
10:17–18	154
11	160
11:2	152, 204
11:3	152
11:4	153
11:6	156, 206
11:7	155
11:7–11	158
11:7–12	152
11:8	155
11:10	150, 211
11:13–15	154
11:18–21	158
11:19	154
11:20	154
11:21–12:10	156
11:22	158
11:23	159
11:23–29	204
11:24–25	155
11:26	155
11:27	155
11:29	147, 155
12	160
12:9	206–7
12:14	152
12:15	158
12:15–19	158
12:19	151, 158–59
12:19–21	205
13	148
13:3	159, 205
13:3–5	204
13:5–10	205
13:9	204, 207
13:11	152
13:13	206

Galatians

Reference	Page
	15, 28–30, 157
1:16	208
3:27–28	55, 188
3:28	25, 29, 34, 54–59, 85, 105, 162, 188
5:19–21	205

Ephesians

Reference	Page
5:30	54

Philippians

Reference	Page
	11, 103, 126
2:6–11	105
4:2–3	103

Colossians

Reference	Page
	10–11
1:15–20	10

1 Thessalonians

Reference	Page
	9
2	9–10
4	10

Ancient Sources Index

2 Thessalonians	9	Augustine, *De doctrina christiana*	
		2.11.16	82
1 Timothy	10–11, 34–35, 77, 166, 168, 170, 177–90	1 Clement	89
1:3	179		
1:3–6	179	Clement of Alexandria, *Stromateis*	
1:3–7	179, 181	3.13.93	55
1:3–9	186–87		
1:4	179–80	Didache	89
1:5	179		
1:6	179	Ignatius, *To Polycarp*	
1:7	179	3:1	180
2:8–15	179, 182, 185–87		
2:9–15	183	Greco-Roman Literature	
2:11–15	52		
2:12	183	Aelius Aristides, *Orations*	
2:14	184	24.22–42	185
2:15	188		
3:4–5	180–81	Apuleius, *Metamorophoses*	
3:15	180–81	9.12	62
4:3	188		
5:3–16	182, 188	Aristophanes, *Ekklesiazousae*	170
5:11–14	186		
5:14	186	Aristophanes, *Lysistrata*	170
6:3	180		
6:3–5	186–87	Aristotle, *Politica*	
6:4–5	181	1252a1–1260a15	170
		1260a12–15	184
2 Timothy	177	1275a2–026	170
Titus	177	Dio Chrysostom, *Orations*	
1:10	179	32.26–27	182
2:3	186	42.1	175
3:4–5	186	43.3	181–82
		47.1	175
Philemon	60	64.3	61
Revelation	26	Epictetus, *Diatribai*	
12–20	203	2.1.31	179
Early Christian Writings		Euripides, *Supplices*	
		435	175
Acts of Paul and Thecla	4, 188–89		
		Herodotus, *Historiae*	
		5.35	62

Lucian, *De syria dea*
6   61

Lucian, *Dialogi meretricii*
5.1–3   61

Lucian, *Fugitivi*
27   62

Lucian, *Juppiter tragoedus*
27   179

Petronius, *Satyricon*
103   62

Plato, *Respublica*   170

Plutarch, *Conjugalia praecepta*
139a–145d   184
142c–d   183

Plutarch, *Demosthenes*
1.1   181
8.7.1   181

Plutarch, *Praecepta gerendae rei publicae*
801e–802f   175
802f   181

Quintillian, *Institutio oratoria*
1.3.83   156
2.11.7   156
2.17.6   156

Seneca, *Controversiae*
2.1   149

Seneca, *Epistulae morales*
114   149

Stobaeus, *Eclogae*
149.7   184

Strabo, *Geographica*
8.6.20   49

Tacitus, *Germania*
19.2   61

Thucydides, *Historiae*
6.39.1–2   181

Xenophon of Ephesus, *Ephesiaca*
5.5   62

Zeno, *Politeia*
57–58

Modern Authors Index

Aland, Barbara 73–74, 76, 84, 87, 93
Aland, Kurt 73–74, 76, 84, 87, 93
Amador, J. David Hester 7–8
Aymer, Margaret 29, 32
Beavis, Mary Ann 9, 58
Benhabib, Seyla 171–73, 176, 182, 190
Bennett, Jane 114, 197
Bennett, Judith 135–36
Betz, Hans Dieter 54, 77–78, 157
Bird, Jennifer 17–18, 133
Briggs, Sheila 11, 18, 57, 60
Brooten, Bernadette J. 3, 6, 8, 16, 61, 135
Buell, Denise K. 23, 33, 113–15, 117, 124, 136, 148, 200, 207
Butler, Judith 61, 100, 106–7, 111, 117
Castelli, Elizabeth A. 8, 56, 101–3, 105, 127
Clivaz, Claire 75, 82, 89
Collins, Raymond 79, 115–16, 136
Colombo, Claire Miller 10–11, 22
Concannon, Cavan 23–24, 34, 107–8, 110, 196, 207
Conway, Colleen 157–58
Conzelmann, Hans 78, 180
Cooper, Kate 4–5, 132
Cvetkovich, Ann 124, 129–31, 133, 135, 138–39
D'Angelo, Mary Rose 11, 184
Deleuze, Gilles 110, 112–14, 197–98
Delobel, Joël 86–87
DuBois, W. E. B. 26–27
Ehrensperger, Kathy 15–17
Ehrman, Bart 85, 87–88, 92
Feinberg, Leslie 130–31

Foucault, Michel 7, 175
Fox, Arminta 9, 10–11, 34, 39, 145, 195–96, 205
Fraser, Nancy 171–73, 187, 182
Gench, Frances Taylor 11–12, 30
Gillman, Florence Morgan 9–10
Glancy, Jennifer 60, 155, 157, 182, 185
Guy, Lindsey 31–33
Habermas, Jürgen 171–73, 176, 182, 189–90
Haines-Eitzen, Kim 81, 87, 92–93
Halberstam, Jack 61, 134–35
Harrill, J. Albert 149, 156–57
Hartman, Midori E. 31, 108, 117, 207
Hearon, Holly 4, 30, 31
Horrell, David 8, 177–78
Horsley, Richard A. 18, 20, 57, 136, 174
Hylen, Susan 12–13
Ivarsson, Fredrik 16, 128
Johnson, Luke T. 177–80, 183
Johnson-DeBaufre, Melanie 9, 51, 101, 109
Johnson Hodge, Caroline 22, 148
Junior, Nyasha 24–25, 28–29
Kahl, Brigitte 15, 17
Katz, Marilyn 168–71, 176
Kittredge, Cynthia Briggs 10–11, 18–19, 21–22, 24, 28, 51, 100, 105–6, 126–27, 149
Kloha, Jeffrey 75–76, 93
Koosed, Jennifer L. 9, 33
Kotrosits, Maia 33, 130
Kraemer, Ross Shepard 2, 4–6, 12, 167
Krause, Deborah 180, 182–83, 189
Landes, Joan B. 168, 171–72, 176

Larson, Jennifer   149, 154–55, 157
Latour, Bruno   100, 109–114, 117, 196–200, 206–7, 210–11
Lopez, Davina C.   7, 157
MacDonald, Dennis R.   54–55, 189
MacDonald, Margaret Y.   167, 178
Marchal, Joseph A.   11, 18, 21, 25, 27, 30–31, 33, 51, 60–61, 101, 103, 108, 124, 126, 135, 137, 150, 157, 195
Marshall, Jill E.   22, 53, 202
Martin, Dale B.   13, 56, 114–16, 128, 133
Martin, Troy W.   7–8
Matthews, Shelly   4, 13, 25–26, 33–34, 54–56, 58, 61, 126, 132–33, 137, 152–53, 195
Miller, Anna C.   10–11, 34–35, 52, 127, 165, 174–76, 181, 183, 195
Miller, Merrill P.   8, 53, 107
Miller, Adam S.   110–11, 206–7
Muñoz, José Esteban   124, 129, 131, 133, 138–39
Nasrallah, Laura S.   22–23, 33, 51, 101, 109
Niccum, Curt   79, 81, 83–84, 86, 202
Ober, Josiah   169, 175
Olbrechts-Tyteca, Lucie   48, 124–125
Økland, Jorunn   12, 17, 34, 77, 90, 132, 167, 196, 202
Osiek, Carolyn   167, 177–78
Parker, Angela   25, 28
Parks, Sara   6–7
Payne, Philip   75, 79–84, 86, 89–90
Penner, Todd   7, 132, 137
Perelman, Chaïm   48, 70, 124–25
Richlin, Amy   2–4, 6, 8, 11–12, 33
Saxonhouse, Arlene   101, 175
Scherbenske, Eric W.   76, 80, 82–83, 88, 90–91
Schmithals, Walter   78, 101
Schüssler Fiorenza, Elisabeth   3, 5, 7–8, 12–13, 18, 24–25, 33, 47, 51, 53, 57, 63, 77, 99–102, 104–5, 108, 112, 123, 126–27, 132, 145–46, 172–73, 178–79, 188
Semler, Johannes   77–78, 88

Shaner, Katherine   11, 23, 185,
Smith, Mitzi J.   24–25, 28–29, 53, 128
Smith, Shanell T.   25–29, 33, 53
Solevåg, Anna Rebecca   183–86
Stowers, Stanley K.   53, 57, 102, 129
Sumney, Jerry L.   108, 145
Tamez, Elsa   11, 29, 51, 183–85
Townsley, Gillian   30, 33, 53, 108
Tupamahu, Ekaputra   31–32
Vander Stichele, Caroline   132, 137, 153, 160
Wire, Antoinette Clark   1–35, 47–59, 63–64, 69–77, 79–81, 83–87, 89, 91–93, 99–100, 102–11, 113–114, 117, 123–29, 131–39, 145–46, 151, 160–62, 165–667, 178, 185, 187–90, 202, 205–6, 209
Witherington, Ben, III   145, 154
Wuellner, Wilhelm   7–8
Young, Iris Marion   168–69
Zamfir, Korinna   170, 174

Subject Index

affective dynamics in interpretation, 2–3, 23, 30, 32–34, 58–59, 88, 129–31, 133–37, 139, 151, 182, 186. *See also* desire; sexual self-control; trauma
agency, 3, 25–26, 29, 33–35, 47, 51–53, 57–58, 62, 92, 100–101, 103–4, 112–18, 166–68, 188–90, 195–211
  nonhuman agencies, 34–35, 100, 112–18, 195–211
  women's agency, 3, 25–26, 29, 33–35, 47, 51–53, 57–58, 62, 92, 101, 104, 166–68, 188–90, 201–2
androcentrism, 3–4, 6–9, 26, 52–53, 56–57, 99, 101, 137, 146–47, 165–67, 170, 172–73, 189–90. *See also* patriarchy; kyriarchy
androgyny, 54–56, 137
apocalyptic, 8, 18, 21, 31, 56, 113, 134–35, 188, 200, 211
assembly/assemblies(*ekklēsia/ekklēsiai*) 1, 10–11, 13–14, 20–21, 23–24, 27–29, 32–33, 47–57, 60–62, 77, 100, 106–7, 117, 123, 127–29, 131–33, 135, 137–39, 165, 174–75, 178, 182, 184, 187, 189, 195, 199, 202, 209–10
authority, 14–15, 28–29, 31, 34, 48–49, 52–53, 63–64, 82, 89–90, 92–93, 102–5, 111, 125–26, 128, 131, 133–34, 139, 146, 148–51, 154–61, 166, 168, 174–75, 178, 180–84, 187, 189, 196, 200, 202, 204, 210–11
authorship, 4, 12, 14, 32, 51, 71, 74, 77, 79, 85, 100, 103–5, 127, 176–82, 187, 190, 196

baptism, 4, 10–11, 22, 25, 29, 54–57, 85, 115–16, 188, 202, 208. *See also* Gal 3:28 in Ancient Sources Index.
butch, 34, 130, 135–37
celibacy, 6, 12–13, 26, 50, 161, 188. *See also* sexual self-control
children, 9, 16, 22, 31, 57, 146–47, 151–52, 158, 161, 179, 184–86, 188
Chloe, 24, 28, 128
Corinthian women prophets, 1, 3–4, 9–10, 12–13, 19–29, 31–32, 35, 48–51, 56–57, 61–62, 92, 123–25, 132–33, 135–36, 139, 145, 161, 195. *See also* women.
Corinthian Women Prophets, The (book), 1–3, 6–9, 12–13, 16, 18–19, 21, 23–24, 47–48, 53, 59–60, 63, 69–73, 76, 78–79, 83–88, 90–91, 99–103, 106, 109, 132, 139, 145, 165–66, 196
creation, 8–9, 11, 54–57, 184–85, 187, 201, 207–10
debasement, 50–51, 62, 123–24, 138
debate, 11, 23, 34–35, 77, 100–101, 103, 108–9, 112, 146, 148, 154, 160, 165, 168, 170–76, 180–82, 185–90, 201
decentering approaches, 24, 29, 31, 34, 51, 63, 110, 135, 147, 195, 201
democratic practices, 52, 100–101, 104, 106–7, 110–14, 117, 165, 168–90
desire, 26, 31, 59, 74, 88, 134, 151, 186
egalitarianism, 11–12, 47, 55–58, 63, 162, 168, 171–73, 176, 181, 187–88, 190. *See also* equality
enslaved people, 11, 13–14, 22–25, 28–29, 49–50, 55, 59–63, 115, 146–47,

enslaved people (cont.)
154–59, 161–62, 165–66, 168, 170–71, 176–78, 181, 184–85, 187–88, 195, 201, 208. See also freed people

enslaving systems, 3, 15, 18, 22–25, 28–29, 57, 60–62, 148–49, 154, 162

ephemera, 23, 29, 34, 84, 123–24, 127–34, 136–39

equality, 29, 79, 83, 91, 112–13, 156, 165, 168–69, 173, 175, 185, 187. See also egalitarianism.

ethnicity, 3, 21–22, 24–25, 28, 32, 34, 60, 62, 108–9, 114, 124, 159, 161, 172. See also racialization and racisms.

feminist approaches, 1, 3–7, 9–19, 22–25, 28, 30–31, 33–34, 51, 53–54, 57–59, 63, 69, 71, 73, 83–84, 90, 92–93, 99–100, 103–4, 106–7, 109, 111, 123–24, 127–28, 131–34, 139, 145–47, 160, 171–73, 176, 189. See also decentering approaches; identification, politics of; intersectional approaches; othering, politics of; reading against the grain; reconstruction (historical); suspicion, hermeneutics of; womanist approaches; women's history

flesh, 15, 54–55, 114–16, 147, 151, 203, 209

freed people, 22, 24, 28, 115, 161. See also enslaved people

gender, 3, 5, 9–12, 15–16, 18–19, 22, 25–27, 30–32, 47, 50, 54–56, 58–63, 70–72, 79, 91–93, 99, 108, 127–28, 132, 134–37, 145, 147, 149–50, 153, 157, 161–62, 165–168, 170, 172–73, 176, 179, 181–86, 188–90, 195–96. See also androgyny; butch; masculinity; sexuality; women
  as a category of analysis, 3, 16, 18–19, 25, 34, 47, 60, 62, 70, 91–92, 108, 132, 145, 161–62, 172, 181, 195
  constructions and ideologies, 5, 15, 18–19, 22, 30–31, 34, 55, 61, 63, 79, 92–93, 99, 108, 127–28, 132, 134–35, 147, 149, 157, 168, 176, 182, 184–86, 195

gender equality. See equality

gender minorities and gendered others, 16, 26, 27, 32, 47, 61, 63, 135, 136–37, 157

gendered divisions and hierarchies, 15, 16, 19, 26, 47, 50, 54, 56, 59–60, 62, 150, 153, 161, 165–68, 170, 172–73, 176, 179, 183–86, 188–90, 196

hair, 25–26, 33, 136–37, 183

haunting, 2, 23–24, 29, 33–35, 103, 107, 109, 114, 123–24, 130–31, 136, 138, 200

head, 27, 29, 34, 48–49, 57, 61–62, 72, 105, 111, 136–37, 201–2

identification, politics of, 13–21, 30, 32–33, 100, 102–4, 132, 135, 146–48, 150, 157, 173, 196

imprisonment, 11, 29, 147, 149, 155

interpolation, 12, 17–19, 34, 73–91, 196

intersectional approaches, 3, 15–16, 18–19, 25–27, 31–34, 47, 53, 57–63, 103, 108, 132, 134, 146–61, 172–73, 180–81, 185–87. See also kyriarchy

Jews and Jewishness, 15, 20–22, 28, 32, 54–55, 70, 147, 157–60, 180, 188, 199, 208–9

Jewish-gentile difference, 20–22, 24, 30, 55, 157, 180, 188, 199

Junia, 29, 161

kyriarchy, 57–58, 103, 108, 132, 146–60, 180–181, 185–87
  defined, 146

lesbian, 129–31, 135–36

marriage, 10, 13, 22, 24, 26, 30, 50, 52, 57, 133–35, 152, 161–62, 169, 185, 187–88, 205

masculinity, 3, 6, 26, 17, 50–51, 61, 101, 137, 148–62, 165–67, 182, 184. See also gender; kyriarchy; patriarchy

network(s), 34, 109–11, 128, 131, 138, 197–201, 208–10

othering, politics of, 3, 10, 14–17, 22, 27, 32, 62, 100–2, 104, 123, 145–46, 148, 156–57, 169, 196 patriarchy, 11, 16–17, 22, 53, 152–55, 160, 168, 180, 187–88, 199. *See also* kyriarchy

postcolonial and decolonizing approaches, 15, 18, 20, 24, 26–27, 34, 17, 104, 162. *See also* Roman imperialism.

posthumanist approaches, 23, 34–35, 100–101, 109–17, 196–211. *See also* haunting

Prisca, 29, 93, 128

prostitutes, 34, 49–50, 60–64, 114–16, 195, 201, 208

public culture(s) and public sphere, 33–34, 52–53, 63–64, 129–31, 137, 165–90, 205

queer approaches, 30–31, 34, 47, 60, 124, 129–39, 145

racialization and racisms, 1, 16, 20–21, 25–33, 53, 61, 124, 169, 172. *See also* ethnicity

reading against the grain, 5, 11–12, 15, 20–23, 30–31, 99, 108, 123, 126–27, 132, 137, 139, 146, 188–89

reception history, 2–34, 47, 52–53, 57–59, 69–93, 108–9, 124–25, 131, 138

reconstruction (historical), 3, 5–11, 22–24, 28, 32, 48–54, 57–58, 63, 69–70, 86, 88, 99–100, 103–12, 123, 127–28, 132, 139, 145–47, 161, 165–66, 179, 189, 195, 201

respectability, politics of, 11, 25–26, 29–30, 33–34, 61, 63

resurrection, 10, 51, 72, 161–62, 201–2, 204, 208–9

rhetorical approaches, 1, 3–14, 16–18, 20, 23–25, 28, 30–31, 34, 48–49, 60, 62–64, 69–73, 86, 99, 101–5, 108–9, 117, 123–29, 132–33, 136–39, 145–62, 165–66, 173, 178–181, 185–187, 189–190, 195–96

Roman imperialism, 1–2, 12–13, 15, 18–20, 22–23, 26–28, 32–33, 57, 61, 78, 103, 109, 111, 137, 146–51, 154–57, 159–60, 162, 174–76, 181, 183–84, 189–90, 198

sexuality, 10, 13, 15–18, 22, 24–34, 47, 49–50, 57, 59–63, 101, 115–18, 127–37, 139, 152–55, 158, 160–61, 172, 184, 188, 205. *See also* celibacy; desire; lesbian; marriage; prostitute; respectability, politics of; trauma

sexual self-control, 10, 26, 49–50, 134–35, 184, 205

sexual vulnerability, 29, 59–61, 63, 129–31, 133, 136, 139, 152, 161, 184

speech practices, 5–6, 25–27, 29, 32, 34–35, 48, 52–53, 58, 64, 74, 77, 89, 103, 105, 107, 112, 136–37, 148–49, 151–52, 154, 156, 158–60, 162, 171, 173–90, 195–96, 198, 202, 205–8

spirit, 29, 50, 53–55, 60, 89, 93, 107, 114–16, 136, 153, 166, 189, 196, 199–200, 206–7, 209

status, 13, 20, 24–26, 32, 34, 50–51, 60–63, 108, 147–49, 154–55, 157–162, 169–170, 181, 189

stigma, 28, 132, 135–36

subordination, 23, 35, 74, 101, 123, 173, 184, 197, 201–3, 210

suspicion, hermeneutics of, 3, 147, 160

textual criticism, 34, 54, 69–93, 174. *See also* interpolation

trauma, 129–31

utopian impulses, 34, 57–59

violence, 14, 16, 22, 61, 107, 130, 147–52, 154–58, 160–61, 198, 200, 208, 211

widows, 50, 134, 153, 161, 185–86

wisdom, 8, 20–21, 49–50, 64, 72, 101, 148, 151–54, 156, 158–60, 162, 175–76, 180–86, 190, 203–6, 210

womanist approaches, 1, 24–30, 53, 145

women. *See also* agency; Chloe; Corinthian women prophets; feminist approaches; gender; Junia; lesbian; Prisca; prostitutes; widows; womanist approaches

women's history, 2–6, 9–14, 18–29, 33–35, 47–63, 70–72, 77, 91–93, 99–102, 104–5, 123–28, 130–37,

women: women's history (cont.)
139, 145–47, 151–53, 159–62, 165–71, 173, 175–79, 182–83, 185, 187–90, 195, 201, 205
women scholars ignored or marginalized, 2, 6–10, 11, 13, 17–19, 28, 47, 53, 58, 79, 83, 84, 133, 145–46
"no women in the index," 2, 6, 8–9, 15, 22
wo/men, 33–34, 47, 58–64, 104–6, 153–54, 159–62
defined, 33–34, 47

www.ingramcontent.com/pod-product-compliance
Lightning Source LLC
Chambersburg PA
CBHW021703230426
43668CB00008B/706